The Spanish
Civil War
IN LITERATURE

The Spanish
Civil War
IN LITERATURE

Edited by Janet Pérez
and
Wendell Aycock

TEXAS TECH UNIVERSITY PRESS

1990

STUDIES IN COMPARATIVE LITERATURE NO. 21
Copyright 1990 Texas Tech University Press

This book was set in 10 on 12 Garamond and printed on acid-free paper that meets the guidelines for permanence and durability of the Committee on Production Guidelines for Book Longevity of the Council on Library Resources. ∞

Designed by Elaine Atkinson

Library of Congress Cataloging-in-Publication Data

    The Spanish Civil War in literature / edited by Janet Pérez and
      Wendell Aycock
          p. cm. — (Studies in comparative literature, ISSN 0899-2193
    ; no. 21)
     ISBN 0-89672-196-5. — ISBN 0-89672-197-3 (pbk.)
     1. War in literature. 2. Literature, Modern—20th century—
    History and criticism. 3. Spain—History—Civil War, 1936–1939—
    Literature and the war. I. Pérez, Janet. II. Aycock, Wendell M.
    III. Series.
    PN56.W3S6 1990
    809'.93358—dc20   90-10999
                                            CIP

Texas Tech University Press
Lubbock, Texas 79409–1037 U.S.A.

Studies in Comparative Literature
Texas Tech University Press

*James Joyce: His Place in World Literature

*From Surrealism to the Absurd

Franz Kafka: His Place in World Literature

Modern American Fiction: Insights and Foreign Lights

*William Faulkner: Prevailing Verities and World Literature

Joseph Conrad: Theory and World Fiction

Albert Camus' Literary Milieu: Arid Lands

Ethnic Literature since 1776: The Many Voices of America,
    Part One and Part Two

Ibero-American Letters in a Comparative Perspective

Classical Mythology in Twentieth-Century Thought and Literature

Shakespeare's Art from a Comparative Perspective

The Teller and the Tale: Aspects of the Short Story

Calderón de la Barca at the Tercentenary: Comparative Views

Johann Wolfgang von Goethe: One Hundred and Fifty Years of
    Continuing Vitality

Women Worldwalkers: New Dimensions of Science Fiction
    and Fantasy

Myths and Realities of Contemporary French Theater

War and Peace: Perspectives in the Nuclear Age

Film and Literature: A Comparative Approach to Adaptation

Literature and Anthropology

The Spanish Civil War in Literature

The Body and the Text: Comparative Essays in Literature
    and Medicine

The Literature of Emigration and Exile

*Out of print

 *Preface*

The purpose of Studies in Comparative Literature is to explore literatures of various cultures and linguistic groups in comparison with one another and to compare literature with other disciplines or fields of study. First published in 1968, volumes of the series originally derived from annual symposia founded by Wolodymyr T. Zyla, under the auspices of the Interdepartmental Committee on Comparative Literature at Texas Tech. In subsequent years, the series flourished, and volumes have been devoted to the study of authors (e.g., Kafka, Camus, Shakespeare), genres (e.g., the short story, science fiction), movements and themes (e.g., surrealism, mythology), and comparative art forms and disciplines (e.g., film and literature, literature and anthropology).

This volume examines literature that arose out of the Spanish Civil War. The idealism that motivated individuals from various countries to form the international brigades for this war is only one of the varying motivations for writers to produce the great amount of literary works devoted to the topic of the war. This literature, much of it written in exile and in various languages, is an appropriate focus for Studies in Comparative Literature. Writers of the following chapters examine works from Spain, France, the United States, Russia, and various countries of Latin America in their commemoration of the fiftieth anniversary of the Spanish Civil War.

CONTENTS

Introduction

Few events of modern times have stirred the emotions and caught the imagination of intellectuals as did the Spanish Civil War of 1936–1939. Discounted by militarists and some historians as little more than a proving ground for Axis armaments utilized in World War II, the internal struggle of the Spanish people has had a literary resonance seldom equalled. Neither of the two much larger conflicts that preceded and followed Spain's civil strife—World War I and World War II—inspired anything near the number of writers who have treated the Spanish Civil War. No necessary correlation exists between the military significance of an event and the quality or quantity of the literature that it inspires, and only the Holocaust offers a parallel with the Spanish Civil War as a source for artistic and literary outpourings. Other connections exist between these two tragic occurrences: Both produced an exodus of refugees from lands falling under the control of fascism; both saw hundreds of thousands of innocent victims die in concentration camps; and both are intimately linked to resultant long-term exile or expatriation. The extensive and significant literature of exile produced by both events is separable only with considerable difficulty from that specifically concerning the causes of exodus, the Civil War and the Holocaust. Unity within the diversity of languages and places of origin of these writings comes from the powerful shock and passion generated by both tragedies.

During most of the forty-year dictatorship of Francisco Franco (1936–1975), the literature written in exile, inspired by Spain's civil conflict, was enormously partisan, with only the pro-Franco or pro-Falangist perspective being published within Spain; dissenting points of view, frequently but not always those of exiles, were silenced or forced to find outlets in other countries. The first several years comprising the conflict and immediate postwar years were subsequently dubbed *triunfalismo*, a period in Spain of self-glorification by the victorious Falangists. During that same interval appeared some of the bitterest indictments of the fascist uprising and Nationalist atrocities, published by Republicans in exile. No impartial or nonpartisan accounts were penned by participants on either side. Many years would pass before persons inside Spain could hear or read the points of view of the losers, or have access to more serene objective appraisals of the national tragedy. Not until the early 1970s, shortly before the death of the dictator, did works of important literary figures in exile receive approval for printing and distribution in Spain. For the most part, works openly critical of the Falange and its allies, portraying the war from a Loyalist perspective or depicting exile from a pro-Republican standpoint, could not circulate freely in Spain until after the death of Franco and subsequent abolition of censorship at the end of 1978. Meanwhile, the Spanish Civil War continued to be a viable and frequent literary theme, not only in Spain but in many other lands. Political circumstances within Spain, combined with the sympathy of intellectuals in much of Europe and the Americas for the Republican cause and the presence of Loyalist exiles in many of the same countries, partially explain the international flood of writings on the Spanish Civil War. There are as yet no serenely dispassionate literary interpretations of this stirring conflict. The half century elapsed has broadened perspectives but has not extinguished the passions inspired by Spain's struggle. Not even scholars are exempt from the emotions generated; within the inevitable—and desirable—multiplicity of literatures and methodologies, powerful sentiments and implicit commitments provide cohesion.

The fiftieth anniversary of Spain's civil conflict has sparked commemorative observances in Spain, the United States, Spanish America, and various other countries. The present volume, another such commemorative undertaking, attempts to view the many literatures of the Spanish Civil War within a comparative and sometimes interdisciplinary framework and to assess the works of specific writers or groups of writers from points of view varying from the stylistic or thematic to the historical, from the standpoint of the newest criticism to that of the sociology of literature and culture. The task of ordering the various essays has not been taken lightly. The form imposed upon content can affect its meaning, and several competing forms suggested themselves. The essays might be grouped according to several binary principles: works by combatants and noncombatants, by Loyalists and pro-Franco writers, by Spaniards and non-Spaniards;

works written during the War and after it, in Spain or in exile. Genre, style, age of writer, or ideology of the critic might also supply hierarchies. In the hope of avoiding implied judgments and maximizing the unity of the national literatures, the editors have opted for an arrangement according to the languages of the several literatures involved, specifically, French, Russian, English, and Spanish. This offers the advantage that readers interested in works by only French or Spanish authors, for example, will find all of the relevant essays grouped together. In addition, this criterion of organization is reasonably objective. Being external to the partisanships involved, it implies no evaluation of relative postures and merits of the writers studied. The reader's right of interpretation is thus not usurped, nor are conclusions anticipated through hierarchy of the essays.

Given the comparative and interdisciplinary nature of the volume and the several languages involved, internal variation is inevitable, despite the strong thematic and historical unity. Diversity is enhanced by the plurality of backgrounds and vocations of the contributors. Although most are professional scholars, academicians, professional critics, or teachers, one, Abe Osheroff, is also an American veteran of the Abraham Lincoln Brigade, who, with three thousand other American volunteers, fought to defend the Spanish Republic. His contribution to this collection carries a different authority than that of the critic: the unique, intransferable perspective of the participant in a major historical event. Clear traces of the passion and conviction that motivated the antifascist volunteers who joined the international brigades to fight for the Spanish Republic remain in Osheroff's "Reflections of a Civil War Veteran." The autobiographical substrata and personal experience of this writer are in frequent evidence, as are his forthrightness, sincerity, and thoroughgoing liberalism. History and literature, personal observations and emotions are inextricably intertwined in Osheroff's impassioned remembrances. Rather than any formal scholastic criticism, his is a partisan reader's response to literature that was just as much a part of history as the events he recalls.

In "Goya's Vision, Malraux's Voice," the authoritative comparatist Edouard Morot-Sir adopts an interdisciplinary perspective that applies the vision of pictorial art to literary conception. Using as his point of departure his own extensive acquaintance with Malraux, Morot-Sir argues, from the French novelist's knowledge of Spanish painting, in favor of the specific presence of Goya's tragic pictures of war in the conception of Malraux's novel *L'espoir*. Beginning with Malraux's understanding of Goya's art, as expressed in other writings by the novelist, Morot-Sir traces the correspondences between the two with particular emphasis on coincidence of aesthetics of line, light, and darkness, the contrast of colors, and the presence of monsters and masks. Specific parallels are drawn between Malraux's rhetoric of ellipsis and Goya's technique of broken strokes in painting. The affinities between the French writer and the Spanish painter are especially strong and visible in their reactions to the sufferings of the Spanish people, a unifying thread woven through many of the works in this collection.

Dealing with the same novel, Malraux's *L'espoir*, Richard Golsan treats this modern classic in terms of its influence on lesser writers, including those of the opposite side. The overwhelming popular success of Malraux's masterpiece led to imitation by some of the most fervent and outspoken fascist intellectuals in France. A major distinction is that the novels of neither Robert Brasillach nor Pierre Drieu la Rochelle deals exclusively with the Spanish Civil War, as had Malraux's, but both authors focus on this conflict at the ends of their novels. Their respective heroes' journeys to Spain to espouse the Nationalist cause are made to coincide with the resolution of all other emotional and political problems. Golsan studies the implicit presence of *L'espoir*, not only on the level of style, but especially on the level of a major theme of the international character of the conflict. Where Malraux had stressed the popular support throughout Europe for the Republican government, these French fascist novels of the Spanish Civil War stress the presence of foreign volunteers on Franco's side. Golsan's analysis focuses upon the presence of fascist ideology in the two novels and its effects upon characterization, events, and values in each.

Christopher Flood prefers to focus upon nonfiction in "Crusade or Genocide? French-Catholic Discourse on the Spanish Civil War." His major sources are essays and journalistic articles, and his theoretical point of departure is provided by Susan Suleiman and John Thompson. In a study that incorporates both historical point of view and elements of the sociology of literature, Flood studies the propagandistic functions of the writings, which attempt to present the Franco revolt as a holy war. His primary interest in ideological discourse presupposes rhetorical and semantic analysis as he proceeds to investigate the semiotics of dissent within the ranks of rightist French Catholics concerning the extent to which the Spanish nationalists' actions were in accord with the long-term needs of Spain or of Europe as a whole.

Alfred Cismaru also emphasizes ideological conflict, although his is internal to one writer. In "Simone de Beauvoir and the Spanish Civil War: From Apoliticism to Commitment," this critic indicates that in spite of strong political convictions, de Beauvoir did not become politically active until late in her life. Her early reluctance to participate in meetings, demonstrations, and the like resulted from her belief in the power of literature to change the world. As the tides of battle by the unarmed Spanish populace against those armed by the Nazis swung more and more in favor of Franco, de Beauvoir began to believe that something more than literature was necessary. Her involvement through petitions, financial contributions, and membership in leftist committees is a response to this moment. Dating de Beauvoir's decided humanitarian solidarity from 1939, Cismaru suggests that it is a direct reaction to her emotional involvement with the cause of the Spanish people.

In "The Writing of History: Authors Meet on the Soviet-Spanish Border," Peter Barta discusses three Communist writers who, with the international brigades, went to Spain during the Civil War: Arthur Koestler, Mate Zalka, and Mikhail Koltsov. The writings are conceived as partisan ideological discourse and are so studied by the critic. Koestler, the only one of the three writers to survive the Spanish Civil War, performed an ideological about-face after writing his *Spanish Testament.* Barta emphasizes the tendentious and propagandistic rhetoric of Zalka's supposed autobiographical writing, as well as indicating the propaganda function of Koltsov's works, adducing textual evidence suggesting that Koltsov and Zalka, as early old-style Communists, were increasingly at variance with Stalinistic ideology and techniques. Disagreement with the operation of the Soviet Communist Party in Spain led to ideological deviations for which Koltsov was executed. Possible roots of future deviation appear in the writing of Zalka, who was killed while in charge of the Twelfth International Brigade. As the sole survivor, only Koestler produced postwar writings documenting the differences in attitude produced by his experiences in Spain, further evincing the power and durability of the emotions generated by the conflict.

Geoffrey Meyers's study "*For Whom the Bell Tolls* as Contemporary History" relates Hemingway's experiences in Spain in 1937 and 1938, his acquaintance with real-life models, and their depiction in the novel. With significant implications for studies of Malraux, Meyers indicates that Hemingway's careful attention to geographical, military, and political detail in the novel has been overlooked by critics, who have preferred to concentrate on the work's romantic and ideological aspects. This distinguished authority illuminates the novel by reference to these historical details, as well as to some thirty fascists, Loyalists, foreign politicians, and soldiers to whom Hemingway refers. Meyers concentrates his explication upon the historical meaning and significance of two crucial passages, chapter 18 and chapter 42, documenting his contention that Hemingway's pro-Loyalist stance did not blind him to the incompetence of Loyalist leaders and to that indecisiveness within the government that facilitated the takeover by Communist disciplinarians. Interweaving historical background, references to Hemingway's other work, and passages from *For Whom the Bell Tolls*, Meyers refutes critics who accused Hemingway of lack of political sophistication and service for Stalin, to demonstrate that *For Whom the Bell Tolls* is both an allegory and an explanation of the Loyalist defeat in the Spanish Civil War.

Charles King, American expert on Ramón Sender, studies the work of the multifaceted Aragonese journalist and novelist, another participant on the Loyalist side in the Spanish Civil War. After a background sketch of Sender's ideological evolution from anarchism to communism, and subsequently to a more libertarian position, King first considers Sender's *Counterattack in Spain*, a propagandistic work written in 1937 while the author was under the influence of Marxism, and then focuses attention on two of Sender's many novels that combine historical accuracy and literary excellence in a personal and original interpretation of the war from his own humanistic point of view. King quotes from English translations of the Spanish originals of these two novels, the first realistic and allegorical, *The King and Queen* (1948), and the second, *Requiem for a Spanish Peasant* (1953), sumultaneously realistic and symbolic. *The King and Queen* portrays the Spanish masses incarnated in a gardener, and traditional Spain incarnated in the duchess, two archetypes who meet in the desolation of war on the level of their common humanity. In *Requiem for a Spanish Peasant*, the war is interpreted as a struggle between the status quo—or old Spain—and change—or new Spain—each again incarnated in a handful of representative characters. Neither the distance offered by allegorical treatment nor the use of a conservative mentality as narrative perspective for the latter novel suffice to erase Sender's passionate *engagement*.

Salvador Jiménez Fajardo concentrates upon the resistance of Madrid during the fall of 1936 and the spring of 1937. The critic focuses especially upon the first and most powerful of Alberti's poems dealing with the besieged city, "Madrid-Otoño," arguing that its central theme is rebirth. His approach incorporates both semiotics and rhetorical analysis, and emphasizes the opposition of birth and death in a search for the origins of what is termed "Alberti's voice of battle." Alberti's passionate commitment to the Republican cause remained intense enough to prevent his return to Spain even after Franco's death, until he was convinced that the movement toward democracy was real. By contrast with Jiménez Fajardo's very intensive analysis, Thomas Devene examines about a dozen recent films that treat the Spanish Civil War from a variety of historical vantage points. Some emphasize the trubulent time immediately before the war itself; others present the years of battle; and still others focus upon the postwar period, often examining the perpetuation of the discord in muted and subterranean strife in human relationships. The numbers and variety of recent vintage films attest to the enduring and passionate interest of Spanish artists and public in the national struggle, an intensity that suffuses all of the works included.

Luis Costa concentrates upon León Felipe Camino Galicia, a major poet of the Spanish Civil War, paradoxically little known in Spain. From 1920 onward, Felipe lived in Spain very little, and three of his years there were spent in jail. Afterward, he lived in exile in Mexico. In "The Failed Ideal in León Felipe's Poetry of the Spanish Civil War," Costa surveys the life and works of this somewhat unlikely intellectual, and studies his aesthetic and ideological evolution. Costa underscores Felipe's loyalty to the Spanish Republic in spite of his long absence from Spain, and the growing bitterness in his poems as the cause of the Republic appeared inevitably lost. The poet's later work is interpreted in the light of his experience during the war. Complementing the exegesis of Alberti's seminal poem, Costa's contribution makes available a significant overview of a long-neglected major poet of the Civil War.

Turning to postwar writers, the respected nineteenth- and twentieth-century scholar Joseph Schraibman studies portrayals of the Spanish Civil War by two women novelists, the well-known Spanish writer Ana María Matute, and the Cuban writer Nivaria Tejera. The novels are similar in that both treat the beginning of the Spanish Civil War from an adolescent girl's perspective, and both are situated on islands, Matute's in Mallorca and Tejera's on Tenerife in the Canary Islands. Schraibman's essay, "Two Spanish Civil War Novels: A Woman's Perspective," reveals other similarities between the two works: both were written at the end of the period of so-called "social realism" in Spain; both present the war as a distant echo of the respective novelists' own youthful experiences; and both have as a key theme the lost father. The possibility of identification of the narrative voice with that of the author provides another parallel between the two works studied.

Janet Pérez's "Behind the Lines: Women Writers in the Spanish Civil War" discusses the preliminary results of a study of some hundred novels by women writers on the Spanish Civil War. The preliminary conclusions are based upon approximately half of that group of novels written by women of different generations, with dates of composition ranging from the time of the war itself until the 1970s. Women writers adhere closely to personal experience for their war narratives but, unlike some male counterparts, seldom glorify or idealize the conflict. Even those who may be classed as ideologues usually concentrate on social and familial concerns. Nearly all present war as hell, and most prefer the reconstruction of small, seem-ingly insignificant moments ignored or scorned by historians. Their sphere is that of the effects of war on the daily and future lives of un-sung and largely unknown individuals, whose collective human his-tory is considered more authentic than the abstract dates and heroes in historians' texts. Psychological and spiritual problems, the varied forms of trial and suffering attendant upon the belligerent state, and the lives shattered long after the conflict's end constitute the preferred focus of women writers.

The death of Franco and the transition to democracy definitively terminated the seemingly endless postwar era for Spain, but rather than consigning the struggle to oblivion, writers and readers in Spain have looked backward with still more avid interest and desire for details. Their thirst for information, combined with the fiftieth an-niversary observances, make this volume especially appropriate. None of the many distinguished specialists included here would claim to have said the last word on this fascinating and polemic event, yet each contribution incorporates the historical advantages of a half century's passage. Occasionally overlapping without repetition, diverging in method without deviating from their single central con-cern, the essays strike a balance between general and specific. As variants of a single major theme reinforced by chronological, geographical, and historical unity and specificity, the several ap-proaches enrich each other, providing further opportunities for com-parison at the same time they furnish the critical apparatus for understanding the many issues and works examined.

Janet Pérez

Reflections of a Civil War Veteran

Abe Osheroff

Spain tore the earth with her nails
When Paris was prettier than ever,
Spain drained her immense tree of blood
When London was grooming, as Pedro Garfías
tells us, her lawn and her swan lakes.
        —Pablo Neruda, "Song to Stalingrad"

It was fifty years ago, yet for those who remember and for those who newly discover it, the Spanish Civil War still exerts a magical power. What was it about that war and the men who fought it that captured the hearts and minds of a whole generation and left so deep a mark on everyone touched by it?

In 1936, the specter of fascism haunted the world. Mussolini had conquered Ethiopia, Japanese militarism had infested China, and Nazi Germany was rearming rapidly. As the gathering storm clouds darkened the sky, fascism struck another blow. The Spanish army rose in rebellion against the legally elected government. Expecting a rapid victory, they had not reckoned with the people of Spain. Workers, peasants, students and intellectuals rallied to the defense of their republic. Although poorly armed, they crushed the rebellion in the major cities of Madrid, Barcelona, and Valencia. Only the intervention of Germany, Italy, and Portugal, and Moorish mercenaries engaged by France saved the rebels. They poured modern arms and thousands of regular army units into Spain and thus transformed the civil war into a war of national independence.

The heroic resistance of the Spanish people gave hope and inspiration to democratic forces all over the world. Madrid glowed like a beacon in the darkness of appeasement and surrender and became the conscience of the world. From that conscience, a new historic phenomenon was born—the International Brigades.

The world communist movement, pursuing the policy of the popular front against fascism, recruited and organized volunteers. Although many recruits were communists, many others were socialists, liberals, and democrats. All were antifascists. There were forty thousand of them from fifty-three countries. For the first time in history, an international crusade of volunteers had assembled to aid an embattled people in its struggle for freedom. And among them were three thousand Americans.

Who were they? Why did they come? Black and white, Jew and Gentile, they came from every corner of the United States. Seamen from the east coast, and longshoremen from the west, miners from West Virginia and farmboys from Iowa, steelworkers from Pennsylvania and meatpackers from Chicago. Furriers, taxicab drivers, artists, writers, students, teachers—a roll call of working, thinking America. Most of them were already veterans of the Great Depression struggles. They had organized trade unions, student organizations, councils of unemployed workers and antifascist demonstrations. Hitler and Mussolini were the incarnation of everything they hated. Spain gave them the opportunity to come to grips with fascism. They took that challenge and they would stain every major battlefield with their blood. Half of the Lincolns remain in Spanish soil.

The Spanish Republicans and the Internationals warned that Guernica, Barcelona, and Madrid in ruins would soon be followed by Warsaw, London, and Rotterdam. Their prophecy was tragically correct. In April 1939, the Nazi Condor Legion marched in Franco's victory parade. Five months later they would be in Warsaw, and World War II, begun in Spain, would engulf all of Europe. Compared to World War II, Spain was a small skirmish. Compared to Hiroshima and Dresden, the bombing of Guernica seemed a "minor act of vandalism," but it shook the world more than any incident in World War II, not because of the power of Picasso's painting, but because Guernica was the first total destruction of an undefended civilian target by aerial bombing. Thus the bombing presaged a new and horrible form of modern warfare soon to come.

The Spanish Civil War brought an explosion of cultural activity. Though many writers felt, as Peruvian César Vallejo, that "the shifts of politics had never depended on what intellectuals said or did," they felt also, as he did, a deep moral, political, and aesthetic need to get involved through their work in active support of one or the other of the ideological positions in conflict.

In Spain, all the ideologies, all the social and political forces, found expression. Culture was alive and well in the midst of a life-and-death struggle to save the Republic. Although not as important as bread and land, culture was one more thing denied to the Spanish people, and once the war broke out, the Spanish masses, mostly illiterate and uneducated, exhibited a greater hunger for culture and knowledge than anyone could have dreamed. Literacy teams went to the fields and trenches to teach peasants and soldiers to read and write. Theaters and concerts played to working-class audiences. One could go on and on, but at the forefront of all this stood poetry. Perhaps poetry was the only thing prepared for the Spanish Civil War.

With very few exceptions, the poets of Spain rallied to the cause of the Republic. Younger poets wrote during breaks in the fighting. Older ones read to the fighting troops or to the rearguard workers in factory and field. Nor was poetic creation limited to known poets. Soldiers who had barely learned to read and write composed and read their first literary efforts to their trench companions. When Republican planes dropped appeals or ultimatums onto the Franco forces, their "bomb" loads often included some poems.

Poetry was everywhere. It became part of the climate in which the war was fought. Even the Franco side used this weapon, and a few of their poets stood out, Gerardo Diego, for example. Poets wrote also in Spain's other languages, Basque, Galician, and above all, Catalan. The total quantity of published poetry was indeed astounding: fifteen to twenty thousand compositions by thousands of different authors. Three quarters of these originated in the Republican zone. In America, we experienced something similar during the Vietnam War, in the antiwar lyrics of rock music, but never on the same scale.

The people of war-ravished Spain spoke and sang in the verse forms of the traditional *romance.* This was basically an oral form of epic poetry consisting of short eight-syllable lines, dependent on assonance and not full rhyme. Why is it that the poem of lyric feeling became the most successful and widespread branch of Spanish literature? A primary reason is that Spain, because of its high rate of illiteracy, had never lost its oral poetic tradition. The new war-inspired poetry was deeply rooted, an extension of the centuries-old folk song. Originating with the peasantry, transformed by strolling minstrels before its adoption by "professional" poets, its general characterics are freedom from idiosyncrasies of highly personal style and above all the power of corresponding to popular taste.

Quickly, the *romance* became an oral newsreel of the streets, the cry of a frightened but heroic people fighting against terrible odds.

Especially in the perilous autumn and winter of 1936, the *romance* strengthened the morale of soldiers and civilians. *Madrileños* sang as they erected barricades against the fascist attack. In November 1936, when the capital appeared doomed to fall, when there was only one gun for every three men, an almost unarmed rabble of civilians sang propaganda verse of the *romance*, and that verse helped inspire them to hold out against waves of *legionarios* and Moors, and to endure the ceaseless bombardment of German and Italian planes.

When in the first days of the war Federico García Lorca was murdered by the fascists in Granada, his Granada, poets of Spain and poets throughout the world knew for whom the bell tolled, and responded to the call of León Felipe:

> And come, poets of the world,
> all the poets of the world,
> all the true poets of the world.
> (Poets with an epic and active sign
> that here we've given to the word and the craft),
> poets of all nations,
> poets of all peoples,
> From large lands
> and from small lands;
> from the white peoples,
> from the black peoples
> from the yellow peoples;
> from the lands that eat with butter
> and from those that eat with oil;
> from those that drink wine,
> from those that drink tea,
> from those that drink beer,
> from those that drink from all the fountains
> and eat at all the tables
>
> but still have a hunger and thirst for justice . . .
> Poets from all the latitudes:
> come here,
> climb up here,
> here, here, here,
> where the politicians can't reach,
> or the bourgeois,
> or the banker,
> or the archbishop,
> or the merchant,
> or the degenerate aristocrat,
> or the buffoon,
> or the beggar,
> or the coward.
> Here, here

> facing great History,
> beneath the light from the stars,
> over the pristine and eternal soil of the world
> and in the very presence of God,
> here,
> let's speak here
> about these REVOLUTIONARY TRANSACTIONS OF SPAIN.
>
> There are two Spains:
> one of forms
> and one of essences.
> One of forms that wear out
> and one of eternal essences.

The finest of Spanish poets were inspired by, and gave inspiration to the heroic Spanish people. They put their work and even their lives on the firing line, and they paid a heavy price. What began with Lorca and ended with the deaths of Antonio Machado and Miguel Hernández was indeed a sorrowful story. Every poet of any consequence—among them Rafael Alberti, Manuel Altolaquirre, José Bergamin, Luis Cernuda, and León Felipe—was either dead or forced to flee into exile. César Vallejo was wrong. That time should always be remembered as a time when poetry did of course make a difference. Though Spanish poets were wiped off the face of Spain, their work, in the words of Carlos Fuentes, "inspired and left a deep mark on Hispanic literature during and after the Spanish tragedy." One has but to read the work of Neruda, Guillén, and Vallejo himself to see that mark.

Still more wrong was British poet Stephen Spender, who was in that war and should have known what it meant to Spaniards to have their dreams turn into a nightmare. Yet fifty years later he wrote, "Of all the tragedies of the war perhaps the greatest was that of the destruction of what was surely a twentieth-century renaissance of all the arts in Spain, particularly by poetry." How myopic this ivory-tower vision of that dirty thing called life! What a disservice to the people's poets, who saw themselves as reflecting and possibly inspiring the tens of thousands of ordinary people who laid down their lives for the political beliefs that animated them. We foreign volunteers, who served in this people's war and sang their songs along with our own, were richly rewarded by the love and gratitude of the Spanish people. This too found expression in their songs. Rafael Alberti wrote:

TO THE INTERNATIONAL BRIGADES

You have come from very far, but what is distance
to your blood which sings without boundary or frontier?
Death is the country which claims you today and forever,
fallen in the fields or cities, death claims you, fallen here.

From one country and another, from the large one, from the small one.
from the one that hardly lends color to the map on the wall;
talking together, simply and anonymously, you have come to join us,
because our roots are in the same dream, because it has nourished us all.

You do not even know the shape and color of our city
where your invincible pledge erects a barricade.
You defend the small piece of earth where you will lie buried,
Meeting death as in a personal encounter, unafraid.

Stay with us, for such is the wish of the very trees, the hillsides,
of each little particle of the all-embracing light.
The same wish moves the sea. You are our Brothers!
At your names Madrid glows, is illumined in the night.
(translated by Katherine Garrison Chapin)

In the Spanish case, the complex relation of literature to history gave rise to more than ten thousand books about the war, its origins, and its aftermath. Most of those books were written by non-Spaniards and range in scope from *Land Tenure in Andalucia in the Eighteenth Century* to the romantic novels of Hemingway and Malraux. Underneath it all is the bedrock of history, the record of human experience. But why bother with the past? Obviously it is one way of getting a job, teaching. It can also provide intellectual titillation, and for some people, diversion from the present. But mainly, it can be used to glorify the past in order to roll back the present, to reinforce the present, or to reform the present and even to project the future. Because of this use, the serious student of history must soon discover that remembrance, discovery and even fabrication all play roles in recording the past. The student will discover too that "to tell it like it was" is neither simple nor easy, but in fact almost impossible. To claim objectivity is to pretend, or to be unconscious of one's inner motivations, prejudices or mindset. This is particularly true of the Spanish Civil War for a number of reasons. It was a labyrinth of ideologies, each with vested interests in how it was recorded. It was fought with incredible passion and ferocity. It was chaotic to the point of making an overall view almost impossible. The participant, the observer, the horde of "tourists," reporters, journalists, poets, and novelists that descended onto the writhing, tortured body of Spain knew very little of the deeply Spanish character of this war. Moreover, with very few exceptions, they came with their own biases and political prejudices. Spanish propagandizing exacerbated the normal fact-fiction problem.

Simone Weill put it very well:

> What is going on in Spain? Over there, everyone has his word to put in, his stories to tell, a judgment to pronounce. Right now, it's in fashion to go on a tour down there, to take in a spot of revolution, and to come back with articles bursting out of your pen. You can't open a newspaper or a magazine any more without coming across accounts of events in Spain. How can all this not be superficial? In the first place a social transformation can only be correctly appreciated as a function of what it means to the daily life of each of those who make up the population. It is not easy to get inside this daily life. Furthermore each day that passes brings new developments. Also, constraint and spontaneity, necessity and idealism are so mixed up that they generate inextricable confusion not only as to the facts, but also in the very consciousness of the actors and spectators in the drama.

Is it any wonder then that myths, legends, and even downright lying should make their way into the so-called historical record? For some of the following questions, the truth is still being contested: Who destroyed Guernica? Who murdered Lorca? What was the nature of the "epic" defense of the Alcazar? Did the POUM (Partido Obrero de Unificación Marxista, a left split off from the Communist party) and anarchists serve France? Did communists betray the Revolution? What was the extent and nature of Soviet aid and the role of the KGB?

The reader may think, "You were there, in the very thick of the fighting. Perhaps you can tell us the truth about that war?" Here I must say that if I limited myself to that experience alone, I could give you a microvision, and a very biased one at that. This is so for several reasons. I was so very young. I knew very little of the language and Spanish culture. I was then a Communist very passionately committed to the fight against Fascism. My only sources of general information were from government and party propanganda, most of which I then believed. The vision of a combat infantryman is limited to the enemy in front and a handful of comrades on either side of him.

My experience in Spain did not qualify me as a historian; that took many years of other experience, breaking with the Communist Party, contemplation, study, dialogue, and perhaps above all, dealing with intelligent students of history in my classes. But there are some truths from that time that I can share. I carried a Russian gun, but wished it were American. I experienced hunger but knew that the civilian population had even less to eat. I saw German and Italian planes in the skies of Spain, and I saw the havoc they played on civilian men, women, and children. I heard Rafael Alberti recite poetry to the troops. I watched young illiterate peasants learning to read and write.

I witnessed a noble, courageous people fighting against overwhelming odds. I experienced their boundless generosity. But above all I remember a time of great love that we gave to and received from this people.

The advantages of the participant as "historian" are obvious. But there are also serious disadvantages. For a person of thought to become a person of action requires the intervention of passion, and that very passion can make one blind to those unpleasant realities that challenge the original thought. But if passion can be blinding, what shall we say of those who lack it, self-blinding to the unpleasant realities of mass hunger, racial and sexual discrimination and exploitation, torture and murder as political instruments, and the possibility of total extinction of life on our planet.

ð

History at its best can tell us only what happened where and when. The why and how are far more elusive, for they involve the subjective aspect of events, the "atmosphere" in which they took place, the way people felt about their lives and times. Their strong feelings (i.e., their passions) were the fuel that drove the locomotive of history. To understand these things we must turn to the art, the music, the poetry and the novels of that time. And also the oral history! The Spanish war as a people's war was the most potent and emotionally engaging focus of the hopes and fears of democratic forces worldwide. But it was also a war in which writers played an important role, inside Spain and internationally, on both sides of the conflict. Many writers put aside their pens and books to spill their blood and give up their lives to defend the Spanish Republic: Ralph Fox, Ralph Bates, John Cornfield, Christopher Cauldwell, and George Orwell, of Britain; Koestler and Gustave Regler, of Germany; Andre Malraux, of France; Ed Rolfe and Alvah Bessie of the United States.

Before dealing briefly with a few of the writers and their works, I will say a few words about literary criticism, and how it should be employed. Formalist critics—such as Barthes—who insist that the text is a self-generating verbal mechanism, independent of cultural contexts, are enraging. Brecht, Sartre, and Thomas Mann are correct when they say that no text lives alone, that the text is very much interrelated with the outside world and the writer's perception of it. Literary discussions, to be meaningful and accessible to more than a few "specialists," should not be confined within the safe and sterile confines of formal analysis—dealing with internal structure, consistency, thematics, tone and symbolism—that dominate the overwhelming majority of academic studies. This, no matter how skillful, is meat-cutting without a carcass. The critic must deal with the difficult, disagreeable, and even dangerous issues of ideology and morality. He must take into account the historic setting in which a work is produced and the diverse problems facing the writer, including his biases and ideological commitment or leanings. He must always remember that literature is by no means the possession of a small group of writers and critics with their own axes to grind, a group that is more or less cannibalistic. Literature should be the possession of its lovers. In the long run they are the best judges.

It is the business of the critic to approach every work with an open mind and in the greatest state of aesthetic receptivity. One has a right to ask of the critic that he allow no bias or preconceived opinion to affect him. At the same time one should also be aware that this is in most cases somewhat utopian or too much to ask. This is particularly true in the case of the Spanish Civil War, a crucible of ideologies and passions.

Yes, the war was many different things to many different people. It answered whatever subjective needs the observer or participant writer brought to it. For the reader this subjectivity and selectivity in choosing or remembering erects barriers that get in the way of making sense of any writing, even of writing about so real and historical an event as the Spanish Civil War.

I have chosen, and want to bring to your attention, the works of a few writers, all of whom were there, two of them as combatants. They were all, whatever their feelings, decent, honest men and independent thinkers who dealt each in his own way with the fact-fiction dilemma, and they resisted ideological constraints and pressure more or less successfully.

George Orwell's *Homage to Catalonia*, became the academic bible of the Spanish Civil War. Those who read Orwell too hastily, and read very little else, think of Orwell as one who "exposed" the Loyalist government and unmasked the Communists. This, of course, made him a reliable witness and very acceptable in an ideologically anticommunist atmosphere. It also brought him under sharp attack from most supporters of the Republic, and this includes the members of the International Brigades, with very few exceptions. Orwell's experience in Spain was limited, extending from December 1936 to May 1937. It covered a small inactive sector of the Aragon front, ending in Barcelona in fighting when government forces clashed with the POUM-anarchist militia. Herbert Matthews says, "Orwell was as brilliant, as honest, as courageous as any man could be; but his politics were completely impractical and his knowledge of what was really happening very slight." Severely wounded, Orwell was pursued by the police and barely succeeded in reaching France. Yet later, from the outside, he could write

> This war, in which I played so ineffectual a part, has left me with memories that are mostly evil, and yet I do not wish that I had missed it. When you have had a glimpse of such a disaster as this—and however it ends the Spanish war will turn out to have been an appalling disaster, quite apart from the slaughter and physical suffering—the result is not necessarily disillusionment and cynicism. Curiously enough the whole experience has left me with not less but more belief in the decency of human beings. And I hope the account I have given is not too misleading. I believe that on such an issue as this no one is or can be completely truthful. It is difficult to be certain about anything except what you have seen with your own eyes, and consciously or unconsciously everyone writes as a partisan. In case I have not said this somewhere earlier in the book I will say it now: beware of my partisanship, my mistakes of fact, and the distortion inevitably caused by my having seen only one corner of the events. And beware of exactly the same things when you read any other book on this period of the Spanish war.

André Malraux headed a group of volunteer French aviators who nearly all got themselves killed at the beginning of the war by flying crates the government picked up second hand, anywhere it could. In Malraux we deal with the problem of the idealist who does not fit into his environment, and, because he is intensely individualistic needs to create his own environment, from the center of which he creates literature. For Malraux this was the life of action. Yet action should be directed toward a just goal, and this presented the dilemma with which Malraux's novel *Man's Hope* attempts to deal. In the words of Magnin (a character in the novel who commands a squadron), "Action . . . always involves injustice," but "it was not in the cause of injustice that he had come to Spain."

Man's Hope has a number of themes: the politics and atmosphere of the Republic, the tragedies involved in fighting, the difficulty of placing personal feelings beneath organizational necessity, and most important, the reasons why the struggle is worthwhile. In the novel, a character says, rather coldly, "What a party wants is to make good, not to find good reasons for its program." For Malraux, this is not good enough; he wants to uncover the good reasons for fighting the war. That these reasons cannot be found in politics is a constant source of comment, and the only answer Malraux can produce is that military necessity and victory unfortunately must come first. García, who is a high-ranking intelligence officer, says to Magnin, "For me, Monsieur Magnin, the whole problem is just this: a popular movement, or a revolution, or even a rebellion, can hold onto its victory only by methods directly opposed to those that gave it victory." Yet this is strange logic indeed, to defend one's aspirations by the very devices that will destroy them, and Magnin is fully aware of the fact: "Organization, discipline—I don't see men giving up their lives for that!" This fundamental paradox of the means to an end lies as bedrock beneath the whole novel. Perhaps this is the reason Malraux textualized his experience in a novel, for only there could he create an environment that could give him peace.

In the introduction to the Grove edition of *Man's Hope*, Herbert Gold compliments Malraux for the great effort he exerted in managing "to transcend the image of himself as shaman in order to think about something else"; by doing so, he accomplished more than Hemingway: "If only Hemingway had been able to forget himself a moment, giving himself time to think about politics." This is somewhat unfair, as *For Whom the Bell Tolls* does contain some penetrating sections on politics, yet there is no doubt that the underlying narrative is shaped mainly by Hemingway's needs. In terms of creating an environment, Hemingway had the advantage of a long-term relationship with Spain. It also encouraged his ideas of masculinity, raw courage and hard drinking. In those parts of his novel dealing with politics, Hemingway was essentially pragmatic: the war had to be won at whatever cost. Tough noncommunist himself, his main character Robert Jordan "was under Communist discipline. Here in Spain the Communists offered the best discipline and the soundest and sanest program for the prosecution of the war." He did not hesitate to attack whoever hampered the war effort inside or outside the Communist Party. Most memorable was his attack on the General Commissar of the International Brigades, Andre Marty, whose purges hurt the morale of those who knew.

Such excursions into politics only break what is essentially a work of romantic fiction, the purpose of which was to commemorate a people he loved and their courageous struggle for justice and freedom. The war itself was not allowed to dominate the author's purpose.

Clearly for Hemingway as for Malraux, it was a vision of man's possibilities that mattered more than the actual circumstances of his existence.

It can be seen that the most famous realist novels produced by the civil war were primarily works that recorded the hopes of their authors. Those hopes were of great merit, and add to the works' appeal, but the novels rest uneasily on the events as they actually occurred. This did not make them intentionally misleading, as is the case with those written for political purposes, but it makes them equally ineffective as documents of the civil war. They recreated the atmospheres that existed in their authors' minds, and could only hint at the collective atmosphere that was such an important part of the struggle.

ॐ

I turn now to two writers who reported on the war from their own personal experiences, Arthur Koestler and Georges Bernanos. Koestler was a Communist when he went to Spain, under orders to write a book from the Republican point of view. The first part of his *Spanish Testament* is clearly written from a Communist perspective. There is no question that the book contains a great deal of truth about fascist terror and the lying nature of facist propaganda. But the book avoids, plays down, or explains away activities by Republicans that might cast a bad light upon them. *Spanish Testament* was published in England by the Left Book Club at a time when Koestler was still a member of the Communist Party, yet it would be over simplification to treat the book as propaganda. On its publication, it was obvious there was a dual nature to the book, an intriguing record of the author's transformation from communist hack at the beginning of the war to his total redefinition of purpose following his release from the Insurgent's Prison in Seville. Koestler wrote later that his time in prison had acquainted him with "a different kind of reality, which had so altered my outlook and values, and altered them so profoundly and unconsciously that during the first days of freedom I was not even aware of it." He had come to realize "that man is a reality, mankind an abstraction; that men cannot be treated as units in operations of political arithmetic because they behave like the symbols for zero and the infinite . . . . that the end justifies the means only within very narrow limits; that ethics is not a function of social utility." He considered that "every single one of these trivial statements was incompatible with the Communist faith that I held." In May 1938, Koestler resigned from the Communist Party.

Georges Beranos was a devout Catholic writer who witnessed large scale mass murder on the island of Majorca in a campaign of terror led by an Italian fascist General and his Spanish cohorts.

> I have seen, seen with my own eyes I tell you . . . . For months in Majorca, killer gangs, swiftly transported from village to village . . . shot down in cold blood for everybody to see, thousands of persons held to be suspect, but against whom the military tribunal could not produce the faintest legal allegation. The Bishop of Palma was informed of this fact. Nevertheless he showed himself to be on the side of the executioners whenever he could—though it was notorious that some of them had the blood of a hundred men on their hands. Will this be the Church's attitude tomorrow?

These two writers represent the interesting phenomenon of conversion, which might occur when truth came into conflict with ideology. The one, finding his truth incompatible with his ideology, renounces communism, the other, a devout Catholic, is horrified by this church's failure to be Christian.

The reaction of writers in Spain to each other sheds some additional light on our subject. In discussions of *For Whom the Bell Tolls*, they disagree:

> George Seldes, correspondent: "It's one of the greatest things written about the war."
>
> Alvah Bessie, volunteer: "I don't think it had anything to do with the Spanish War."
>
> Hemingway, author: "Greatest thing I ever wrote. All true, every word of it. I don't understand politics—it hurts my head."

Of *Volunteer in Spain*, by John Sommerfield, who died defending Madrid, George Orwell says

> Mr. Sommerfield was a member of the International Brigade and fought heroically in the defence of Madrid. *Volunteer in Spain* is the record of his experiences. Seeing that the International Brigade is in some sense fighting for all of us—a thin line of suffering and often ill-armed human beings standing between barbarism and at least comparative decency—it may seem ungracious to say that this book is a piece of sentimental tripe; but so it is. We shall almost certainly get some good books from members of the International Brigades, but we shall have to wait for them until the war is over.

Cyrus Connally responds, "John Sommerfield was there to fight for an idea. It is fortunate for us that he was also an excellent writer."

In 1952, the Veterans of the Abraham Lincoln Brigade published an anthology of civil war writing called *Heart of Spain*. The editor was writer Alvah Bessie, a good, honest, and brave man. In the introduction he wrote:

> We would particularly like to explain our reasons for the omission of work by Hemingway. His talent and personal support he rendered to the Loyalist cause were shockingly betrayed in his work *For Whom the Bell Tolls* in which the Spanish people are cruelly represented and leaders of the International Brigades maliciously slandered. The novel in its total impact presented an unforgiveable distortion of the meaning of the struggle in Spain. Under the name and prestige of Hemingway important aid was given to humanity's worst enemies.

Fortunately, the book had a very small circulation. Alvah lived to regret it. And Hemingway was big enough to forgive him eventually.

CONCLUSION

It remains difficult to separate myth from reality when dealing with the tension, the urgency, and the life-and-death drama of those tragic but noble years.

Shall we ever be so free of the politics of the Spanish Civil War that we can judge its literature only by aesthetic criteria? And should we ever do so? Those who read it must always remember the six hundred thousand who died, the one million thrown into concentration camps, and the four hundred thousand forced into exile.

We fought the good, if not the perfect, fight and we lost. Fascism conquered, but it never convinced. Lorca, Machado, Hernández, Alberti, and all the others dead or exiled, are still with us. This occasion is witness, and last year three hundred campuses commemorated the fiftieth anniversary of the Spanish Civil War.

Dialogues between Painting and Narrative: From Goya to Malraux

Edouard Morot-Sir

In his essay "Néocritique," André Malraux made a very justifiable plea to his future critics: The unique duty of criticism is to give a new presence to a work of art, that is, to make sensible its values and to show that that kind of artistic presence is actually a more or less powerful interrogation that establishes a unique and original relation between the world and the artist's language or voice. Thus I shall try to elaborate the power of the presence that *L'Espoir*, translated into English as *Man's Hope*, has kept today for our readings half a century later as a permanent memorial to the Spanish Civil War.

Indeed, as Camus said, Malraux's novel is an inspired *reportage* on the Spanish Civil War, written in a few months in the middle of this tragic conflict. It is also a historical *chronique* addressed to future historians, and a historical vision based upon facts experienced by the author or documented directly. Historians have paid tribute to Malraux's objectivity, even when small events are blown out of proportion. Furthermore *L'Espoir* is a grandiose epic fresco, a sort of one-sided *Iliad*, with new Trojans fighting for the survival of their city. Finally, it is a concrete political and revolutionary ethic, a meditation on human fate, a lucid analysis of human action, its nobleness and its servitudes, an act of faith in Man's dignity.

All those readings are possible and advisable. They can be mixed. However *L'Espoir* is more than any of those linguistic and artistic achievements. Malraux told Gaetan Picon that beyond its specific characters (narration, characterization, thematization) a novel was a challenge to life, an act of recreation competing with life itself (Picon, 38). It is why I strongly believe that *L'Espoir* should be read ultimately as an *Orphic and Pindaric poem* of hope and a song of victory. It is an act of entire admiration addressed to Spain, and in a paradoxical way the poem incarnates the voice of Spain herself, affirming her dignity and her life as Hope. Alvear, one of the heroes of *L'Espoir* says to the Italian Scali, a former historian of art: "Il y a un espoir terrible et profond en l'homme . . . ,"[1] and he immediately associates that universal hope with the feeling of revolt and indictment. Hope is Humanity itself in the deepest expression of its nature. The English translation of the title "Man's Hope" is in a way pleonastic, because, for Malraux, Humanity *is* interrogating hope; it is what Spain is saying to her people and to the world in that first part of her Civil War. Apocalypse is not only the Book of Revelation, it is the Book of Hope. Apocalypse and Hope express the two sides of the same experience of life as creation.

In French hope is designated by two words, *espérance* and *espoir*. The first word is often chosen to suggest the metaphysical aspect of hope. For example, *espérance* was the term preferred to designate one of the three "theological virtues," with *foi* and *charité*. *Espoir*, in contrast, is usually reserved to limited hopes within the human world. Malraux's choice of *espoir* against *espérance* is highly significant in its implicit rejection of Christian theology. It means that when humanity is reduced to its own world, *espoir* is the *agnostic experience per se*. Then the three medieval virtues are one and the same: *Espoir* is human faith, and *charity* finds another denomination, *fraternity*, that is hope in action, that is Spain herself.

For Malraux, Spain is not a geographical and historical entity. It is a cultural force, which finds its deepest moments of creation in art. At the same time, it is the essence of the Spanish people. The occurrence of the word people (*peuple*) means that, in 1936, even when Malraux thinks that the alliance with the communists against fascism is a historical fatality, he does not believe that the Marxist duality *bourgeois/prolétariat* is basic. If for him the word *people* referred to some social group, it would be to the *peasants*. One will remember that Magnin, the main personification of Malraux in *L'Espoir*, mentions his strong attraction to the peasants. The peasant who accompanies him to show the hidden place of a fascist airfield takes on a symbolic value. I do not hesitate to say that in that period of revolutionary fighting Malraux was a premature gaullist. In 1933 he was saying that the French people feel threatened, not in their class, but in their existence as nation.[2] The people are the real mediators between individuals—whatever their social function may be—and the nation is the eternal value of hope. In *L'Homme précaire et la littérature* he declares that the true topic of *Brothers Karamozov* is Evil. One could say that the true topic and the true hero of *L'Espoir* is Spain as a unique and universal incarnation of hope.

In 1938 the first critics of *L'Espoir*, all of them, made the famous antinomy "*Etre et Faire*," translated wrongly as "Action and Reaction" (a better translation could be "Being and Acting"), the central theme and structure of *L'Espoir*. From an ethical point of view, those critics were right. However, most of them forgot the artistic antinomy that inspires the work itself, dominates the agnostic world of art since the Renaissance, and is at the core of modernity: *Seeing and Hearing*, with their two complementary manifestations, Light and Darkness, Sound and Silence. When Malraux says "Tout est signe" (*La Condition humaine*, 452), he means that all human experiences are sensorial marks, images developing themselves into pairs in the world of the Imaginary.[3] He said also, "Notre siècle, comme le 13ème siecle, est un siecle d'images."[4] Among images the visual and the aural ones dominate our agnostic culture. Consequently, the arts that become prevalent for our period will be painting and literature, the art of vision and the art of voice, both looking for the other.

Thus one will not be surprised if Malraux, writing in French on behalf of Spain, and seeking to restore her authentic voice, chose as intercessor a Spanish artist, not a writer, but a painter, and for him the true Spanish artist, Francisco de Goya y Lucientes. In *La Métamorphose des dieux* he notes that painting became the privileged art of demiurgy (337). Later, he underlines what has been, since the eighteenth century, the great complicity between painting and the novel: "C'est la fiction qui fait de la peinture un art majeur."[5] In 1938, many critics noticed a certain presence of Goya in *L'Espoir*, but without exploring it, quoting also Velásquez and El Greco. I would like to recognize, however, the perspicacity of Georges Altman and Marius Richard, who compared Goya's *The Third of May 1808* to the execution of Hernández at the fall of Toledo.[6]

Malraux turned himself to the world of literature to find a second accoucheur who would help him to give to the voice of Spain its thematic projection: Miguel de Unamuno. *L'Espoir's* pages devoted to Unamuno's complex behavior during the first months of the Civil War are well known, but too often are interpreted as a subtle condemnation of the philosopher of *The Tragic Sense of Life*.

Malraux denounces the weak conduct of Unamuno as pure intellectual, but he does not refuse his ideas as such. Far from it! I do not hesitate to state that, among the thinkers who preceded Malraux immediately, and whom he knew well, Unamuno was closer to him than essayists like Spengler or Frobenius. Unamuno added to Goya's visions a theoretical voice, even if vision remains more powerful and convincing than speculative declarations. Dialogues in *L'Espoir,* as exchanges of ideas and intellectual clarifications, are always surrounded and permeated by visions that give to abstract expressions their ultimate fascination. Ideas are subordinated to images; they help to build a myth, not the contrary. That is why, in my own judgment, when Unamuno's presence can be felt, Goya remains for Malraux the great mediator, his paintings and drawings permitting the novelist of *L'Espoir* to find the right style and to express the fundamental quality of Spain.

I will make one last remark before analyzing in detail the Goya/Malraux correspondences. In a rather ironical way, E. Gombrich said that the true Malraux's myth was that of humanity being a super-Picasso, creating ceaselessly new forms.[7] There is an element of truth in this remark, all the more so since Goya was one of Picasso's most admired painters. Nevertheless, in Malraux's perspective, Goya inaugurated our modern period, whereas Picasso was living at its end and was already possessed by the demon of chance: with him, human values had become occasions for superb free plays; hope was dissipated into imaginary games. By contrast, Goya taught the modern world that there was no hope without metaphysical anguish, that is the consciousness of the human condition. The sense of value is felt tragically by the modern spirit, for which moral dignity and artistic dignity are one and the same. Malraux terms that modern experience the "rupture of consciousness," meaning that for the modern man, in order to be conscious, he must experience a rupture between mankind's creations and the world as first and unknown creation. Goya was a moralist as "the prophet of irremediable" (*Drawings from the Prado,* 43). He was the first artist who expressed that moral and artistic rupture and who found the proper techniques and themes to express it. He was the right model to follow. He crucified himself on the cross of history, whereas Picasso was an unbound and clownish Goya-Prometheus condemned to convert art into a fantastic parody of itself. In *L'Espoir* as well as in other works, Malraux remains in spiritual kinship with Goya.

It is important to remember that in 1939 Malraux alluded to the project of giving a continuation to *L'Espoir,* on a larger scale, he said, less political, more metaphysical. Later the same year he wrote that he had changed his mind: "I am giving up on the second book on Spain: its themes will be transferred to the French book; problems of war, life, and death are not national . . . " (*Via Malraux,* 256). Yes, indeed, but they are felt through nations, through national voices.

When Malraux could not stay within national borders, he gave up the form of the novel and wrote meditations on art in a dialogue transcending nations and times, but without abolishing them.

Goya takes a central place in Malraux's meditation on art. He is omnipresent in *Les Voix du silence* and in the three volumes of *La Métamorphose des dieux*, where there are many references to Goya's works and their specific signification at the dawn of the modern ages. Furthermore, Malraux devoted to Goya a very important essay in 1947, *Goya, les dessins du Prado*.[8] In 1950, the essay was extended and received a new title, *Saturne, essai sur Goya*. A new edition in 1978 was titled *Saturne, le destin, l'art et Goya* (English translation, *Saturn*, by C. W. Chilton). One could object to my present purpose by saying that *L'Espoir* precedes all those writings by almost ten years. My answer is simple. First André Malraux began his reflections on art very early, actually during the twenties; in the thirties he was already working on what he called then "the psychology of art." Second, a brief allusion in a letter to Eddy du Perron in 1929 suggests that as early as *La Tentation de l'Occident*, Malraux was conscious of Goya's art and its originality:

> "Plus ça va et plus je me rends compte de mon indifférence foncière a l'égard de ce que les bonnes gens appellent 'l'art du roman' . . . il y a des gens qui ont quelque chose à exprimer et qui ne font jamais des chefs d'oeuvre (Montaigne, Pascal, Goya, les sculpteurs de Chartres) parce qu'on ne domine pas une passion qui attaque le monde; et il y a ceux qui 'font des objets.'"[9]

The enumeration in the middle of which Goya appears is revealing by itself. He is assimilated to the greatest French moralists and to the medieval sculptors. He is understood already as an artist whose passion is to challenge the world, to accuse it, to condemn it. In the Preface to *Saturne* Malraux will say again,

> Goya, like Pascal, was famous for his talent, but a genius only to posterity. His genius lies not only in having broken with the demand for harmony and having taken horror for his province, it lies in having discovered a style the equal of the great religious styles.

Goya is mentioned in other series. Among them let us quote "Goya, Van Gogh, Dostoevsky" (*Voices of Silence*, 417) and this sort of abridged Imaginary Symposium: "Dante, Shakespeare, Cervantes, Michel Angelo, Titian, Rembrandt, and Goya" (*Voices*, 489). May I do what Malraux would not have dared to do, at least explicitly, and to complete that enumeration, add his name, as Malraux the novelist-curator-coordinator of the Imaginary Museum-Library?

Why is such a unique place reserved to Goya? Malraux answers, "Goya foreshadows all modern art. His task is to cry aloud the anguish of man forshaken by God" (*Voices,* 88), and to show that behind the most sinister situation, "there is a sort of call for hope" (André Malraux, 18). Nevertheless, there are two more direct reasons for Malraux's choice. First, when one speaks of Spain threatened again by a new destructive force, the Goya of *The Third of May 1808* would be the most natural mediator. Surely Velásquez, El Greco, and others belong to the spirit of Spain as did Goya, but they are not as typical, and they cannot be identified with Spain's coming to modernity. Second, André Malraux recognized in Goya his elder brother, and in Goya's works, a unique experience of artistic fraternity. When reading and rereading simultaneously *L'Espoir* and *Saturne*, confronting also all those enthusiastic references to Goya in his works on art, I had a very strong feeling that it was like I was listening to Malraux's inner voice trying to formulate his own conceptions of art and his thematic or technical decisions concerning his own works.

Goya never looked for an aesthetics of beauty. He opposes himself to Raphaël and Poussin. His feverish and impatient brushstroke does not aim at masterpieces. It seeks metaphysical *density*. In the following sentence Malraux sums up Goya's ideal as well as his own ideal, while writing transposes the movement of the brush on the white sheet: "Goya did symbolize, he exposed [in French *il révéle*], using a broken, breathless, manner [in French *écriture*] which made all the drawings of his time seem decoration" (*Saturn,* 125). In the first lines of *Saturne* Malraux declares, "His dream, his reality, his style, even that break in the pencil-line [I would prefer to say: brushstroke] by which his workmanship can be recognized at first glance—all were his own creation"(*Saturn,* 125). Such is the way to obtain density: by break. Malraux says *brisure* (rupture) and even more often *déchirure* (rent).

That broken style leads to the art of accents or demonstrative gestures. Malraux notes that the art of the painter and the art of the novelist are the same (*Voices,* 295). They experience details as accents and put them within ensembles conjured up by imagination. It is a style of sketch. Goya rejects the continuous line, the arabesque that expresses the confidence in a united universe under the supervision of God, and he eliminates the "*contour*" of persons and objects. Animate or inanimate beings should not be separated from the background, nor projected in a sort of front of stage in the guise of the Renaissance painters telling their stories, or of the nineteenth-century novelist producing his characters in front of descriptions. For Goya, painting in its totality is a matter of tension between forward and backward planes: "Bursting into anger over 'lines,' he muttered that there was really no such thing and that all he was aware of was 'advancing and retiring planes'" (*Drawings*, 33). Effects of density and tension, of emptiness and fullness, result from the movement of planes contrasting each other, as empty place calls for plenitude. Goya is the master of dissonance: dissonance is the only possible perception, the true rendering of beings and things in a world separated from God.

Beyond the contrast of colors, any kind of dissonance belongs to the basic opposition of white and black: "Although among the greatest colorists [Goya] was to observe that 'in Nature there is only black and white'" (*Drawings*, 37). Thus the tension between planes is rendered ultimately by the conflict of light and darkness. Actually, "in Goya there is not light, only lighting" (*Drawings*, 35); that is to say, the power of lighting is trying to spread against the fundamental power of eternal darkness. Malraux tells us that Picasso admired Goya's "black paintings," and he recognized in Goya the great poet of Western shadow. After Titian and Rembrandt, Goya made of darkness a haunted world where white carries on an uninterrupted fight against permeating black. A remark in *The Voices of Silence* gives the key to that mysterious action of the broken brushstroke between black and white. After evoking Michaelangelo, Titian, Rubens, and Rembrandt, linking humanity with the universe, Malraux adds to his list Goya, "flinging [men] his gift of darkness"; then he concludes, "As for the art of today—does it not tend to bring to men only that scission of consciousness, whence it took its rise?" (*Voices*, 602).

Such is the secret link that unites Goya's technique of the broken gesture of the brushstroke to the sense of primeval darkness. In its inner tension between humanity and the world, consciousness, in its own permanent tearing, is the modern spirit of interrogation. Goya's paintings opened on a world of disharmony and ignorance, a world of reason oriented toward the Unknown; they were metaphysical agnostic experiences. In a tragic paradox, they turned toward transcendence at the very moment when they felt their separation, their extreme solitude. Goya's universe is unable to reach serenity. It is fatally a world of war for which the only way to freedom is destruction (Cf. *Voices*, 358–59).

Two manners of being express, at the same time, the fight of art against the created universe, and human victory in its defeat itself: monsters and masks. Monsters make visible and free humanity from its inner demons. As they typify, masks are the true intercessors of the Unknown; they constitute a true style by itself between dream and reality; they are not covering a face; they are actual expressions of life and death; they are Saturnian creations. As state director of the Absurd, Goya replaced the Great Opera of the Renaissance by a dramatic carnival of masked monsters presided over by Saturn, God of metamorphoses and fascination. One could add that Goya announced the novel of the modern ages. Referring to Baudelaire's formula applied to Goya, Malraux says, "Sans doute tout personnage est-il un monstre viable; tout grand roman l'est bien davantage, malgré tous les plans de l'auteur" (*L'Homme précaire,* 139–40).

Must we apply that expression of "*monstre viable*" to *L'Espoir?* Must we see in *L'Espoir* a verbal expression of Goya's *Disasters of War,* of his last drawings, and more specifically of the two paintings into which Goya incarnated Spain in her revolutionary spirit, her sense of sacrifice and her hope: *The Second* a n d *The Third of May 1808?* Everybody, André Malraux included, prefers *The Third of May* to *The Second of May,* feeling that the insurrection against Napoleon's Mameluks keeps the conventional aspect of war paintings, of powerful warriors on their horses; rebels look so little compared to Napoleon's soldiers! Maybe Goya intended to emphasize that contrast, and to attract attention to the less visible and the most admirable. It has been said that *The Second of May* is a painting without a central hero. The people of Spain, the masses, are the true protagonists. However, I do not plan to play the Devil's advocate. I agree that *The Third of May* has a metaphysical dimension that it is difficult to find in *The Second of May.* Let us listen to Malraux; references to *The Third of May* appear and reappear in his works on art and in interviews. The following are some of his most typical comments:

> This is one of the most dramatic paintings which exists. But when we look at it we do not look at an execution. (Suarès, 153)

That theme is also underlined in *L'Intemporel.* It is not a shooting, "it is spots reunited along a certain order" (150).

Those spots constitute an autonomous universe,

> it arouses a secret exaltation (151).

> it is an appeal to the world (152).

> . . . The arms of the man shot . . . do not hang down, they are stretched upward; like a modern novelist Goya knew that laughter can express the anguish of a condemned man better than tears (Saturn, 125).

> Is *The Shootings of May Third* superior to *The Dos de Mayo,* its companion picture, because it is better painted or not, rather because implicit in it is a vision of Spanish common cause of martyrdom, and of that secret fire which glows in the gaze of Goya's monsters? (*Voices,* 590).

> ". . . *The Third of May* is a lay crucifixion. It evokes the fraternity of the victims, a Christian world without Grace. . . . Though the ideas behind *The Shootings of May*

Third are Justice, the People, and the Nation the attitude of the victims bring to mind a Crucifixion; that dark underworld in which Goya's art struck root has nothing in common with the brave new world of Rationalism. (*Voices*, 122)

Malraux gave the most elaborate reading of *The Third of May* through the voice of Picasso in *La Tête d'obsidienne.*

Guernica l' [Picasso] avait mené à étudier les *Fusillades du 3 Mai.* "Le ciel noir, il n'est pas un ciel, il est du noir. L'éclairage, il y en a deux. Un qu'on ne comprend pas. Il éclaire tout, comme un clair de lune: la sierra, le clocher, les fusilleurs qui devraient être à contre-jour. Mais il éclaire bien plus que la lune. Il n'a pas sa couleur. Et puis, il y a l'énorme lanterne par terre, au centre. Elle, qu'est-ce qu'elle éclaire? Le type aux bras dressés, le martyr. Vous regarderez bien: elle n'éclaire que lui. La lanterne, c'est la Mort. Pourquoi? On ne sait pas. Goya non plus. Mais Goya, lui, iL sait que ça doit être comme ça."

[André Malraux answers:] "J'ai toujours eu l'impression d'un tableau envoûté. Envoûté par quel surnaturel, je ne sais pas."[10] Malraux refers to the *V* of Churchill and de Gaulle. Nevertheless the universality and transcendence of *The Third of May* remains that of Spain, because "the voice which fills his deepening silence was no longer his own; it was the lost voice of Spain herself" (*Drawings*, 18)

Finally, let us quote the most fascinating remark in *Saturn*:

The Third of May 1808 and some of the *Disasters* call to mind Dostoïevsky's great novels. The two artists were suddenly cut off from men by the irremediable (and the House of the Deafman would be a fitting habitation for the Karamazoffs . . .). Dostoïevsky's novels were, and still are, narratives, but they become a sermon obscurely and vehemently expressed as all modern prophecy is. What is a prophet, if he is not a man who speaks to others in order to . . . give them the world of Truth? (*Saturn*, 113–14)

In the following paragraph, Malraux alludes to the Christian sculptors he already mentioned in his letter to Eddy du Perron in 1929, and he concludes, "Like them Goya meant to find again the sacred language."

Now is the time to ask ourselves if *L'Espoir* does not belong to the same cultural and artistic constellation, and thus, the time to become conscious that the same creative forces inspire *The Third of May*, Goya's last works, and Malraux's *L'Espoir*.

Is it not puzzling that a painter was chosen as a model by a writer? For Malraux, nothing is more normal than that sort of intercommunication between the arts, and especially, in our culture, between painting and literature. Each one is, in one way, the metaphor of the other; each one teaches the other how to express itself through a different code and different practical rules. Malraux expects that the spectator will hear the voice by which lines and colors find their unity as well as that reader will look for the vision that can crown a noisy

swarm of words. More than any other novelist of the twentieth century, Malraux took seriously that confrontation and challenge between painting and literature, one aspiring to become the other in its
own originality and through the contrast of instant and continuity.

If my hypothesis is correct, the critic must find in *L'Espoir*'s composition and development the presence of Goya's techniques and
themes, but transposed into the universe of language, which is made
of meaningful sounds. My analysis will be conducted at four main
levels: the literary projection of Goya's broken style, the transpositions of the *Disasters of War* and *The Third of May*, the sketching of
the world of sounds, and the awareness of Space as the fight against
the primitive darkness.

Malraux's critics agree that his art is controlled by a rhetoric of the
ellipsis, but they never go back to the source of that stylistic decision.
Actually, Malraux practised all sorts of techniques that give to the
microtext or the macrotext its density and concentration—techniques such as abruption, suspense, paradox and hyperbole, which
should be added to ellipsis. The Malrucian fragmentary vision of
framing events and characters have already been studied,[11] as well as
his will to change the usual form of statement by which short or long
texts tend to express knowledge and information into the powerful art
of interrogation. There is no need to repeat what has already been
well said. Nevertheless, I would like to go deeper into that stylistic
analysis and show how, with Goya's leadership, Malraux has broken a
rhetoric dominated by the ideal of continuity into a rhetoric of accents, how he has substituted for the art of binding propositions in
harmonious chains, *the art of apposition,* as if words, sentences, para-
graphs, chapters were subsisting as independent units, condensed
universes of discourse, different and yet analogous. From moment to
moment, language closes up within itself instead of pretending to
communicate with the absolute reality of God. To take another
favored Malrucian word, every moment of language is a metamor-
phosis seeking to be different from any other one. It is why any perception is more than a fragmentation: It is a "*déchirure,*" a tear, a
rupture conscious of itself. Objects and beings witness that experience of break within language. For example, Malraux sees trees
tearing up the sky (*La Voix royale,* 161). By the very fact that they are
aspects of consciousness, characters are tensed ruptures between
themselves and the world, and inside themselves. Goya's broken
brushstroke is transposed into the broken voice of human consciousness, of which language is the unfaithful projection. Condemned to
the principle of continuity that governs grammars and logics of the

human languages, especially Western languages, the true writer, seeking his inspiration in the painter's works, applies his creative energy to the destruction of language, but in that enterprise he is limited by the requirement of communication. The Malrucian movement and assembling of words experiences then a living paradox. It consists in breaking verbal continuity, but respecting its coherence. Malraux calls accent that stylistic experience as emphasis and rupture. Such is also the meaning of the omnipresence of superlativism, which underlines the uniqueness of events and beings and takes them out of their serial existence or their group. It is a way to break the flux of narratives and closing of society.

Examples of that technique can be sampled upon each page of *L'Espoir*. We may quote two:

> Pour la première fois, libéraux, hommes de l'U.G.T. et de la C.N.T., anarchistes, républicains, syndicalistes, socialistes, couraient ensemble vers les mitrailleuses ennemies.[12]
>
> . . . et pour la première fois au monde, les hommes de toutes les nations mélés en formation de combat chantaient l'Internationale.[13]

In Malraux's works, everything happens for the first time in a unique rupture of consciousness. That rupture is symbolized by the famous antinomy "*Etre et Faire*" (Being and Acting). Actually, Malraux refers to the rupture between being and acting, and to their interactions. That also explains in the novel the breaking between narrative description and reflection. There are a few important chapters devoted to reflection as conversations between characters, but every personage in himself (I do not say "herself" because there are no women in *L'Espoir* except by collective reference) is torn out between his action and the perception of it. Ultimately, the rupture of consciousness is experienced at the pure intellectual level. Malraux does not put his thoughts into logical order, into demonstrations. He throws them as sparking independent units. Communications through conversations are simply exchanges of thought, rebounding echoes. Aphorisms are found everywhere. Here are just a few samples: "Le courage est un problème de organisation,"[14] and the famous "*Toute action est manichéenne. Et toute politique.*"[15]

The break of language is the perfect means to express the disasters of war, to use Goya's terms. All kinds of war atrocities are present in *L'Espoir*. One will never forget the visit to the hospital and its dreadful details, the sufferings of Jaime when he is blind, the description of Madrid when the city is bombed by Franco's airforce. Almost every page expresses a kind of Goya's horror. There is that lucid, pitiless and general remark with its sinister bearings: "si la torture apparaît souvent dans la guerre, c'est aussi—parce qu'elle semble la seule réponse à la trahison et à la cruauté."[16] The sequence of the flamethrower is by itself a superGoya. I quote only one fragment:

> La gerbe d'essence crépitante avançait pas à pas, et la frénésie des miliciens était multipliée par ses flammes bleuâtres et convulsives qui envoyaient gigoter sur les murs des grappes d'ombres affolées, tout un déchaînement de fantômes étirés autour de la folie des hommes vivants. Et les hommes comptaient moins que ces ombres folles, moins que ce brouillard suffocant qui transformait tout en silhouettes, moins que ce grésillement sauvage de flammes et d'eau, moins que les petits gémissements aboyés d'un brûlé.[17]

I am not the first one to have noticed that the execution of the prisoners after the fall of Toledo is authentic *Third of May.*

> ... Le plus affreux, des prisonniers, c'est leur courage. ... On s'habitue, à droite à tuer, à gauche, à être tué. ... Avec le même mouvement que celui des fusils qui se lèvent, il lève le poing pour le salut du Front populaire. C'est un petit homme chétif, qui ressemble aux olives noires. Hernandez regarde cette main dont les doigts seront avant une minute crispés dans la terre ...[18]

Painting refers indirectly to sounds. Every Goya picture or drawing "speaks" in its own manner. One is forced to "hear" the cry of the little guy of *The Third of May* or the tumultuous crowd of the *Burial of the Sardine:* sound accompanies vision. Nevertheless language has a superiority over painting: it can refer directly to sounds; it can describe them. Malraux the novelist takes advantage of that situation that relates language and hearing, but with the Goya style of the broken brushstroke. *L'Espoir* is full of what I propose to call *audiosketches.* André Malraux is almost obsessively heedful of war's noises combined with the noises of nature, with human voices, and with music as the supreme contemplative art. In *L'Espoir* the reader hears the multiple voices of Spain, very often expressed in striking foreshadowings either separately in their pure aural existence, or associated with the visual or the olfactive world. Here are a few samples:

> Le canon battait régulièrement comme le coeur de cette foule au-dessus des minces coups de fusil qui partaient de toutes les fenêtres et de toutes les portes, au-dessus des cris, de l'odeur des pierres chaudes et de bitume qui montait de Madrid.[19]

> La fenêtre était ouverte: accompagnant le roulement des gros osselets d'Espagne, un martèlement entra, aussi net que celui des fers de chevaux, mais ordonné comme celui des battoirs et des forges: c'était le piétinement assourdi des troupes.[20]

> ... [Alvear] lisait avec lenteur, avec un sens du rythme d'autant plus saisissant que la voix était sans timbre, aussi visible qu'une source. Le bruit assourdi des pas de fuite dans la rue, les détonations lointaines, tous les bruits de la nuit et du jour que Scali sentait encore collés à lui, semblant tourner comme des animaux inquiets autour de cette voix engagée déja dans la mort.[21]

> ... Une explosion toute proche fit sauter les porte-plumes sur la table. Les tuiles retombèrent sur les toits éloignés, et sous la volée des pas d'un groupe qui fuyait. Il y

eut une seconde de silence, puis un cri extraordinairement grinçant raya la nuit; puis le silence.[22]

. . . Shade écoutait de toute son attention ce son venu de très loin dans le temps, sauvagement accordé au monde du feu: il semblait qu'après une phrase périodiquement prononcée, la rue entière, en matière de réponse, imitait le battement des tambours funèbres: Dong-tongon—Dong.[23]

. . . Les femmes pleuraient sans un geste, et le cortege semblait fuir l'étrange silence des montagnes, avec son bruit de sabot, entre l'éternel cri des rapaces et le bruit clandestin des sanglots.[24]

The audiosketch is everywhere in the powerful accent of microexpression. Nevertheless, it is always part of the larger and deep rhythm of the succession of scenes. Here are two typical examples: The last chapter of "*Etre et Faire*" begins this way: "Un chant de merle s'élève, reste suspendu comme une question—un autre lui répond. Le premier reprend, pose une question, plus inquiète, le second proteste furieusement, et des éclats de rire passent à travers la brume."[25] Malraux tells us that the blackbirds are Siry and Kogan of the first International Brigade. The Brigade is attacking the Moors, and finally breaks their lines. The chapter ends: "Ebloui, un merle chante. Quelque part dans la brume, Kogan qui saigne sur les feuilles mouillées, un coup de baïonnette dans la cuisse, répond pour les blessés et pour les morts."[26] Music, as expression of hope, triumphs over the destructive noises of war. Any reader will remember the last chapter of *L'Espoir* which is a homage to music as the purest expression of consciousness.[27] Here is *L'Espoir*'s final paragraph:

Ces mouvements musicaux (Beethoven's) qui se succédaient, roulés dans son passé, parlaient comme eût pu parler cette ville qui jadis avait arrêté les Maures, et ce ciel et ces champs éternels. Manuel entendait pour la première fois la voix de ce qui est plus grave que le sang des hommes, plus inquiétant que leur présence sur la terre: —la possibilité infinie de leur destin; et il sentait en lui cette présence mêlée au bruit des ruisseaux et aux pas des prisonniers, permanente et profonde comme le battement de son coeur.[28]

For Manuel and thus for the author, music expresses hope as the highest moment of human consciousness, and it is the voice of Spain, identified with life and its rhythms, covering all the noises of war and giving them their profound sense.

Nevertheless the universe of sounds, in its chaotic manifestations or its harmonious ecstasies, is itself dominated by the universe of vision. The opposition sound/silence refers to the eternal tension of light and darkness, day and night, which inscribes Humanity onto the Cosmos, and makes of Mankind's consciousness a paradoxical vision aspiring to the peace of night. There Malraux is more Goya than ever! He says that Saturn as fire was waiting for Goya; one could add that Saturn was also expecting Malraux to sing the metaphysical profundity of that transtemporal moment when the world was just darkness and light.

   Maybe the most tragic situation of Humanity is to be killed in full lighting. A foreign *miliciano* asks Hernández: "Crois-tu qu'on fusille avec des phares? Et sans attendre la réponse: —Etre fusillé pendant qu'un phare t'éclaire . . . "[29] It is obvious that, in writing those lines, Malraux had in mind the lantern of *The Third of May*. Light is the consciousness of Death. It also changes the world into dramatic scenery: "Dans la pleine lumière des lampes électriques, Madrid, costumée de tous les déguisements de la révolution était un immense studio nocturne."[30] There is no light without darkness. As in Goya's paintings and drawings, the brilliance of light emerges from the darkest depth of the background. Malraux speaks of a light coming from elsewhere, but it does not come from God; it bursts out of the original darkness. Light is a double experience of death and life, of threat and fraternity, of anguish and hope. Readers of *L'Espoir* cannot forget the extraordinary moment in the airplane when it is pursued by a D.C.A. spotlight: "La fraternité des armes remplit la carlingue avec cette lumière menaçante: pour la première fois depuis qu'ils sont partis, ces hommes *se voient*."[31] One of the best examples of the menacing aspect of light and fire joined together is a vision of Madrid burned down by fascist planes—a great Goya's vision!

> Dans une grande déchirure des rochers venait d'apparaitre l'autre versant de la Sierra; au-dessus de Madrid peu visible dans l'étendue grise, d'immenses fumées sombres montaient avec une lenteur désolée. Manuel savait ce qu'elles signifiaient. La ville disparaissait derrière son incendie, comme les navires de guerre derrière les rideaux de leurs fumées de combat. Venues de brasiers nombreux dont n'apparaissait pas le moindre rougeoiement, les colonnes de fumées montaient se désagréger jusqu'au centre du ciel gris; tous les nuages semblaient nés de cet immense foyer déployé dans le sens de la marche, et les souffrances accumulées sur la fine ligne blanche de Madrid entre les bois emplissaient le ciel immense. Manuel s'aperçut que même le souvenir de la nuit était emporté par le vent lent et lourd qui apportait l'odeur des brasiers de Cuatro-Caminos et de la Gran Vía.[32]

Unlike to fire, night permits the deepest experience of fraternity. As Malraux says in the first chapter of *L'Espoir*, "la nuit n'était que fraternité."[33] Night is also invitation to participate to the cosmos: "Ils causent. La nuit s'installe sur le champ, solennelle, comme sur toutes les grandes étendues."[34] On certain rare occasions night is felt as "sérénité géologique."[35] More often, as in Goya, the calmness of the night is torn out by the violence of a menacing light which looks for you or destroys you. Here is another example of fire when daylight is made of a tumult of flashes and sounds—another Goya's vision:

Dans la nuit pleine de cris assourdis, de bruits de course, de détonations, d'appels et d'écroulements étouffés au-dessus du roulement ininterrompu de la bataille, un couvent, s'effondrait parmi les décombres; des fulgurations le parcouraient comme des bêtes, sous un bouillonnement de fumée grenat. Il n'y restait personne. Piquets de miliciens, gardes d'assaut, services de secours, regardaient, fascinés par la trouble exaltation des flammes, la vie inépuisable du feu. Assis, un chat gris, levait la tête.[36]

There is no need to multiply quotations, for Goya is there in every page of *L'Espoir*, present in style and in vision. The movement of the phrase responds to the movement of the brush; it is the same rupture of line, the same interpretation of light and darkness, as if light were the consequence of burning fire emerging from the Unknown. It is not by chance that in 1947, Malraux, meditating upon Goya, cites especially *The Third of May*, the *Burial of the Sardine*, the *The Madhouse*, the *Colossus*, *Saturn*, the *Dogé* the *Communion of San José de Calasanz*. However, Malraux, who thinks that he is the prophet announcing the end of modern ages when Goya voiced its beginnings, does not make of literature a simple copy of painting. Literary originality consists in the double experience of vision and hearing. Humanity is just uproar and booing, a plenitude of discordant noises. Music only is close to the tranquility of silence. Painting is made of visions that are fires rending the peace and depth of darkness. Literature then attempts to compete with painting, but using meaningful sounds. It invites the eyes and the ears to cooperate through the broken rhythm of language, and to give to human consciousness its fullest accomplishments. Malraux's art plays a double metaphysical game where vision aspires to be felt as a voice, and articulated sounds to be converted into visions.

NOTES

1. Malraux, *L'Espoir* (Paris: Gallimard, 1937), p. 318; the English translation, *Man's Hope*, was made by Stuart Gilbert and Alastair Macdonald (New York: Random House, 1938).

2. Cf. John Romeiser, *Critical Reception of André Malraux's* "L'Espoir" *in the French Press: December 1937–June 1940* (University, Mississippi: Romance Monographs, 1980), p. 34.

3. Cf. *L'Intemporel* (Paris: Gallimard, 1976), p. 371.

4. Malraux, *L'Homme précaire et la littérature* (Paris: Gallimard, 1977), p. 23. "Our century like the 13th century is a century of images."

5. La Métamorphose . . .., p. 338. "This is a fiction which made of painting a major art."

6. Cf. Romeiser, *Critical Reception* . . .., pp. 135–36. Romeiser notes that those critics may have been impressed by a major Goya exhibition at the Orangerie in Paris, in January 1938. Thanks to the courtesy of Wildenstein and Co., I was able to get a copy of the catalogue of that exhibition. Actually the catalogue is entitled "Peintures de Goya des collections de France," and gives a list of thirty-one works, mostly portraits. It contains none of the works Malraux will mention in *Saturne*. A preface is written by René Huyghe, then curator of painting at the Louvre Museum. Huyghe connects the genius of Goya and the originality of the Spanish spirit. He writes: "One will find there the undefinable unity which joins those works together, that anguished, tragic, or only bizarre accent, that fervent or pathetic intensity that

conveys such a powerful Spanish smell. One has often exposed the contradictions of that people (in French: *race*) extreme in everything, which divides itself in such a singular way between the ecstasies of mysticism and the truculent manifestations of realism . . . . It was thus necessary that to find a full translation of herself, Spain waited for the ages of individualism and the dawn of twentieth century."

7. Cf. *Etre et Dire*, ed. by Martine de Courcel (Paris: Plon, 1976), p. 228.

8. Editions d'art Skira; English translation: *Goya, Drawings from the Prado*, trans. Edward Sackville-West (Oxford University Press, 1947). This essay was reprinted in *Le Triangle d'or* (Paris: Gallimard, 1970) under the title *Goya en noir et blanc*.

9. "The more it goes, the more I realize my total indifference toward what the good people call 'the art of the novel'. . . . there are people who have something to express but who never produce masterpieces (Montaigne, Pascal, Goya, Chartres's sculptors) because one cannot control a passion which attacks the world; and there are those who 'make objects.'" Letter of April 20, 1929, quoted by André Vandegans, *La Jeunesse littéraire d'André Malraux* (Paris: J.-J. Pauvert, 1964), p. 284, and by Christiane Moatti, *Les Personnages d'André Malraux, Le Predicateur et ses masques* (Paris: Les Publications de la Sorborne, 1987), p. 34; my translation.

10. "Guernica had led him (Picasso) to study *The Third of May*. 'The dark sky, this is not a sky, it is blackness. Lighting, there are two. One which one does not understand. It lights everything, like moonlight: the sierra, the steeple, the soldiers who should be against the light; but it lights much more than the moon does. It has not its color. And then, there is the lantern on the ground, enormous, at the center. It, what does it light: The guy with his arms raised up, the martyr. You will look well at it: it lights only him. The lantern, this is Death. Why? One does not know. Goya neither. But Goya, he knows that that should be like that.' André Malraux answers: 'I have always the feeling of a bewitched painting. Bewitched by what Supernatural?'" *Miroir des Limbes* (Paris: Gallimard, 1976), p. 755; my translation.

11. See in particular Paul Raymond Coté, *Les Techniques picturales chez Malraux, Interrogation et métamorphose* (Edition Naaman de Sherbrooke, 1984); Philippe Carrard, *Malraux ou le récit hybride: essai sur les techniques narratives dans L'Espoir* (Paris: Minard, 1976); and Edouard Morot-Sir, "André Malraux's Aesthetics: The Problematic of Universals," *Twentieth Century Literature* 24:3(Fall 1978), "Agnosticism and the Gnosis of the Imaginary," *New York Literary Forum* 3(1979), "Imaginaire de peinture et imaginaire romanesque dans l'oeuvre d'André Malraux," *Cahiers de l'Association internationales d'études françaises* 33(1981).

12. *L'Espoir*, 22. "For the first time, liberals, members of the U.G.T. and of the C.N.T., anarchists, republicans, trade-unionists, and socialists joined in an attack on the common foe and his machine-guns . . . ." (*Man's Hope*, 22).

13. *L'Espoir*, 278. "For the first time, the strains of the Internationale were raising from men of every nation united in battle together" (*Man's Hope*, 278).

14. *L'Espoir*, 205. "To give it (the army) courage is a question of organization" (*Man's Hope*, 206).

15. *L'Espoir*, 386. "Every true revolutionary is a born manichean. The same is true of politics, all politics" (*Man's Hope*, 392).

16. *L'Espoir*, 300. "If torture is so prevalent in war, a reason—another reason—is that it seems the only apt rejoinder to treachery and cruelty" (*Man's Hope*, 300).

17. *L'Espoir*, 132. "Sizzling, the shaft of fire gained foot by foot, and sudden, sputtering bursts of bluish flame chequered the walls with a fantastic rout of dancing shadows as the milicianos turned and twisted in their frantic saraband; it was as though a horde of phantoms were capering with glee around the madness of the living men. And somehow the living forms seemed more spectral than those wildly capering shadows, less palpable than the stifling fog across which solid shapes showed flat as stencils, less real than the angry hiss of fire and water and the weak, whimpering cries of a burnt man" (*Man's Hope*, 131).

18. *L'Espoir*, 256. "The most appealing thing about the prisoners was their courage . . . . They were getting into routine; those of the right—on killing, those on the left on being killed . . . . He was a puny little man with a complexion the color of black olive. Simultaneously with the movement of the rifles brought up to the shoulder, he raised his fist with the Popular Front salute. Hernandez watched the uplifted fist; a moment hence those fingers would be clenched on earth" (*Man's Hope*, 258–59).

19. *L'Espoir*, 4. "Like heart-beats of the serried crowd, there came at regular intervals the boom of the cannon, drowning the thin patter of shots from doors and windows, reverberating through the tumult of voices and the heavy fumes of heated stones and tar pouring up from Madrid" (*Man's Hope*, 35).

20. *L'Espoir*, 274. "The window was open: Accompanying the click of the big Spanish bones came a sharper noise like hammering, as distinct as the beat of horses' hoofs [sic], but with the regular rhythm of flails and forges. It was the dull tread of marching troops" (*Man's Hope*, 277).

21. *L'Espoir*, 315. "Alvear read the lines slowly and with a feeling of their rhythm all the more impressive because his voice was toneless, senile as his smile. Muffled footsteps scattered into the distance, far-off explosions, and all the sounds heard from dawn to dusk that still were haunting Scali's memory seemed circling now like startled animals round that voice already committed to death" (*Man's Hope*, 321).

22. *L'Espoir*, 336–37. "An explosion in their immediate neighborhood made the pens jump on the table. There was a noise of tiles falling on distant roofs, the scurrying footsteps of a crowd running for shelter. Then, after a moment of silence, a scream, sudden and intolerably shrill, jarred the darkness. Then silence fell again" (*Man's Hope*, 343).

23. *L'Espoir*, 380. "Shade strained his ears to catch the sound which seemed to come from some far-off prehistoric age, congruous with this world of fire. After a phrase rhythmically recurring, it seemed that everyone in the street was uttering a response which imitated the clang of funeral gongs: Dong-Ding-A-Dong" (*Man's Hope*, 387).

24. *L'Espoir*, 474. "The women were weeping quietly, and the procession seemed to be fleeing the eerie silence of the mountains, its noise of clattering hoofs and clogs linking the everlasting clamour of the vultures with the muffled sound of sobbing" (*Man's Hope*, 485–86).

25. *L'Espoir*, 326. "A blackbird's song rose through the air in seeming interrogation—and drew an answer. It came again with a note of growing uneasiness; a furious protest followed, then a burst of laughter through the fog" (*Man's Hope*, 330).

26. *L'Espoir*, 332. "A blackbird broke into ecstatic song. Somewhere in the mist, Kogan answered for the wounded, for the dead" (*Man's Hope*, 338).

27. It seems that Malraux adopts the Schopenhauer's philosophy of music when he writes: "Comme la musique supprime en lui la volonté . . ." (497), poorly translated: "Now that the tension of his will relaxed . . ." (*Man's Hope*, 609).

28. *L'Espoir*, 498. "As the strands of melody took form, interwoven with his past they conveyed to him the self same message that the dim sky, those ageless fields and that town which had stopped the Moors might, too have given him. For the first time Manuel was hearing the voice of that which is more awe-inspiring than the blood of men, more enigmatic even than their presence on the earth—the infinite possibilities of their destiny. And he felt that this new consciousness within him was linked up with the sounds of running water and the footfalls of the prisoners, profound and permanent as the beating of his heart" (*Man's Hope*, 510–11).

29. *L'Espoir*, 225. "Can you believe that the firing squads used search-lights? Without awaiting the reply he burst out: 'Imagine being shot with a spotlight on you! . . .'" (*Man's Hope*, 225–26).

30. *L'Espoir*, 47–48. "Bathed in the bright glare of its street-lamps, disguised in its revolutionary dress, Madrid looked like an enormous night scene in a film studio" (*Man's Hope*, 42).

31. *L'Espoir,* 272. "It was their comradeship which has brought them into that cabin filled with the menacing light; for the first time since they began their flight, those men could see each other" (*Man's Hope,* 274).

32. *L'Espoir,* 404–5. "Through a great rent in the rocks of the Sierra the farther slopes had just come into view. From Madrid, scarely visible across the grey expanse, pillars of dense black smoke were slowly, mournfully spreading across the sky. Manuel knew only too well what that smoke meant. The city was veiled in the shroud of its conflagration as warships are veiled in swirling banks of battle-smoke. The smoke was rising from buildings whence no glow of fire was visible, towering in columns frayed out across the murky sky. And all the clouds seemed to have welled up from the unseen furnace, progressing like an army on the march in the direction of their drift. Above the thin white line of the beleagured city, nestling in its woods, brooded an infinite distress, a holocaust of agony, filling the whole immensity of heaven. And to Manuel it seemed that even the memory of the night was being borne away by the slow, stagnant breeze, that brought to him the reek of the smouldering fires of Cuatro Caminos and the Gran Vía" (*Man's Hope,* 409).

33. *L'Espoir,* 18. "The darkness was all fraternity" (*Man's Hope,* 11).

34. *L'Espoir,* 83. "As they talked on, the advancing night flooded the flying-field, with a grave, unfathomable gloom" (*Man's Hope,* 80).

35. *L'Espoir,* 218. "Geological tranquility" (*Man's Hope,* 219).

36. *L'Espoir,* 338. "The darkness was loud with muffled cries, echoes of racing feet, explosions, calls for help and the long-drawn crashes of falling buildings, sounding above the never-ending din of battle. A convent was collapsing in a cataract of toppling masonry, over which sleek scarlet flames were scurrying, like hungry beasts of prey, through the red rolling smoke. The building had been evacuated and *milicianos,* Assault Guards and first-aid parties were watching the scene, fascinated by the exultant havoc of the flames, their irrepressible vitality. A grey cat on the curb raised his eyes to watch" (*Man's Hope,* 343–44).

WORKS CITED

Carrard, Philippe. *Malraux ou le récit hybride: essai sur les techniques narratives dans L'Espoir.* Paris: Minard, 1976.

Coté, Paul Raymond. *Les Techniques picturales chez Malraux, Interrogations et métamorphose.* Paris: Edition Naaman de Sherbrooke, 1984.

Gombrich, E. *Etre et Dire.* Ed. Martine de Courcel. Paris: Plon, 1976.

Langlois, Walter. *Via Malraux.* The Malraux Society, 1986.

Malraux, André *L'Espoir.* Paris: Gallimard, 1937.

———. *Man's Hope.* Trans. Stuart Gilbert and Alastair Macdonald. New York: Random House, 1938.

———. *La Condition humaine.* Paris: Gallimard, Bibliothèque de la Pléiade, 1976.

———. *L'Intemporel.* Paris: Gallimard, 1976.

———. *L'Homme précaire et la littérature.* Paris: Gallimard, 1977.

———. *La Métamorphose des dieux.* Paris: Gallimard, 1977.

———. *La Voix royale.* Paris: Grasset, 1930.

———. *Goya, Francisco de. Drawings from the Prado.* Trans. Edward Sackville-West. New York: Oxford University Press, 1947.

———. "Goya en noir et blanc." *Le Triangle d'or.* Paris: Gallimard, 1970.

———. *Saturn.* Trans. C. W. Chilton. London: Phaidon Press, 1957.

———. *The Voices of Silence.* Trans. Stuart Gilbert. New York: Doubleday and Co., 1953.

———. *André Malraux.* Paris: Editions de l'Herne, 1982.

———. *Miroir des Limbes.* Paris: Gallimard, 1976.

Moatti, Christiane. *Les Personnages d'André Malraux. Le Predicateur et ses Masques.* Paris: Les Publications de la Sorbonne, 1987.

Morot-Sir, Edouard. "André Malraux's Aesthetics: The Problematic of Universals." *Twentieth Century Literature* 3:24, pp. 413–30.

———. "Agnosticism and the Gnosis of the Imaginary." *New York Literary Forum* 3 (1979), pp. 85–124.

———. "Imaginaire de peinture et imaginaire romanesque dans l'oeuvre d'André Malraux." *Cahiers de l'Association internationales d'études fracaises* 3 (1981).

Picon, G. *Malraux par lui-meme.* Paris: Editions du Seuil, 1966.

Romeise, John. *Critical Reception of André Malraux's "L'Espoir" in the French Press: December 1937–June 1940.* Oxford, Miss: University of Mississippi Press, Romance Monographs, 1980.

Suarès, Guy. *Malraux, celui qui vient.* Paris: Librairie Stock, 1975.

Vandegans, André. *La Jeunesse littéraire d'André Malraux.* Paris: J.-J. Pauvert, 1964.

Countering L'Espoir: *Two French Fascist Novels of the Spanish Civil War*

Richard J. Golsan

Because of its well-deserved reputation as one of the great novels of the Spanish Civil War, Andre Malraux's *L'Espoir* has largely overshadowed other fictional treatments of the conflict written in French. These works include critical successes such as Claude Simon's *Le Palace* (1962) and Henry de Montherlant's *Le Chaos et la Nuit* (1963), both written long after the fighting was over, as well as more contemporary works appearing within a few years of the publication of Malraux's masterpiece.[1] In the latter category are two novels published in 1939, Robert Brasillach's *Les Sept Couleurs* and Pierre Drieu La Rochelle's *Gilles*. Brasillach and Drieu were among the most fervent and outspoken fascist intellectuals in France during the interwar years and the Occupation, and therefore it is not surprising that their novels favor Franco's cause and espouse values very different from those championed in *L'Espoir*. *Les Sept Couleurs* and *Gilles* nevertheless reflect the impact of Malraux's masterpiece both in their thinly disguised efforts to imitate certain aspects of the style of *L'Espoir* and in their attempts to counter some of its major theses. This is not to say, however, that these fascist novels are purely derivative works. *Les Sept Couleurs* and *Gilles* provide valuable insights into French Fascist ideals and aesthetics as well as the French Right's perception of the conflict in Spain. They also express to varying degrees the contradictory extremes of unbridled hope and the sense of imminent catastrophe which characterize much of historically conscious fiction written in France in the thirties.

Although neither *Les Sept Couleurs* nor *Gilles* focuses exclusively on the Spanish Civil War, the conflict is granted a privileged status in the novels, both in terms of narrative economy and the development of the hero. The segments in Spain occur at or near the end of the

works, and bring into sharp contrast and final confrontation the
political, social, and ideological issues which inform the narratives.
The hero's arrival in Spain and commitment to the Nationalist cause
in both *Les Sept Couleurs* and *Gilles* coincides with the resolution or
transcendance of all his emotional, political, and spiritual quandaries.
In this sense the Spanish episodes bring to conclusion the heroes' *Bildungsroman*. In Brasillach's novel, the protagonist, François Courtet,
finds in Spain a way out of a love triangle as well as a privileged terrain
on which to fight for the fascist ideals that motivate him. Drieu's
hero, Gilles, finds in the Spanish conflict an escape from the
decadence of French society and the dead end of politics in France.
He also discovers a place where he can translate into action the fascist
ideals he had embraced on the morrow of the right-wing–inspired
riots of February 6th, 1934, treated in the Parisian episodes of the
novel. So complete is the transformation or regeneration of the two
men in Spain that both are given new names. François Courtet becomes the cheerful, courageous Francesco Herbillo[2] of the Spanish
Legion while Gilles is the mysterious Walter, agent for an international and mythical fascist conspiracy. Like the phoenix, both men rise
from the ashes of their past lives in France to discover and fully express their new identities in Spain.

While the tone and perspective of the Spanish segments of *Les Sept
Couleurs* and *Gilles* are hardly reminiscent of *L'Espoir*, it is precisely in
these segments that the impact of Malraux's work and especially his
style are most evident. Brasillach makes frequent use of *reportage* in
his novel, interspersing episodes from Courtet/Herbillo's life as a
volunteer for Franco with newspaper accounts of political and social
aspects of the war. These highly propogandistic and pro-Nationalist
documents, attributed to a certain Pierre Raynaud of *La Revue Grise*,
are actually drawn from Brasillach's *Histoire de la guerre d'Espagne*
(1939) which he coauthored with Maurice Bardèche, and his
memoirs of the interwar years, *Notre avant-guerre* (1941). The articles
are clearly intended to give a sense of immediacy and urgency to the
conflict, a device used in *L'Espoir* in the reporter Shade's dispatches on
the fighting. Moreover, the pro-Franco slant of these documents
counters the pro-Republican sentiments expressed in Shade's articles.
Although Brasillach strongly disapproved of Malraux and his novel,[3]
it is clear that he considered Malraux's narrative technique effective
enough in certain instances to be emulated.

Drieu's novel, too, imitates aspects of the style of *L'Espoir*, a novel
which Drieu had earlier criticized[4] despite his admiration and
friendship for its author. Mary Jean Green has remarked on his use of

Malraux's technique of interspersing scenes portraying various forms of action "with conversations bringing out the wider significance of these actions" (Green, *Fiction,* 237). This is especially true in the Balearic Islands episode, in which Gilles discusses the meaning of the fascist struggle and its goals with other pro-Franco volunteers in the interim between firefights with the Republicans. In earlier scenes in Barcelona in which Gilles links up with and then murders the Communist agent Van der Brook, Drieu offers his own version of Malraux's cinematic style. He emphasizes light and dark effects, the movement of shadows, sudden shifts of focus, and so on. As in Malraux's fiction, the illusion of authenticity in portraying the Spanish City is established through the use of what one critic describes as "filmic sleight of hand."[5] In an effort to create a sense of immediacy and danger, Drieu frequently introduces a series of questions intended to heighten the tension and confusion of a scene. Walking along the Republican held streets of Barcelona with Van der Brook, Gilles speculates "Jusqu'où iraient-ils? Etaient-ils suivis?" (Drieu 1939, 615). To readers of *L'Espoir* and other novels by Malraux, this is a familiar technique.[6]

The impact of *L'Espoir* on *Les Sept Couleurs* and *Gilles* is evident not simply on the level of style, but in the fascist novels' efforts to counter one of the central themes of Malraux's work as well. Among the many characters in *L'Espoir* are volunteers for the Republic from virtually every European country. Malraux's intention in introducing these characters is first of all to stress the international dimension of the conflict. More significantly, however, he wishes to emphasize the groundswell of popular support throughout Europe for the beleaguered but legitimately elected Popular Front government. In an effort to counter Malraux's implicit claim, Brasillach and Drieu in their novels stress the presence of foreign volunteers on Franco's side. François Courtet in *Les Sept Couleurs* is not the only French volunteer for the Nationalists, nor are these French volunteers the only foreigners present. Italian and German Legionnaires are introduced, all of whom have come to fight in the new "wars of religion." In implying they have *chosen* the fight for fascism, however, Brasillach ignores the fact that Hitler's and especially Mussolini's troops in Spain were hardly all volunteers.[7]

Drieu in *Gilles* is even more insistent on the idea of strong European popular support for Franco. Traveling through dangerous Republican-held territory on the Balearic Islands, Gilles is rescued by an Irish volunteer and his Polish companion. It is these men, O'Connor and Zabuloski, and not the Spaniards themselves, who along with

Gilles are later granted the privilege of discussing and assigning meaning to the fascist struggle in Spain. In giving these foreign volunteers such an exalted role and essential function in the narrative, Drieu is assigning them an importance which far exceeds the real value of men such as these to Franco's cause. As is the case with Brasillach, Drieu's efforts to counter one of the central theses of *L'Espoir* leads him to create situations which are simply not in keeping with what really happened in Spain.

If their efforts to contradict *L'Espoir* lead Brasillach and Drieu to play loosely with history in their novels, ultimately so do their attempts to express the fascist prejudices, beliefs and ideals which animate their heroes. These include a rabid anticommunism and an outspoken hostility toward the corruption and decadence of liberal bourgeois culture. They also embrace an obsession with virility, youth and force and a nostalgia for a primitive Christian past combined paradoxically with an intense admiration for some of the most striking manifestations of a highly technological modernity.

Both in *Les Sept Couleurs* and *Gilles*, the Republicans and their allies fighting in Spain are identified simply as "Reds," although it is quickly evident that this title embraces essentially everyone who opposes fascism. Whether they be foreign Communist agents, Loyalist soldiers, liberals, or simply anonymous individuals in a Republican crowd, these characters are invariably dishonorable and frequently prime examples of the worst ravages of decadence. In *Gilles* the Communist agent Van der Brook is a liar and physically repulsive to boot. He is "[un] gros Hollandais qui ressemble exactement à une caricature de bourgeois dans un journal communiste" (Drieu, 614). In *Les Sept Couleurs*, Loyalist soldiers are implicitly lacking in honor since, unlike their fascist counterparts, they refuse to broadcast the names and status of fascist prisoners-of-war to their families in Nationalist Spain to let them know they are alive. International volunteers for the Republic are also dishonorable, in that most are unemployed laborers who have come to Spain for money, or workers too cowardly to resist pressure from their union to volunteer. Drieu reserves his harshest criticisms for the loyal citizens of the liberal Republic. Attending a town council meeting or walking down the streets of Republican-held Ibiza, Gilles notices the same decadent figures he had observed previously in Paris: aging, obese politicians, corrupt Freemasons, homosexuals, drug addicts and so on. Individuals of a similar ilk presumably inhabit Republican Spain in *Les Sept Couleurs* as well, although their presence can only be inferred. Siegfried Kast, a German volunteer for the Nationalists had earlier joined the Nazi Party to fight "decadent" elements such as Jews and homosexuals in his own country, and it is logical to suppose that he has joined Franco's cause for much the same reason.

Old age, obesity, sexual perversion and drug addiction are not the only marks of decadence which Brasillach and Drieu's fascist heroes seek to combat in Spain. Intellectualism and culture itself are also favorite targets, since they corrupt the individual and sap him of his strength. In *Les Sept Couleurs* Siegfried Kast is fond of quoting Georing's statement, "Quand j'entends parler de la culture, je prends mon revolver . . ." (Brasillach, 102). For the German volunteer, literature, philosophy, music and the arts are simply *pourriture* (Brasillach, 97).[8] In Drieu's novel, Gilles, too feels nothing but contempt for the arts and intellectual activity in general, since he knows from past experience in Paris that activities along these lines cannot resolve his dilemmas. His tastes now run to the brutal, the simple, the primitive. Completely indifferent to life's subtleties, he is a far cry from the intellectuals who fight for the Republic in Malraux's novel. In fact, his attitude toward men of this sort is best summed up in Francoist general Millan Astrays famous cry: "Death to the intellectuals."[9]

If the Fascist vision which animates Brasillach and Drieu's heroes is in part defined in negative terms, it certainly has its more positive sides as well. In *Les Sept Couleurs* and *Gilles* it is associated with a youthful, virile exuberance, courage, and a taste for discipline and force. Courtet/Herbillo is characterized as enthusiastic and joyful in Brasillach's novel while a Spanish volunteer for Franco is youthful, disciplined and courageous. In *Gilles* the fascist fighters the protagonist encounters on the Balearic Islands are *beau gars* who give off a "forte ordeur d'homme," and their faces are "sévère" and "mâle" (Drieu, 655). In both novels these men are not simply admirable, they are exemplary. They represent a whole new order of men. In *Les Sept Couleurs*, Brasillach goes so far as to claim they are the next evolutionary phase of the human race, the *uomo fascista* (Brasillach, 156).[10] Combining the best qualities of the contemplative with the active, the ancient with the modern, they are defenders of the primitive and warlike Christianity of the Middle Ages and proponents of the technologically advanced fascist states. In Drieu's novel, Gilles, in fact, belongs to a secret, international conspiracy which seeks to unite the Catholic Church with Fascist Italy and Nazi Germany and assure their common triumph in Europe. He is a *moine-soldat* striving to follow in the footsteps of Joan of Arc, "catholique et guerrière" (Drieu, 677). Rather than fight his battles with a sword, however, he faces his enemies with a machine gun, a product of modern technology he describes as "sacred" (Drieu, 660).

Like a medieval crusader or a Renaissance condottiere,[11] Brasillach's model, Siegfried Kast, has come to Spain to join in the "wars of religion." He is at the same time, however, a "technician" of war (Brasillach, *Les Sept,* 216) in the service of the modern totalitarian state. The "research" he does while aiding the Nationalists will assure the military supremacy of his own country, and eventually the triumph of fascism in Europe.

The juxtaposition of the old and the new that characterizes the heroic ideals proposed by Brasillach and Drieu inform their novels in other ways as well. As Mary Jean Green has noted, in *Les Sept Couleurs,* it is expressed in the novelists' effort to provide a classical frame for contemporary subject matter (Green, *Fiction,* 163–64). Each section of Brasillach's novel describing the adventures of his fascist heroes is introduced by an epigram taken from Corneille's *Polyeucte,* and the love triangle in *Les Sept Couleurs* is clearly inspired by a similar triangle in Corneille's tragedy. In the last segment of the novel, Courtet's wife, Catherine, who is going to Spain to bring her wounded husband home, compares him and his fellow fascist warriors directly to Polyeucte and another well known Cornelian hero, Horace (Brasillach, 244). Brasillach's intention in making these comparisons is evidently to further emphasize the nobility of his heroes and the grandeur of their destiny.

Unlike Brasillach, Drieu does not stress similarities between his fascist protagonist and Corneillian heroes, nor is he interested in classical models of this sort. His novel is marked nevertheless by a comparable obsession with melding the old to the new, in this case the primitive to the modern. Robert Soucy defines this technique in terms of Drieu's "modernist antimodernism," and he argues that it derives from the novelist's willingness to ascribe what is usually associated with the primitive to the modern (Soucy, 924). Thus violence, brutality and the excessive use of force are labeled "modern" and those who employ these methods to achieve their ends are commended for their "modernity." As Soucy notes, Drieu had earlier praised Lenin and Hitler for their "modern" approach to political means, and, in the 1939 novel, the hero displays a similar primitivistic modernity while witnessing the execution of Republican prisoners. At first moved to pity (a decadent emotion) he thinks better of it, reminding himself that he is not an "amateur" (Drieu, 669) but a professional in the service of the champion and chief proponent of "modern" virtues, fascism.

Less idiosyncratic conceptions of the modern and the primitive are joined in Gilles's relationship with his mentor Carentan. In his life-style, tastes and experiences, an excellent example of "modern" man, Gilles nevertheless shares the beliefs and prejudices of the reactionary Norman peasant. Like Carentan, he despises the "scientific" spirit of the twentieth century and the materialistic society modern technology has produced, despite his admiration for some of that technology's more frightening and murderous products, such as the machine gun mentioned earlier. Throughout the novel he retires to Carentan's primitive hut in the Normand countryside whenever he is overwhelmed and disgusted by the modern world, and there he is rejuvenated by the old peasant's reactionary wisdom. Gilles's bond with Carentan is in fact the strongest and most positive personal bond presented in the novel, and one can only conclude Drieu wishes the reader to believe that modern man's salvation is assured only if he adopts such a primitivistic perspective.

The problem with this philosophy is, of course, that if one embraces such an outlook one turns ones' back on the complex realities and problems of contemporary society, and this is precisely where both Drieu and Brasillach run into difficulties depicting the Spanish conflict. In their efforts to turn the Civil War into a struggle with modern weapons over exalted but anachronistic values, they completely ignore the real social, economic and political issues over which the war was fought. Such problems as agrarian reform, the role of the Catholic Church in Spanish politics and the Army's relation-ship to the Republic are not even mentioned. In *Les Sept Couleurs* and *Gilles* the discussions are never allowed to descend to such mundane and practical concerns. The result in Brasillach's novel is that all so-cial and economic distinctions are glossed over, along with the realities of daily existence.[12] Even the Civil War itself hardly seems real, since Brasillach's protagonists are never shown fighting, suffering and dying on the battlefield. Like the Corneillian heroes to whom they are compared, they state their views, espouse their cause with eloquence, and then leave the Spanish stage at the end.

In *Gilles*, the problem is more complex. Drieu is not averse to depicting bloodshed, as the episodes in Ibiza show, but his passion for anachronistic values leads him to distort and indeed to falsify the realities of the Spanish War and the European situation in general. Jean-Guy Rens notes that Drieu sends his hero to Spain to rediscover his youth and that of civilization, to preserve the virile faith of the middle ages, and help create an aristocracy of the spirit. In fighting for Franco, however, he serves none of these ends, since the Spanish general's primary concern was the preservation of the status quo, with its privileged, indolent upper classes, its entrenched Catholic hierarchy, and its complete indifference to a dynamic aristocracy of the spirit (Rens, 239). A similar refusal to face the facts is also evident in the goals, ambitions, and even the existence of the secret international fascist conspiracy to which Gilles/Walter belongs. As Mary Jean Green points out, the existence of a supranational organization seeking to assure the union of the fascism and the Catholic Church is completely unlikely and in fact utterly absurd, given the political realities of 1939 (Green, *Fiction*, 237). The fascist states and Nazi Germany in particular were certainly not seeking to wed their ideologies to Roman Catholicism, nor were they interested in encouraging revolutions from the Right in the interest of promoting other independent and powerful fascist states. Both Nazi Germany and Fascist Italy were interested exclusively in expanding their respective empires.

In both *Les Sept Couleurs* and *Gilles*, then, the Spanish conflict provides the ingredients for creating an idealized reality where the forces of light and dark, good and evil confront each other unambiguously. Such a Manichean vision, moreover, lies at the heart of much Right Wing writing about the war produced at the time, be it fascist or reactionary Catholic. Paul Claudel's pro-Nationalist poems, essays, and letters, for example, stress similar dichotomies while ignoring the real motives and intentions behind German and Italian involvements in Spain.[13] The reasons for these distortions in the novels of Brasillach and Drieu are perhaps many and complex, but one reason seems clear. In a section of *Notre Avant-guerre* dealing with the Spanish Civil war (which is quoted in its entirety in *Les Sept Couleurs*) Brasillach speaks of the war as having succeeded in transforming the "long opposition" between fascism and anti-fascism "en combat spirituel et matériel à la fois, en croisade véritable" (Brasillach, 206). He also speaks of the Spanish conflict as having provided the opposition with forceful, galvinizing images which lend it its "religious coloration" and are capable of stirring men to act (Brasillach, 207). It is this latter function of mythmaking in the Sorelien sense which Brasillach and Drieu seek to imitate and perpetuate in their novels.[14] The audience to be brought together, to be mobilized by such images, however, is not the Spanish people but European people as a whole. By 1939, the war in Spain was decided and the final showdown between fascism and antifascism in Europe was at hand.

Finally, myths have a way of escaping the narrow confines of their creator's intentions, and this is certainly true of the political myths

presented in *Les Sept Couleurs* and *Gilles*. The novels may or may not
have succeeded in rallying some Europeans to fascism, but the myths
they project do convey the aspirations as well as the deep-seated fears
of their creators. Both Brasillach and Drieu's narratives provide insights into the novelists' dreams of a new *homo fascista*, or "Hitlerian
man," as Drieu was later to call him, and a New Order founded on
fascist modernity and medieval Christianity. However, they also
reveal both writers' sense of an imminent and final conflagration, in
short, their premonition of apocalypse. This sentiment is expressed
subtly in *Les Sept Couleurs* by Courtet, who despite his conviction that
Nazism is invincible, curiously wishes to rush to Germany to see
Hitler's Reich before its fall (Brasillach, 170). Gille's apocalyptic
leanings are more persistent and intense, and manifest themselves in
a number of ways in different situations. Despite his faith in a fas-
cist/Catholic Utopia of the future, he cannot escape the feeling that
the fundamental reality of all things is destruction and death. Watching Republican prisoners being led off to be executed, Gilles observes,
"C'est cela, mon époque. Et c'est cela, la vie de l'humanité, toujours."
(Drieu, 668). On a personal level death becomes a temptation the
fascist idealist must repeatedly struggle against and to which he finally
succumbs.[15] At the end of the novel, after earlier refusing to flee an
arena which is now surrounded by enemies and from which there is
no escape, Gilles rushes off to kill and be killed.

Why these extreme expressions of hope and despair in both novels?
The answer is possibly that despite their political commitments,
Brasillach and Drieu were sensitive and acute observers of their times.
The thirties in Europe as exemplified in the Spanish Civil War was a
decade of extraordinary turmoil, of utopic dreams and terrible,
catastrophic disappointments. As faithful expressions of these contradictions, *Les Sept Couleurs* and *Gilles* transcend the narrow and
frightening constraints of the fascist ideology which informs them to
become valuable testaments of their time.

NOTES

1. A good example of this omission can be found in Frederick R. Benson's *Writers in
Arms*, a general study of the literature of the Spanish Civil War. The only French novel discussed is *L'Espoir*. Right Wing fictional responses are dismissed because of "their inferiority
in literary terms" (xxiii) and presumably this includes the two fascist works under discussion
here. The novels of Montherlant and Simon are also ignored.

2. A footnote in the text of the novel explains that "Herbillot" is François's mother's name.

3. For Brasillach's attacks on Malraux and *L'Espoir* in the pages of the fascist periodical *Je
suis partout* and *Action Française*, see Brassié 153–57.

4. See Green 1986, 236.

5. For a discussion of Malraux's cinematic style and filmic sleight-of-hand, see Rowan 31–33.

6. The most famous example of the use of this technique in Malraux's fiction is in the opening passage of *La Condition humaine* in which the terrorist Tchen stands over a bed in which his intended victim is sleeping. The passage begins "Tchen tenterait-il de lever la moustiquaire? Frapperait-il au travers? L'angoisse lui tordait l'estomac" (Malraux, 315).

7. Danielle Vieville-Carbonel notes that Brasillach preferred to think of the combatants in Spain as volunteers for the most part, *chevaliers* and *généreux* fighting in a new "crusade" (Vieville-Carbonel, 235).

8. Kast is not the only character in the novel hostile to cultural and intellectual activity and those who devote themselves to such pursuits. Patrice Blanchon, François's contemporary and the central figure in the German episodes of *Les Sept Couleurs,* believes that people are always interesting "à condition qu'ils ne soient pas des intellectuels" (Brasillach, 31).

9. The slogan was shouted at Miguel de Unamuno at a meeting at the University of Salamanca in October 1936. For a discussion of the circumstances surrounding Millan Astray's outburst, see Thomas, 501–4.

10. Brasillach's discussion of the *uomo fascista* in *Les Sept Couleurs* also appears in *Notre avant-guerre* (Brasillach, 205).

11. Brasillach's choice of the Renaissance mercenary as a precursor for the fascist warrior is curious and ultimately contradictory. He apparently wishes to present a classical model for his modern hero and stress the latter's courage and skill by comparing him with the former. But the Condottiere remains a mercenary, selling his services to the highest bidder. He is by definition *not* wedded to a particular belief, cause, or ideology. See Ralph, 33.

12. For a discussion of the "distanced" narrative voice in Brasillach's fiction and the writer's deliberate ignorance of economic realities in *Les Sept Couleurs* and other novels, see Green, 82–89.

13. See Flood, 13–14.

14. In his introduction to Sorel's *Reflections on Violence,* Edward A. Shils defines the Sorelian myth as the "value system and picture of the world of the fraternal band" (21). Sorel himself defines such myths as "historical forces" (49) essential to "provoking any revolutionary movement" (57). The impact of Sorel's thought on Brasillach is obvious from the passage cited. For a discussion of its influence on Drieu's thinking and the latter's early association with the Sorelian *Cercle Proudhon,* see Roth, 123, 245–47. For a recent analysis of Sorel's thought and his conception of myth in particular and its impact on French Fascism, see Kaplan, 59–73.

15. Gilles's suicide has been described as a sort of self-fulfillment (Kaplan, 106) or self-resolution (Green, *Fiction,* 243). It has also been analyzed as a mystic-religious self-sacrifice pulling together a number of Christian and pagan themes and structures that inform the text (Dugaste-Porte, 57–62).

WORKS CITED

Benson, Frederick. *Writers in Arms.* New York: N.Y.U. Press, 1967.

Brasillach, Robert, and Maurice Bardèche. *Histoire de la guerre d'Espagne.* Paris: Plon, 1939.

———. *Notre Avant-guerre.* Paris: Plon, 1941.

———. *Les Sept Couleurs.* Paris: Plon, 1939.

Brassié, Ann. *Robert Brasillach, ou encore un instant de bonheur.* Paris: Laffont, 1987.

Drieu la Rochelle, Pierre. *Gilles.* 1939. Paris: Folio, 1973.

Dugaste-Porte, Francine. "Drieu la Rochelle: La parabole espagnole." *RECIFS* 3 (1981): 51–63.

Flood, Christopher. "French Catholic Writers and the Spanish Civil War: The Case of Claudel." Texas A&M University, College Station, Texas, 17 October 1986.

Green, Mary Jean. *Fiction in the Historical Present: French Writers and the Thirties*. Hanover: The University Press of New England, 1986.

———. "Towards an Analysis of Fascist Fiction: The Contemptuous Narrator in the Works of Brasillach, Céline, and Drieu la Rochelle." *Studies in Twentieth Century Literature* 10, n.1(1985): 81-97.

Kaplin, Alice Yeagar. *Reproductions of Banality: Fascism, Literature, and French Intellectual Life*. Theory and History of Literature 36. Minneapolis: University of Minnesota Press, 1986.

Malraux, André. *La Condition humaine*. 1933. Reprint. Paris: Editions Grasset et Editions Gallimard, 1976.

———. *L'Espoir*. 1937. Reprint. Paris: Editions Grasset et Editions Gallimard, 1976.

Montherlant, Henry de. *Le Chaos et la nuit*. Paris: Gallimard, 1963.

Ralph, Philip Lee. *The Renaissance in Perspective*. New York: St. Martin's, 1973.

Rens, Jean-Guy. "L'Espagne les yeux fermés." *Espagne/écrivains/guerre civile*, 237–40. Ed. Marc Hanrez. Paris: Pantheon Press, Les Dossiers H, 1975.

Roth, Jack J. *The Cult of Violence: Sorel and the Sorelians*. Berkeley: University of California Press, 1980.

Rowan, Mary M. "Asia out of Focus: Decoding Malraux's Orient." *Witnessing André Malraux: Visions and Re-visions*. Ed. B. Thompson and C. Viggiani. Middletown, Conn.: Wesleyan U. Press, 1984.

Simon, Claude. *Le Palace*. Paris: Editions du Minuit, 1962.

Sorel, Georges. *Reflections on Violence*. Trans. T. E. Hulme and J. Roth. Glencoe, Ill.: The Free Press, 1950.

Soucy, Robert. "Drieu la Rochelle and Modernist Anti-Modernism in French Fascism." *Modern Languages Notes* 95(1980): 922–37.

Thomas, Hugh. *The Spanish Civil War*. New York: Harper and Row, 1977.

Vieville-Carbonel, Danielle. "Le Cas de Brasillach." *Espagne/écrivains/guerre civile*, 231–36. Ed. Marc Hanrez. Paris: Pantheon Press, Les Dossiers H, 1975.

Crusade or Genocide?
French Catholic Discourse
on the Spanish Civil War

Christopher G. Flood

The positions adopted by French Catholic writers, intellectuals, and publicists on the subject of the Spanish Civil War have been discussed in general terms by a number of historians, and there have been more detailed studies of individual cases.[1] The principal lines of division are therefore well known. In the first instance, as René Rémond observes, the vast majority of French Catholics showed sympathy for the Nationalists and accepted a straightforward explanation of the conflict in terms of a struggle by defenders of the Church against forces pledged to the destruction of all that was sacred (Rémond, 177). Conservative political preconceptions, already sensitized by tensions in France, combined with horror at the news of widespread anticlerical atrocities in the Republican zones of Spain in the early days of the war and reinforced a perception of the Popular Front in Spain as a harbinger of international communism in its onslaught on Christian civilization. By the same token, Franco was taken to be waging a just war, indeed a holy war, to create a social order compatible with the furtherance of the Church's mission to the Spanish people. Although the majority remained faithful to this view throughout the war, a minority of French Catholics came rapidly to doubt the sanctity of the Nationalist cause in the light of reports of atrocities committed against Republicans, the presence of the Moorish auxiliaries, or the participation of the German and Italian forces on Franco's side. Apart from the *Esprit* group, very few were committed to defense of the Popular Front itself. Most of the dissenting minority were Christian Democrats of various shades, seeking a more neutral, evenhanded approach, as they denounced the errors of the Government side, but equally rejected identification with the savage methods, the hypocrisy, and the absence of compassion shown by the Nationalists.

This discussion is not designed to chart the history of the two factions again. Rather it focuses on certain features of the controversy that which have not hitherto been discussed by historians. The features in question relate to the discursive construction of meanings within this particular field of ideological confrontation. Within the limits of the present discussion, one can offer only a sketch of the type of approach that is being considered and the ways in which it relates to literary concerns. That approach will draw not on works of fiction, but on articles, essays, and other nonfictional campaigning material. Nevertheless, all of the texts involve narratives, in the sense that they implicitly or explicitly tell a story, which purports to be a true story, a history, of the conflict in Spain, its antecedents and anticipated outcome. Sometimes they also tell a story about other writers who are deemed to have recounted those events in a manner that is worthy of positive or negative comment. There is nothing particularly subtle about these texts, but focusing on the fact that their arguments are woven around a story reveals an interesting illustration of ideological discourse that will often ride on the back of a simple narrative. The narrative naturalizes such a discourse and gives it force by virtue of its structural fit with a schema assimilated by the reader in the course of exposure to fables and other fictions from childhood onwards.

Whether or not the narratives focus on individual characters, such as Franco himself, they all feature entities that fulfill *actantial* functions analogous to those found in fictional stories. They favor a certain type of syntagmatic structure and certain forms of rhetorical or stylistic redundancy that are equally found in the novel. Consequently, a narratological model developed to account for characteristics of prose fiction can be relevant also to discussion of the type of texts in question here. In Susan Suleiman's work, for example, on the subject of the ideological novel as a literary genre, many of her analytical categories can be applied with little modification. That takes us only part of the way, however, since Professor Suleiman adopts an excessively narrow definition of ideological discourse as a type that "refers explicitly to, and identifies itself with, a recognized body of doctrine or system of ideas" (2). The only alternative, she implies, is to adopt one of the more all-embracing Marxist definitions. In fact, the choice is far wider than that. A preferable theory is John B. Thompson's, which synthesizes a number of non-Marxist and Marxist strands of thought. For Thompson, "to study ideology is to study the ways in which meaning (signification) serves to sustain relations of domination"

(Thompson, 130–31). Ideology enacts this function by legitimating the dominance of particular groups through appeal to traditional, charismatic or rational-legal forms of authority; by consciously, or more often unconsciously dissimulating the sectional nature of the interests that it serves; and by reifying transitory historical states of affairs to present them as if they were natural, permanent, and necessary. Thompson's argument is that, because ideology is manifested through discourse, analysis must not only include sociohistorical study of the forms of domination that it seeks to sustain or establish, but must also pay attention to the actantial, the argumentative, and even the syntactic structures of the narratives in which ideology is expressed.

Suleiman's and Thompson's models complement each other, and when taken together, they offer a fairly comprehensive framework for the analysis of texts relating to the war in Spain, though due allowance must obviously be made for the distinction of form between the ideological novel and the ideological tract, because the former emphasizes demonstration by concrete (fictional) example, while the latter relies more heavily on argumentation. Whereas the narrative discourse of the novel—the telling of a story—will normally be enormously richer than that of the tract, the interpretive discourse explaining the meaning of the story in the light of explicit or implicit general principles will normally be far richer in the tract than in the novel. Either way, however, the writer is presenting a message that purports to be the truth, but that the critic takes to be something less.

In the case under consideration here, we have the interesting situation of ideological dissentious within an overarching framework of apparent consensus. Notwithstanding the relative politeness with which they attacked the positions of fellow-Catholic opponents, there was extremely bitter conflict among French Catholics over the issue of how far the Spanish Nationalists were acting in accordance with the long-term spiritual and temporal needs of the Spanish people, or, indeed, of Europe as a whole. There was apparent community, however, in their shared adherence to the doctrines and institutions of the Catholic Church. Although while they did undoubtedly share religious beliefs and doctrinally conditioned patterns of thought that imposed certain boundaries on the debate, the intertwining of political with religious issues in Spain also highlighted crucial differences of meaning and emphasis that Catholicism itself held for these writers. Thus, the conflict over interpretation of the meaning of events in Spain was also the site of what Pierre Bourdieu would term a symbolic power struggle to impose the legitimate

definition of Catholicism in the modern world.[2] In pursuit of this
unavowed and perhaps unrecognized objective, each writer on each
side would capitalize on all of the symbolic assets at his disposal, including selective testimonial references to allegedly factual reports on
the war, declarations by eminent churchmen, theological sources,
papal encyclicals, and the Scriptures.

Some material pertaining particularly to the construction of the
pro-Nationalist position illustrates the general points considered in
this chapter. Some attention is due also to the partial deconstruction
of that position by Catholic opponents, but the scope of this chapter
does not encompass the more positive aspects of the dissenters' positions—the stories that they might have wished to tell about the direction in which Spain ought to have moved if circumstances had been
different. The main sample of representative texts on the pro-
Nationalist side is drawn from writings by Paul Claudel, Henri Massis, Rear-Admiral Henri Joubert, and François Maret, and the brief
treatment of arguments raised by the dissenting minority will be a
synthesis based on writings by figures such as Jacques Maritain,
François Mauriac, and Georges Bernanos. The texts form an intricate
network in which the writers frequently make explicit or tacit reference to each other's arguments.

What was the story of the war, as conceived by the supporters of
Franco? And what was it intended to legitimate? There were, of
course, secondary narratives on the Nationalist side with variant
structures, but the central story of the war, with the Spanish nation as
an entity syncretizing the *actantial* functions of subject, object and
receiver of the object, conforms to what Suleiman would categorize as
a positive, exemplary, apprenticeship structure, which is a form of the
Bildungsroman. It is the story of a quest in which a central figure or
entity (the Spanish people in this case) is prompted by an *actantial*
sender (God) to search for authentic selfhood (religious, social, and
political in the case of Spain). In the course of the search, a transition
is made from passive ignorance to decay (the state of Spain on the eve
of the war) through an ideologically instructive process of trials and
testing against opposing forces (the war against the Republicans) to
eventual self-knowledge and the prospect of dynamic action in the future (the anticipated Catholic, Nationalist regime). Thus, the aims of
the story were to legitimate the war itself, to legitimate the role of the
Church in Spain, and to justify a certain form of socioeconomic and
political order for Spain once the war had been won. All of this was
intended to rally or consolidate Catholic conservative support for

Franco's cause in France, and, no doubt, to apply indirect pressure on the policy decisions of the French government.[3]

If the starting point for the process of self-discovery was the outbreak of the war, the meaning of the conflict must necessarily include its antecedents, which were presented in such a way as to justify the military rebellion against a legally elected government, and to rationalize the stance of Catholics, including the writers, in support of Franco. Here, as elsewhere, the narrative was created by inclusion and combination of sets of information that supported the thesis and by exclusion of information that did not. The chronological focus was on the period from the inception of the Second Republic in 1931 to the weeks immediately following the Nationalist uprising in July 1936. The texts show a series of mutually reinforcing elements, the function of which is to displace moral responsibility for the bloodletting from the Nationalists to the Republicans and to identify the Republic as a whole with the actions or ideas of its most extreme left-wing constituents—an identification that was further reinforced by the writers' *pratique de l'amalgame* in treating all of the governmental forces in the war as Reds or anarchists, regardless of their differing complexions in reality. Conversely, the army and the Church were represented as the two bodies that had remained as bearers of the true Spanish values.

The construction of this binary scheme involved a selective condensation of the history of the Republic from 1931 onward, according to a teleology that presented the events of those five years as an inexorable, nightmarish development, culminating in the anticlerical atrocities and the quasi revolution occurring in the Republican-controlled regions immediately after the military uprising. The upheavals in the Republican zone were claimed to be of such magnitude that they testified to a conspiracy planned long in advance. In other words, it was implied, the final, antireligious, revolutionary upheaval was about to happen anyway as a climax of what had already been taking place under the Popular Front and earlier governments. Thus, the military insurrection itself, besides being explained as a last desperate effort to stem the tide of chaos and tyranny, was subtly downgraded and minimized as a cause of the war, all the more so because there was no mention of the failed military coup four years earlier nor of any of the other disruptive activity from the right under the Republic. The reader was tacitly invited to infer that the civil war was really started by an extreme left-wing conspiracy, not by the Nationalist generals. Joubert, Claudel, and Maret each convey this impression in their own form of argument, while Massis, in a hagiographic account of an interview with Franco, uncritically quotes the latter's claim to have seen documentary evidence of such a conspiracy by the left.[4]

If these references to the immediate past serve as a basis for the claim that Franco was fighting a lawful defensive war and that he was defending the Church from barbaric persecutors, there was also a longer historical perspective that conveyed the implication that Spain was intrinsically, essentially Catholic and that the secularism or dechristianization of the more recent past were merely short-term aberrations. In Claudel and Massis, who had both shown the same pattern of thinking in relation to France during World War I, the present conflict marks the renewal of the spirit of Spain's golden centuries, a reaffirmation of national identity and vocation.[5] Similarly, for Maret, Spain is the sleeper who reawakes, whereas Joubert merely has to quote from the collective letter published by the Spanish bishops asserting the revival of national fervor in tandem with a return to the Christian freedom of former times.[6] In this perspective, the crusade, a contemporary counterpart of the battle for Jerusalem or the *Reconquista*, becomes a temporal expression of the recovery of an alienated, stolen part of the self. The idea emerges, for example, when Massis describes the conflict as "cette reconquête de l'âme qui s'opère en même temps que la reconquête du sol, cette fièvre de création qui se mêle à l'oeuvre de sang et de mort" (*Chefs*, 156). Moreover, the extent to which French Catholics could build on a well-tried narrative scheme—and one that offered them a compensation for the frustration of hopes which they had cherished for their own country in 1914—was apparent in their attribution to Spain of precisely the role that they had projected for France in that earlier war. Through the cleansing, expiatory effects of sacrifice and the exaltation of heroism in a holy cause, Spain was to become an exemplary beacon of the faith in an otherwise benighted age. So, for example, in May 1939 Claudel was still referring to "la sainte terre espagnole, maintenant purifiée, par-dessus les ruines," or to the prospect of "l'Espagne régénérée, revenue à ses traditions et à son rôle de champion de la chrétienté" ("Hommage"). Likewise, Massis could be found describing Spain as "la suprême réserve morale de l'Occident" offering its young people the vision of a new age (*Chefs*, 175).

It is important, however, not to lose sight of the fact that the meaning of the story was not restricted to the religious struggle against forces identified with militant atheism. In the binary scheme of the narrative and of the interpretive discourse accompanying it, Spanish Nationalism also represented the renewal of traditional civilized values in opposition to anarchism and communism. The legitimation of the social cause could be encoded in the most general terms of reified, timeless abstractions, as it was in the pro-Nationalist manifesto, "Aux intellectuels espagnols" (drafted by Claudel and signed by numerous right-wing notables, including Massis and Joubert).[7] There, the claim was to be above politics and to defend values such as justice, order, brotherhood, authority, tradition, the family, and property—the foundations of any civilized society—against barbarism, violence, and class hatred. Yet, the signatories could not have been entirely unaware that this was an ideological veiling of the particular with the general. In the Spanish context, these supposedly neutral, self-evident concepts corresponded to the prospect of a nondemocratic, antiparliamentary political system, restrictions on civil rights, and a social character that, for all its pious paternalism, posed no significant threat to dominant economic interest groups in the country. In fact, this was what the majority of the signatories would also have wished to see in France. But what is more interesting is that, in the discourse of Catholic pro-Nationalists, the political and the socioeconomic were often infused with the religious, hinting at a utopian sacralization of social life, so that it would not be too much of an exaggeration to suggest that in the distant background of the imagination, the millenarian narrative of temporal and spiritual glory following apocalyptic battles against the forces of the Antichrist may have unconsciously overdetermined these stories of the future Spain with its own structure of crisis-judgments-salvation.[8]

It was unfortunate that there were Catholics who pointed to flaws in the plot. From the animosity that they aroused, we may suspect that they intruded on the charmed circle of belief in a far more insidious way than non-Christians whose thinking did not include even the notional possibility of a holy war. It is true that when Jacques Maritain gave a historicophilosophical definition of the concept of the holy war that disqualified the conflict in Spain, he was not on promising ground, given the impossibility of conclusive empirical proof one way or the other (Maritain, "De la guerre sainte," 21–27). Henri Joubert's refutation of Maritain, though less erudite and less well argued than Maritain's article, could still call on a leading Spanish theologian or the collective statement by the Spanish bishops to increase the symbolic force of his case (Joubert, 22–26, 36–45). Furthermore, Joubert and others were not above defending the dominance of their interpretation by recourse to more conventional polemical techniques of denigrating the credibility of the opponent to devalue his position. Joubert uses turns of phrase, such as "ce philosophe d'étiquette catholique" or "cet ardent converti, catholique

un peu bruyant," and other innuendos to cast doubt on the or-
thodoxy of Maritain's Catholicism (Joubert, 7, 41). Likewise, using
the binary scheme of interpretation, Joubert could suggest that, objectively, Maritain's refusal to accept the thesis of the holy war
betokened sympathy for the Reds, notwithstanding his claims to the
contrary (Joubert, 21). Other Christian democrats received similar
treatment from other pro-Nationalists, many of whom had crossed
swords with them in the past over other issues.[9] Bernanos, of course,
could not be pushed into the Red camps so easily, but his own eyewit-
ness account in *Les Grands Cimetières sous la lune* could be faulted on
the grounds that his comfortable location on Majorca had given him
a naïvely narrow perception of the issues at stake.[10]

Nevertheless, the dissenting minority had embarrassing facts to
raise against the thesis of the Nationalist crusade. They drew attention to Nationalist atrocities, especially those visited on the deeply
Catholic Basque regions, including the bombing of Guernica and
Durango. They pointed with distaste to the use of Moorish
auxiliaries, which was, after all, something of a paradox, since the
medieval crusades had been fought against Islam. The presence of the
Germans was also difficult to reconcile with the notion of a holy war
at a time when the Nazis had been actively repressing the Church in
Germany. Nor was it helpful to the pro-Nationalists that Maritain,
Mauriac, and others should campaign for mediation between the two
sides to try to stop the war, however little chance there might be of
success, or that the binary scheme should be attacked by the dissenters
in a variety of other ways as they pursued their own different conception of what it meant to be Catholic.[11]

How did the pro-Nationalists defend their story? One important
factor was the symbolic advantage of being able to draw far more
heavily than the dissenters on testimonial references to high-ranking
ecclesiastical figures. Especially among the Spanish clergy, sympathy
for the Nationalists was the dominant tendency within the upper
strata of the Church, including the (somewhat cautious) Vatican.[12]
The French writers, in turn, vouched for the lucid judgment of the
Spanish bishops, and ratified the latter's somewhat disingenuous
claims that there was no element of economic interest or political
prejudice in their commitment to the Nationalist cause.[13] Another
factor was that, amid the welter of conflicting reports on events in
Spain, pro-Nationalist Catholics were drawn naturally to journalistic
and other sources that selected information to present Nationalist actions in a favorable light, and those of the Republicans in the opposite
way. For example, on the basis of such reports, the bombing of

Guernica and Durango could be flatly denied, and the accounts of the bombing attributed to the Reds' making propaganda to cover their own scorched-earth tactics.[14] On the other hand, if outright denial was not feasible, it was possible to minimize and disconnect Nationalist abuses, while reprojecting the charges back on the Republicans. Thus, it could be acknowledged that the Nationalists had been guilty of occasional outrages without any system or pattern behind them, while it was asserted that systematic extermination was a necessary product of the ideologies of the left (See, for example, Maret, 228, note 1). Yet another alternative was simply to ignore the allegations, as did Joubert, Maret, and Claudel on the issue of the German and Italian presence.[15] Finally, the overall effect of much of the pro-Nationalist discourse was to split the opposing arguments and deal with each item individually, but to pay no attention to their aggregate weight. As Claudel and Joubert showed, it was even possible to elude the problem of the Catholic Basques by following the Spanish bishops in suggesting that by fighting for the Republic, the Basques were objectively colluding with communism. With the basic, binary division maintained, the call for mediation could also be rejected on the grounds that there could be no compromise with forces pledged to destroy Christian civilization.[16]

This account may be concluded by recalling some of the wider considerations that colored the pre-Nationalist Catholics' perception of the war. First, the outcome of the conflict could be decisive in restoring the dominance of Catholicism in one of the countries where it had been eroded over a long period by liberal secularism, and more recently by atheistic Marxism, with its evangelical universalist aspirations similar to Catholicism's. In that sense, Spain could be a valuable example for other countries, including France. Equally, it could be hoped that the establishment of an authoritarian conservative political regime, maintaining an inegalitarian socioeconomic order based on private ownership, tempered by Catholic compassion once the subversives had been neutralized, would not only serve Spain but also be an example for France. Furthermore, Spain would mark a reassertion of the traditional alliance between the Church and the political right, at the expense of the Christian Democratic and other more radical groups that had gained strength in the more open climate of the late 1920s and early 1930s. If the Nationalists triumphed in Spain with the blessing of the Spanish episcopate, it would be a victory also for the French Catholic right over the Christian Democrats in France. Furthermore, although Franco's Catholic supporters in France might find his collusion with Germany and Italy distasteful, their fear of the spread of Soviet influence far outweighed their antipathy toward the two fascist powers.[17] The uncompromising determination with which the pro-Nationalist campaigners defended their story of the war is an indication of how high the stakes appeared to be. But above all, perhaps, it is a striking testimony to the power of the ideological imagination.

NOTES

1. For general discussion, see, for example Maryse Bertrand de Muñoz, *La Guerre civile espagnole et la littérature française* (Paris: Marcel Didier, 1972), especially pp. 93–116; René Rémond, *Les Catholiques dans les années 30* (Paris: Cana, 1979), pp. 175–203. For individual cases, see, for example, Bernard E. Doering, *Jaques Maritain and the French Catholic Intellectuals* (Notre Dame: University of Notre Dame Press, 1983), pp. 85–125; Christopher G. Flood, "French Catholic Writers and the Spanish Civil War: The Case of Paul Claudel," forthcoming in proceedings of the Exile Conference on the Literature of the Spanish Civil War, Texas A&M University, 15–18 Oct. 1986.

2. See Pierre Bourdieu, "Genèse et structure du champ religieux," *Revue française de sociologie* 12(1971): 295–334; and *Ce que parler veut dire* (Paris: Fayard, 1982).

3. The propagandistic function of the writing, therefore, is a paradoxical combination of *agitation* (aggressively subversive, oppositional, in relation to the Spanish Republic and, indirectly, to its counterpart in France) and *integration* (in favor of conformity and stability in a permanent setting under the new order). See A. P. Foulkes, *Literature and Propaganda* (London: Methuen, 1983), pp. 10–11 and passim.

4. See Henri Joubert, *La Guerre d'Espagne et le catholicisme* (Paris: SGIE, 1937), especially pp. 16–26; Paul Claudel, "L'Anarchie dirigée," in *Oeuvres complètes*, vol. 16 (Paris: Gallimard, 1959), pp. 270–74 (first published in *Le Figaro*, 27 Aug. and 13 Sept. 1937); François Maret (pseud. Frans van Ermengem, a Belgian art and literary historian, who participated in debate in France). *Les Grands Chantiers au soleil* (Paris: Sorlot, 1938), pp. 219–22; Henri Massis, *Chefs* (Paris: Plon, 1939), p. 147 (the meeting with Franco took place in July 1938).

5. See Claudel, "La Solidarité d'Occident," *Le Figaro,* 29 July 1938, and "Aux martyrs espagnols," in *Oeuvre poétique,* edited by Jacques Petit, Bibliothèque de la Pléiade (Paris: Gallimard, 1967), pp. 568–69 (first published as preface of J. Estelrich, *La Persécution religieuse en Espagne* (Paris: Plon, 1937); Massis, *Chefs*, p. 174. For their hopes of France during the Great War, see, for example, Massis, *Le Sacrifice* (Paris: Plon, 1917); Claudel, *La Nuit de Noël 1914,* in *Théâtre,* vol. 2, ed. Jacques Madaule and Jacques Petit, Bibliothèque de la Pléiade (Paris: Gallimard, 1969), pp. 573–92, to be read in conjunction with Claudel, letter to Piero Jahier, 30 Jan. 1915, in Henri Giordan, *Paul Claudel en Italie* (Paris: Klincksieck, 1975), p. 155; and for the wider context, Jacques Fontana, *Attitude et sentiments du clergé et des catholiques français devant et durant la guerre de 1914–1918* (Lille: Université de Lille III, Atelier de reproduction des thèses, 1973), especially pp. 50–162.

6. See Maret, *Les Grands Chantiers*, p. 231; Joubert, *La Guerre d'Espagne*, p. 40.

7. See Comité Intellectuel de l'Amitié entre la France et l'Espagne, "Aux intellectuels espagnols," reprinted in *Occident,* 10 Dec. 1937, with list of early signatories. For reference to Claudel's authorship of the manifesto, see, for example, *Journal,* vol. 2, ed. François Varillon and Jacques Petit, Bibliothèque de la Pléiade (Paris: Gallimard, 1969), p. 207.

8. For examples of sacralizing discourse, see Massis, p. 156 (on Franco's social policy "que l'Espagne s'impose avec amour" to be accomplished "dans un sentiment de réparation, de justice, pour que le travail, ce devoir imposé par Dieu, soit assuré comme un droit"); Maret, p. 232.

For the structure of apocalyptic narratives, see Bernard McGinn, *Visions of the End. Apocalyptic Traditions in the Middle Ages* (New York: Columbia University Press, 1979), pp. 1–36.

9. See, for example, Marcel Grosdidier de Matous, "L'Erreur de François Mauriac," *Occident*, 10 July 1938. This article is a compendium of the accusations which appeared frequently in *Occident* and other pro–Nationalist newspapers. Mauriac is accused of watering down Catholicism, compromising with antireligious forces, flirting with the left, giving the impression that the rich are all evil, etc. Under the title "L'Ennemi le plus dangereux," the same issue of *Occident* contains a report of a speech by Serrano Suñer, attacking Maritain. See Rémond, pp. 175–203, for numerous extracts from articles by Mauriac and other Christian Democrats concerning Spain, and passim for their controversies with the Catholic right on other issues. Also, for an interesting collection of articles on the war by another Christian Democrat, Francisque Gay, see his *Dans les flammes et dans le sang* (Paris: Bloud et Gay, 1936).

10. See Maret, p. 219, forming part of an attempted refutation of Georges Bernanos, *Les Grands Cimetières sous la lune* (the latter is reprinted in Bernanos, *Essais et écrits de combat*, vol. 1, ed. Michel Estève, Bibliothèque de la Pléiade (Paris: Gallimard, 1971), pp. 353–575.

11. The Comité Français pour la Paix Civile et Religieuse en Espagne, which conducted the campaign for mediation, was cofounded by Jacques Maritain with his friend, Alfredo Mendizabal (see Doering, *Jacques Maritain*, p. 110 for background). The most comprehensive expression of Maritain's position on the war, including the argument for mediation and democratic self-determination, is his preface to Mendizabal's *Aux origines d'une tragédie: la politique espagnole de 1923 à 1936* (Paris: Desclée de Brouwer, 1937), pp. 7–57. The preface subsumes "De la guerre sainte."

12. For the position of the Church hierarachy, see Bertrand de Muñoz, *La Guerre civile espagnole*, pp. 101–2; and Anthony Rhodes, *The Vatican in the Age of the Dictators, 1922–45* (London: Hodder & Stoughton, 1973), pp. 122–30.

13. See Claudel, "L'Anarchie dirigée" in its entirety; and Joubert, pp. 39–40. For discussion of the political tendencies and the substantial economic interests of the Spanish Church, see Hugh Thomas, *The Spanish Civil War* (London: Penguin, rev. ed., 1965), pp. 51–57; and Frances Lannon, "The Church's Crusade against the Republic," in Paul Preston, ed., *Revolution and War in Spain, 1931–39* (London: Methuen, 1984), pp. 35–58.

14. See Joubert, pp. 32–33 (based on claims in Estelrich, *La Persécution religieuse en Espagne*, p. 135 and passim); also Flood, "French Catholic Writers and the Spanish Civil War," for discussion of Claudel's position within the wider context of his views on the Basque question. See David Wingeate Pike, *Les Français et la guerre d'Espagne* (Paris: PUF, 1975), pp. 217–35, for an account of the conflicting reports on Guernica, the Nationalist cover-up, and Catholic responses in France.

15. Massis, on the other hand, quotes Franco's claim that he has no obligations to Germany, because the Germans are aiding him on a purely commercial basis, without any strings attached (pp. 148–49). The question of how this cynical opportunism matched the idea of the crusade was not raised. See Flood, "French Catholic Writers and the Spanish Civil War," for a discussion of the same question in Claudel's private correspondence.

16. See Joubert, pp. 41, 43; Claudel, "L'Anarchie dirigée," in *Oeuvres complètes*, vol. 16, pp. 273–74; Estelrich, p. 134.

17. See, for example, Charles Micaud, *The French Right and Nazi Germany, 1933–1939* (New York: Octagon, 1964).

WORKS CITED

Bernanos, Georges. "Les Grands Cimetières sous la lune." Reprinted in *Essais et écrits de combat*, vol. 1. Ed. Michel Estève. Bibliothèque de la Pléiade. Paris: Gallimard, 1971.

Bertrand de Muñoz, Maryse. *La Guerre civile espagnole et la littérature française.* Paris: Marcel Didier, 1972.

Bourdieu, Pierre. *Ce que parler veut dire.* Paris: Fayard, 1982.

———. "Genèse et structure du champ religieux." *Revue française de sociologie* 12 (1971): 295–334.

Claudel, Paul. "L'Anarchie dirigée." In *Oeuvres complètes,* vol. 16. Paris: Gallimard, 1959.

———. "Aux martyrs espagnols." In *Oeuvre poétique.* Ed. Jacques Petit. *Bibliothèque de la Pléiade.* Paris: Gallimard, 1967.

———. *Journal,* 2d. ed. Ed. François Varillon and Jacques Petit. *Bibliothèque de la Pléiade.* Paris: Gallimard, 1969.

———. Letter to Piero Jahier, 30 Jan. 1915. In Henri Giordan, *Paul Claudel en Italie.* Paris: Klincksieck, 1975.

———. *La Nuit de Noel, 1914.* In *Théâtre,* vol. 2. Ed. Jacques Madaule and Jacques Petit. *Bibliothèque de la Pléiade.* Paris: Gallimard, 1969.

———. "La Solidarité d'Occident." *Le Figaro,* 29 July 1938.

———. "Hommage." *Occident,* 30 May 1939.

Comité Intellectuel de l'Amitié entre la France et l'Espagne. "Aux intellectuels espagnols." Reprinted in *Occident,* 10 Dec. 1937.

Doering, Bernard E. *Jacques Maritain and the French Catholic Intellectuals.* Notre Dame: University of Notre Dame Press, 1983.

Estelrich, Juan. *La Persécution religieuse en Espagne.* Paris: Plon, 1937.

Flood, Christopher. "French Catholic Writers and the Spanish Civil War: The Case of Paul Claudel." Forthcoming in the Proceedings of the Exile Conference on the Literature of the Spanish Civil War, Texas A&M University, 15–18 Oct., 1986.

Fontana, Jacques. *Attitude et sentiments du clergé et des catholiques français devant et durant la guerre de 1914–1918.* Lille: Université de Lille III, Atelier de reproduction des thèses, 1973.

Foulkes, A. P. *Literature and Propaganda.* London: Methuen, 1983.

Gay, Francisque. *Dans les flammes et dans le sang.* Paris: Bloud et Gay, 1936.

Grosdidier de Matous, Marcel. "L'Erreur de François Mauriac." *Occident,* 10 July 1938.

Joubert, Henri. *La Guerre d'Espagne et le catholicisme.* Paris: SGIE, 1937.

Lannon, Frances. "The Church's Crusade against the Republic." In *Revolution and War in Spain, 1931–1939.* Ed. Paul Preston. London: Methuen, 1984.

Maret, François. *Les Grands Chantiers au soleil.* Paris: Sorlot, 1938.

Maritain, Jacques. "De la guerre sainte." *NRF,* July 1937.

———. Preface to *Aux origines d'une tragédie: la politique espagnole de 1923 à 1936,* by Alfredo Mendizabal. Paris: Desclée de Brouwer, 1937.

Massi, Henri. *Chefs.* Paris: Plon, 1939.

———. *Le Sacrifice.* Paris: Plon, 1917.

McGinn, Bernard. *Visions of the End. Apocalyptic Traditions in the Middle Ages.* New York: Columbia University Press, 1979.

Micaud, Charles. *The French Right and Nazi Germany, 1931–1939.* New York: Octagon, 1964.

Pike, David Wingeate. *Les Français et la guerre d'Espagne.* Paris: PUF, 1975.

Rémond, René. *Les Catholiques dans les années 30.* Paris: Cana, 1979.

Rhodes, Anthony. *The Vatican in the Age of the Dictators, 1922–45.* London: Hodder & Stoughton, 1973.

Suleiman, Susan R. *Authoritarian Fictions. The Ideological Novel as a Literary Genre.* New York: Columbia University Press, 1983.

Suñer, Serrano. "L'Ennemi le plus dangereux." *Occident,* 10 July 1938.

Thomas, Hugh. *The Spanish Civil War,* rev. ed. London: Penguin, 1965.

Thompson, John B. *Studies in the Theory of Ideology.* Cambridge: Polity Press, 1984.

Simone de Beauvoir
and the Spanish Civil War:
From Apoliticism to Commitment
Alfred Cismaru

In 1936 Simone de Beauvoir was twenty-eight years old. If we compare the extent and the intensity of her activities in other areas, her noninvolvement in politics until the beginning of the Spanish Civil War emerges as a strange phenomenon. It is clear that in her case, as in the case of her mentor Jean-Paul Sartre, who was three years older, there was no commitment in the cradle; nor really during their adolescent or student years, nor as budding writers and philosophers, nor even after 1933 when Hitler rose to power. It was not until Franco's troops landed in Spain in July 1936 that the two Existentialists became aware that the advancement of a cause required less sympathy than action.

For the country itself, de Beauvoir had a particular penchant. Prior to the start of the hostilities, she and Sartre had visited Spain with great enthusiasm. She reports in *La Force de l'âge* that they did not have much money at the time. Sartre converted into *pesetas* the little that was left from a small inheritance; they knew that they were going to have to rough it in Spain, but they simply had to go. Recalling the voyage years later, de Beauvoir is not above becoming quite lyrical in the description of general and specific reactions.

> Nous imaginions que chaque lieu, chaque ville avait un secret, une âme, une essence éternelle et que la tâche du voyageur était de les dévoiler . . . pas seulement dans leurs musées, leurs monuments, leur passé, mais au présent, à travers leurs ombres et leurs lumières, leurs foules, leurs odeurs, leurs nourritures. (de Beauvoir, *La Force,* 87)

Afterward, she goes on to say that she agrees with André Gide, who, in *Prétextes,* had declared that drinking a cup of Spanish chocolate was the same as holding all of Spain in one's mouth (De Beauvoir, *La Force,* 87–88).

Such luscious recollections notwithstanding, she and Sartre went through the country in the manner of superficial tourists. The fact is that museums, churches and other monuments interested them much more than the pulsating upheavals of the country's political existence under a leftist government that they supported, but that was subject to considerable and insurmountable problems. One afternoon, for example, while searching for a cathedral they wished to see, they noticed that the streets were suddenly deserted. They continued to walk, and then they chanced upon groups of people hotly debating issues they did not quite understand because they did not speak Spanish. They saw police cars and arrests being made, but they proceeded to find the cathedral and visited it leisurely. Only in the evening, while deciphering as best they could a local newspaper, did they realize that a general strike had been declared, that union militants had been arrested in the afternoon, and that the crowds they had noticed were deliberating whether or not to attack the police and free the militants. De Beauvoir was mildly ashamed of having missed the whole affair: "nous étions présents et nous n'avons rien vu. Nous nous consolâmes en pensant à Stendhal et à sa bataille de Waterloo" (De Beauvoir, *La Force,* 89), referring, of course, to the well-known episode in *La Chartreuse de Parme,* in which the protagonist watches a most important historical event without understanding at all what is going on.

It was no different in Seville. There de Beauvoir and Sartre witnessed an attempted military coup: When General Sanjurjo arrested the mayor of the city, a Spanish-speaking friend explained that troops had occupied all the strategic points in the area as part of a major plot to overthrow the Republic. Years later, de Beauvoir recalled that although there were many soldiers in the street, and much armament, "tout était paisible; les monuments, les musées, les cafés accueillaient tranquillement les touristes" (De Beauvoir, *La Force,* 119). She does not even wonder why she and Sartre did not feel involved, did not attempt to find out more about the event, did not fear at all the possible success of the military.

The two Existentialists practiced such detachment in France as well. They deluded themselves that it was especially through writing that history could be shaped, perhaps even controlled. Of course, writing was their life, their business, de Beauvoir's even more than Sartre's. The latter, in fact, had considered joining the Communist Party at one point, but ultimately opted against it. It will be recalled that André Gide's Communist Party affiliation lasted only until his brief stay in Russia was over. Even before that, however, reports of

Stalin's reign of terror filtered through, and many French intellectuals began to have second thoughts about the Communist alternative. A Spanish friend of the Sartre–de Beauvoir couple, Michel del Castillo, was to explain later:

> I say, very simply, that if bloodshed is absolutely necessary in making history, I would rather someone else did the history-making. Does this mean that nothing matters to me? No! No one can withdraw from the issue that easily. In spite of ourselves, we are plunged into history, and sooner or later we are forced to take sides. But there is a great deal of difference between taking sides and joining a party. (viii–ix)

Whereas Sartre also decided not to join, Simone de Beauvoir refused even to entertain the idea. Political commitment that took time away from writing was wrong, she concluded, and journalistic writing was beneath her. She believed firmly that it was possible to promote one's political views through the practice of solid literature, that in fact it was through the latter that one attained the reputation required for the exercise of influence in the political arena.

Before 1936, whenever more committed friends reproached de Beauvoir for her attitude of noninvolvement, she would respond that, were she to engage in speeches or participate in meetings or demonstrations, no one would pay much attention because she was not sufficiently well known. She and Sartre went even further in their aloofness by refusing to vote, when the occasion arose, in local or general elections. She writes in *La Force de l'age:*

> il ne nous vint pas à l'idée de défiler, de chanter, de crier avec les autres. Telle était, à l'époque, notre attitude; les événements pouvaient susciter en nous de vifs sentiments de colère, de crainte, de joie: mais nous n'y participions pas; nous restions spectateurs. (224)

De Beauvoir's sympathy for communism and left-wing causes notwithstanding, writing was foremost in her mind, and her commitment to it was paramount. One commentator went even further, speculating that she and Sartre did not really wish society to change and acquire all the aspects they dreamt of, because then they would have been deprived of the enjoyment of dabbling in a literature of *contestation:*

> Sartre even went so far as claiming that his opposition Aesthetics needed . . . objects of attack, for without them literature would not be very important. So as a writer he did not mind the continued existence of this detestable society and it could be said that he came close to implying that if the bourgeoisie did not exist it would have to be invented. (Whitmarsh, 12–13)

De Beauvoir, of course, was easily influenced by Sartre, and it was only much later in her life that she looked back at her apoliticism and regretted it, at times to the point of making fun of it. Such regret and mockery can be found in *Memoirs of a Dutiful Daughter* (de Beauvoir, 34), for example, and in an interview with Madeleine Chaspal (Francis and Gontier, 393).

De Beauvoir's belated regret sheds little light on the reasons for which she skirted the responsibility requirement of a true Existentialist. The simple explanation that it is customary for most people to preach one thing and to practice another is tempting, but the complexity of de Beauvoir's personality and of the movement to which she lent her name make it even more tempting to see a less apparent exegesis. Could it be, for example, that both she and Sartre, inwardly at least, considered political activity to be at odds with their spiritual growth as philosophers with a mission that went beyond the minute and temporary effervescence of historical bubbles? So long as there was no war, so long as Fascism remained only a threat, might they not make better use of their time—by concretizing their ideas in published writing, for example, directing their thoughts to both the elites with whom they identified and the masses whose support kept them in the limelight?

Writing was no easy task. For the most part, Sartre created while de Beauvoir explained and defended that creation. Both his philosophical flights and her explanation and illustration of them were extremely time-consuming. There were, to be sure, mundane activities as well. There were liaisons, parties, time spent drinking, a great deal of travel. But above all there was writing: day and night, on holidays, while waiting for and on board planes, on trains, and even in the subway, whether seated or standing. Above all they wrote in the cafes, where often they were permitted to remain between closing and opening hours, in order to continue to fill page after page with the surges of their minds.

Words came easily most of the time, like avalanches prey to the gravitational pull. The hand moved effortlessly, and the fingers would no longer hurt after hours of writing. That was the time when expression, far from betraying thought, reinforced it with the throbbing substance of life. Seeing the black words on the white page was the same as caressing a child, palpable and growing, and enhancing the initial pleasure of conception and the later satisfaction of gestation. The reward was immediate and direct.

In contrast, political involvements would have provided only a precarious and uncertain gratification. There would have been more physical and furious action, but attainment of goals would have remained dubious; whereas the pleasure of writing derived only from the writers. Large readership was a bonus, not a must, and at any rate they saw their readership growing rather fast. It was understandable, therefore, that Sartre and de Beauvoir should chose to write about commitment rather than actually to become *engaged*.

Their apolitical stand was shaken thoroughly when Franco landed in Spain. At first de Beauvoir did not worry much about the Republic. It had lasted already for five years, and although there would always be reactionaries who would fight against it, it was an entrenched reality, its victory plausible, if not certain. Nearly all of her friends shared her optimism. They all were touched by the epic struggle of the people against the better armed and more disciplined army supported by the Fascists in Italy and the Nazis in Germany. Recalling those days almost three decades later, she wrote, "La guerre d'Espagne m'a émue," yet, still wishing to hang on to her apoliticism, she added, "mais je ne pensais pas qu'elle me concernat directement" (de Beauvoir, *La Force,* 33).

Almost immediately, however, guilt set in, more and more devastating as Franco won battle after battle and the fall of the Republic became almost certain. It became first difficult and then impossible for de Beauvoir and Sartre to find excuses for their inaction.

> Pour la première fois de notre vie, parce que nous prenions profondement à coeur le sort de l'Espagne, l'indignation n'était plus pour nous un exutoir suffisant; notre impuissance politique, loin de nous fournir un alibi, nous désolait. Elle était totale. Nous étions isoles, nous n'etions personne: rien de ce que nous pouvions dire ou écrire . . . n'aurait le moindre poids. (de Beauvoir, *La Force,* 298)

Some of de Beauvoir's friends went to Spain and attempted to join the Republican combatants on the field of battle, but there was not enough armament. Simone Weil, for example, crossed the Spanish border and asked for a machine gun and duty in the militia. Instead, she was given a job in a kitchen, and promptly dropped a huge pot of boiling water on her feet. Colette Audry, who went to Barcelona in order to fight, was told that her role would be limited to making speeches on France's sympathy for the Republican cause. When she returned to France, she expressed her deep disappointment that she had not had an active role, because no speech, no matter how vigorous, replaces a gun; no one really had cared to listen to speeches.

De Beauvoir had no desire to go to Spain. She cried when others went, both because she knew that it was futile to do so, and because she realized that her makeup precluded such extreme action. She abandoned her position on the sidelines, however, and used all her influence to persuade members of the Popular Front Government of Léon Blum to abandon neutrality and send arms, if not troops, to aid the Republic. Those were useless efforts as well, because the

timid Léon Blum followed a position of nonintervention. Recalling
later the distressing days when she watched Spain fall into fascist
hands, her memory was both tersely factual and poetically sentimental.
She wrote:

> Dans les villes et les villages les miliciens, faute d'armes, faisaient l'exercice avec des
> bâtons: il y avait de nombreuses femmes dans leurs rangs; elles étaient aussi ardentes à
> se battre que les hommes. Contre les chars d'assaut de Franco, les *dinamiteros* lançaient
> des grenades et des bouteilles enflammées. L'héroisme d'un peuple aux mains nues allait
> barrer la route aux troupes . . . que jetaient contre lui la Propriété, l'Eglise, la Finance:
> c'était une épopée bouleversante. (De Beauvoir, *La Force,* 283–84)

At the time she jots down these recollections, she is deeply hurt and
angry at herself for not having done a great deal more than watch. Actually, she does not quite understand the rather placid attitude of her
youth when confronted with the historical happenings taking place so
close to France. She is all the more astonished because

> aucun pays ne nous était plus proche que l'Espagne. . . . Nous avons partagé la liesse
> du premier été republicain, sous le soleil de Madrid; nous nous étions mêlés à la joyeuse
> effervescence de Seville, après la fuite de Sanjurjo, quand la foule allumait dans les
> cercles aristocratiques des incendies que les pompiers n'éteignaient pas. Nous avions vu
> de nos yeux la grasse arrogance des bourgeois et des curés, la misère des paysans. . . . Je
> me rappelle un dîner, dans le restaurant espagnol dont j'ai parlé et que fréquentaient
> exclusivement des républicains. Une jeune cliente espagnole se leva soudain et déclama
> un poème à la gloire de son pays et de la liberté; nous ne comprenions pas les mots—un
> de nos voisins nous en indiqua le sens général—mais nous fûmes emus par la voix de la
> jeune femme, par son visage. Tous les convives se dressèrent et crièrent: "Vive la
> Republique espagnole!" Tous croyaient à son prochain triomphe. La Passionaria avait
> jeté aux fascistes un cri de défi: "*Non passaran!*" qui retentissait à travers tout l'Espagne.
> (de Beauvoir, *La Force,* 283–84)

Being apolitical, then, appeared more and more of a travesty. Both
de Beauvoir and Sartre began to attend meetings asking for Blum's approval of arms shipments to Spain. They got together with other intellectuals and signed manifestos, and petitions, and raised money for
those who wished to join the International Brigades and go to Spain
to fight. Writing began to be a secondary undertaking, for what was
happening in Spain was being echoed in Germany, and most leftists
started to review their priorities and their specific role as Leftists in
contemporary historical developments. Madrid was being bombed,
the Guernica massacre shocked even some of the rightists in France,
Bilbao was about to fall, and within the Reich there was nothing and
no one anymore to stop Hitler. In the midst of all this there was one
last defense for de Beauvoir's individualism: she became ill and the
doctors ordered her to take three weeks off in the south of France.

In this context, one is reminded of a little-known short story by an almost Existentialist, Albert Camus, whom the Sartre–de Beauvoir couple first befriended and with whom they quarreled later. Jonas is the name of that story, and it deals with a successful painter by the same name. He would like to devote his life to art, but he has a family, social obligations, and, alas, disciples. Circumscribed, cornered by society, his creativity suffering, he withdraws to his attic to devote all his time to painting. He has his meals brought there and refuses to see anyone, even those closest to him. After a while, his last canvas is discovered, signed with the word *solitaire*. Only the t in it might be a d, looks like a d, and there is really no way of telling for sure whether Jonas made a definitive decision, or hesitated until his very last breath.

When Simone de Beauvoir returned from her medical leave, she brought with her a reasoned, deliberate and solid commitment to leftist causes, one that remained with her for most of the rest of her life. She recalled the transformation that took place then in tragically lyrical phrases:

> Je me sentais coupable. . . . Le remords me poignait. . . . Il n'est pas possible d'assigner un jour, une semaine, ni même un mois à la conversion qui s'opéra alors en moi. Mais il est certain que le printemps 1939 marque dans ma vie une coupure. Je renonçais à mon individualisme, à mon antihumanisme. J'appris la solidarité. (*La Force*, 367–68)

WORKS CITED

Beauvoir, Simone de. *La Force de l'âge*. Paris: Gallimard, 1960.
———. *Mémoires d'une jeune fille rangée*. Paris: Gallimard, 1958; Memories of a Dutiful Daughter. Trans. James Kirkup. London: André Deutsch, 1959.
———. *Tout compte fait*. Paris: Gallimard, 1972.
Castillo, Michel del. *The Disinherited*. Trans. Humphrey Hare. New York: Alfred A. Knopf, 1960.
Francis, Claude, and Fernande Gontier. *Les Ecrits de Simone de Beauvoir*. Paris: Gallimard, 1980.
Whitmarsh, Anne. *Simone de Beauvoir and the Limits of Commitment*. Cambridge: Cambridge University Press, 1981.

The Writing of History: Authors Meet on the Soviet-Spanish Border

Peter I. Barta

Three authors who went to Spain during the Civil War—Arthur Koestler (a Hungarian-born British writer), Mate Zalka (a Hungarian-born writer who became a Soviet citizen), and Mikhail Koltsov (Soviet-Russian writer)—were connected with both the International Brigades and the Communist Party of the Soviet Union. Each of them gained considerable prominence in the East or in the West, but, significantly, not in both. Koestler is all but unknown in Eastern Europe, while Zalka and Koltsov are not well known in the West. Their writings voice certain explicitly ideological discourses that are regulated by the culture in which they circulate.[1] For the West, the Soviet works appear as propaganda; for the East, the whole Koestler *oeuvre* was, until recently, regarded as provocatively anti-Soviet because of the writer's ideological shift in the years after he wrote the *Spanish Testament*.

The texts produced by these, and other, writers in the Spanish Civil War resulted in a historical portrait. All writing is rooted in ideology, but the degree of explicitness varies. Koltsov's, Zalka's and Koestler's works, like most literature about the period, are clearly "partisan" and, as regards general historical awareness of the Spanish Civil War, this confirms what Orwell, somewhat pessimistically, predicts in *Homage to Catalonia*: "Future historians will have nothing to go upon except a mass of accusations and party propaganda" (141).

The focus in this study on ideology, rather than on the person of the writer, is justified by the greater significance of the author-function than that of the author. The individual texts under discussion are mere paroles of the langue of an ideological discourse. In the works of the Soviet authors, and in Koestler's *Spanish Testament*, the first-person voice is generated from an ideological matrix with which the author-function is in agreement, but with which the actual person of the author, in fact, is not.[2]

Arthur Koestler was the only one of the three writers to survive the Spanish Civil War, its aftermath and the decision to challenge Stalinism once he became disillusioned with it. Because of his volte-face in outlook, Koestler's writings are of pivotal importance: the author-function is determined by mutually contradictory ideological discourses in the *Spanish Testament* and *Darkness at Noon*. In the latter work, a broad enough hermeneutic horizon is available against which to view the dominating discourses of the political system that is determined to "purge" the protagonist, Rubashov. He typifies the fate of people like Koltsov and Zalka whose implied personal challenge of Stalinism never reached the author-function in their writings. It was, however, partially because of *their* experiences that Koestler's ideological shift occurred.

Numerous Western volunteers came together in Spain within the ranks of such organizations as the Stalinist International Brigades or the socialist, but anti-Soviet, militia of the Spanish POUM. Soviet participants, including the writers, were commissioned by the Communist Party of the Soviet Union to join the Brigades. Motivating the Westerners was a conviction that the struggle of the Spanish Republic against Franco's forces, backed by Nazi Germany and Italy, needed to be supported morally, financially and militarily. Many shared George Orwell's feelings:

> When I came to Spain, and for some time afterwards, I was not only uninterested in the political situation but unaware of it. I knew that there was a war on, but I had no notion what kind of a war. If you had asked me why I had joined the militia I should have answered: 'To fight against Fascism,' and if you had asked me what I was fighting for, I should have answered: 'Common decency.' (*Homage*, 54)

In addition to a struggle between "Democracy and Fascist Totalitarianism," as the rhetoric of the 30's and 40's would have it, there also occurred a confrontation between the various wings of the Spanish Republican forces and the Soviet-backed foreigners who came to fight against the phallangists. This particular aspect of the complex dynamics of the Spanish Civil War was at the time, and has been since, frequently overlooked. Hemingway, for instance, seemed unaware of the role of some of the foreigners in the International Brigades. He said: "I don't understand much about politics . . . but I know what Fascism is. The people here are fighting for a good cause."[3] The issue was, in fact, considerably more complex than this quotation suggests.

The International Brigades were organized by the Comintern which was, in reality, operated by the NKVD—the Soviet Secret Police. The internal operation of the Brigades was styled after that of other Soviet armed party units. These were typified by excessive alertness about supposed spies, iron discipline and total un-scrupulousness in the execution of the dictates of the party line.[4]

Numerous Spanish republicans were resentful about the nature of the Soviet support they received. Manuel Azaña, a leading intellec-tual and politician, and Largo Caballero, a left-wing socialist who headed the Spanish Government until he was ousted by the Moscow-supported Communists, were quite explicit about their fears of an eventual Soviet takeover.[5] Whereas Western news correspondents, writers and other sympathizers joined the International Brigades of their own free will, the Soviet participants were, of course, agents of the Communist Party. For instance, it is clear, as Frederick R. Bensan points out, that the role of the war correspondents of *Pravda* and *Iz-vestiia*, Mikhail Koltsov and Ilia Ehrenburg, was, primarily to par-ticipate in undercover operations (89). The Soviet Union, moreover, was not a country that ordinary civilians could leave of their own free will. The published Soviet accounts of Mate Zalka's sudden decision to travel to Spain to join the International Brigades, motivated by his—the former GPU officer's—abhorrence of the crimes committed against humanity there, sounds rather tendentious. It distorts the fact that it was the party that assigned people deemed as thoroughly reliable to go to Spain.[6]

The clandestine manner of Zalka's being *delegated* by the Com-munist Party of the Soviet Union to go to Spain becomes clear from the published memoir of a friend:

> "You know, I fooled you. I am going to Spain and not to China." This piece of news did not surprise me too much. After all, what mattered was not where he was going to, but why he was going. From this new confession I grasped only how secretive all the things were he was carefully and gradually telling me about. But even when I understood it all, I did not guess that I was not familiar with all the details: Zalka would have to fight in Spain under a pseudonym.[7]

If Zalka, like many of the European and American participants in the International Brigades, had been the bona fide volunteer that his published biographical materials wish to suggest, surely he would not have been instructed to use the name Pal Lukacs, instead of Mate Zalka.[8]

Arthur Koestler was sent to Spain on both of his visits by Willi Muenzenberg, who headed the propaganda section of Comintern in Paris. On his second trip, Koestler's job was to start a Soviet controlled Press Agency in Spain.[9] Koestler's *Spanish Testament* and Koltsov's

Ispanskii dnevnik exhibit some noteworthy similarities. Both books have been praised for their well-written and informative accounts of the war in Spain.[10] More interesting, however, is the Stalinist author-function from which both works are generated. Koltsov's *Ispanskii dnevnik* covers events between August 3, 1936 and July 8, 1937; the individual entries appeared on the pages of *Pravda*. A contemporary Soviet critic K. Zelinskii, summarizes the usefulness of the entries:

> The workers who pack food and warm clothing for the Spanish children, the lorry drivers, who hurriedly put the sacks onto ships and freight trains, the railway-workers, weavers, writers—we all, who with our whole heart live now with the Spanish people, we all want concretely to experience people, events, place names. Koltsov unfalteringly brings these facts to light. Having read about them, few of our people stay calm. You think: there would be the place of our. . . .who? Any one of the thousands of committed proletarians who had completed the great Stalin's school. (11 Nov. 1936, translation mine)

It is unnecessary to discuss how the above passage and the general projection of political events in *Ispanskii dnevnik* distort the facts, in portraying the Soviet people as united behind the party which, driven by the purest of motives, rushes out to help the oppressed of the world.

Koestler's *Spanish Testament* is much more subtle propaganda—it was, after all, written for Western readers. But in many essential details it resembles Koltsov's diaries: information that does not prove one's point is distorted or simply dismissed (Conquest, 740). Koestler reports the bombardment of Madrid by Franco's air force. As is customary in Soviet-style press reports of enemy attacks on the country's allies, in Koestler's account only women, children, hospitals, and proletarian homes are bombed. One cannot help wondering how it can be that men and middle-class businesses and homes do not get damaged as well. It is also ironical how Koestler's comments in the *Spanish Testament* about phallangist and Nazi totalitarianism also hold true for Stalin's Soviet Union.

> . . . the document goes on, page after page; it is astonishing what the German official propagandists have the effrontery to put before the reader, secure in the fact that the banning of foreign newspapers deprives him of all the opportunity of checking up on their statements. The propaganda designed for France and England is not so crude in its methods.[11]

Of course, Koestler was more aware of the similarity between the German and Soviet propaganda machines than most people at the time, even if he chose not to acknowledge this publicly.

Koltsov, Koestler and, very probably, Zalka too—loyal servants as they were of Moscow—belonged to the old guard of the Communist Party and they had, by the time of the Spanish Civil War, ceased to approve fully of the party line under Stalin.[12] Both Koltsov and

Koestler left documentary evidence of their growing disapproval of Stalin-style communism. Zalka, to my knowledge, did not write anything except letters in Spain. He was in charge of the Twelfth International Brigade under the pseudonym of General Lukacs, and was killed by an enemy bullet in June, 1937. He became, incidentally, well acquainted with Ernest Hemingway.[13] There seems to be very little doubt that, if Zalka had returned to the Soviet Union, he would have been a prime candidate for liquidation.[14] The fact that he had associated freely with Westerners, in addition to being a foreign-born citizen of the USSR, would have been sufficient reason. In *Ispanskii dnevnik*, Koltsov also hints at possible difficulties Zalka might have experienced upon his return to Moscow for deviating in his writing from the Stalinist norms of socialist realism:

> Lukacs gave an order: the paintings should be brought out of the church lest they should be destroyed there. We admired together the naïve and passionate painting of the fifteenth-century unknown artist: the saints reminded one of both torreadors and caballeros in love. "There is in Moscow some Hungarian writer called Mate Zalka; if he should get to this hidden nook, to these fabulous places, and were to write down what he saw and submit it to the publisher, he would be thoroughly reprimanded for being so much attracted to the exotic"—I said to him.[15]

The artificially cheerful tone of the above passage is in sharp contrast with the kind of reprimand Koltsov himself experienced upon his return. He was arrested in Moscow in 1938 and was sentenced to imprisonment in exile for allegedly being the agent of Lord Beaverbrook.[16] He was executed, presumably in 1942. Koltsov was one of the many victims of Stalin's show trials.

Even as the International Brigades started arriving in Spain, the Purge Trials were getting under way in Moscow. Several old Communists like Zinoviev, Radek, Bukharin and Rahorsky were being arrested and executed. The Soviet intervention in Spain came in extremely handy for Stalin. He could publish his open letter in *Mundo Obrero*: "the liberation of Spain from the yoke of the fascist reactionaries is not the private concern of the Spaniards alone but the common cause of progressive humanity" (Mitchell, 77). Thus parading as a fervent advocate of democratic values, he managed to keep the loyalty of many Western supporters of the Soviet Union. Stalin's use of such hackneyed terms as "progressive" (=good), and "reactionary" (=bad) is an essential ingredient of the two-dimensional ideological underpinning of the writings of Zalka and Koltsov, and Koestler in his communist phase.

Koltsov left evidence that he made it quite clear, while still in Spain, that he was unhappy about the way the Soviet Communist

Party operated. Thus, Koltsov, the man, ceased to be at one with the author-function behind his diaries. Koestler spent time with him in Valencia in January, 1937. This is how he recalls Koltsov's comments about the Moscow trials:

> When Koltsov. . . had turned out the lights, the other two heard his voice, strangely flat in the darkness: "Attenzione, Agence Espagne. Tomorrow, in Moscow, starts the trial of Piatkov, Radek, Sokolnikov, Muralov and accomplices; we are all expected to report the reactions of the Spanish working class." (Quoted from Weintraub, 131)

The bitterness of these remarks suggests the same disillusionment with the dominating ideology as does his state of mind shortly before his arrest in Moscow. He said to Ehrenburg: "But what will remain of me after I have gone? Newspaper articles are ephemeral stuff. Even a historian will not find them very useful, because we don't show in our articles what's going on in Spain, only what ought to be happening."[17]

Unlike Koltsov, Koestler was not a Soviet citizen, and his famous breach with Stalin's brand of communism was not followed by a death sentence.

Koestler's resignation from the party was marked by a speech in which he declared harmful truth to be better than a useful lie (Lang, 161). This statement reveals a loss of faith in an ideology according to which the individual is irrelevant in the face of historical determinism that, in turn, justifies all crimes. In his *Invisible Writings, An Autobiography,* Koestler explains that the real guilt shared by those people arraigned in the Moscow Trials is "having placed the interests of mankind above the interests of man, having sacrificed morality to expediency." He continues, "now they must die, because their death is expedient to the Cause, by the hands of men who subscribe to the same principles" (Koestler, 479). Viewing his former authorial self from the premises of a different ideology, Koestler now found unacceptable the perspective of the *Spanish Testament,* in which the narration of events had been distorted through an author-function generated from a Stalinist frame of thought. He therefore withdrew all the publication rights for the book.[18]

The author-function produced from this new ideological position of "liberal humanism," connects *Dialogue with Death* with *Darkness at Noon,* notwithstanding the altogether different subject matter. *Dialogue with Death,* which incorporates parts of the *Spanish Testament,* is autobiographical, whereas *Darkness at Noon* is fiction; the former takes place in Spain and the latter in Moscow. Both concentrate on the private self of the protagonist, however:

> on how the human soul comes to terms with itself in total isolation in the face of death. The tendentious historical and political analyses attempting to give Marxist

explanations for events in Spain in the *Spanish Testament* yield their place to the reckoning the individual has with himself in the prison cell.

Some thematic components unite the two novels. The atmosphere and the physical environment of the Lyublyanka prison strongly resemble those of Koestler's cell in Seville (Weintraub, 138). This also indicates that Kostler no longer pretends to be blind—as he did in the *Spanish Testament*—to the affinities between totalitarian systems, be they phallangist or Stalinist. The most important connection between the novel summarizing the Spanish experiences and the novel on the Moscow Trials is that *Darkness at Noon,* in effect, offers the conclusion of the life history of many of the Soviet Communists Koestler associated with in his communist phase. Rubashov—although a fictional character—combines essential features of people Koestler knew—most notably, Radek, Bukharin and Koltsov. He had met these men in Moscow in 1933 and was struck at the time by how much the inner struggle within the Communist Party had exhausted them (Levene, 13). Koestler learned about Koltsov's disenchantment with Moscow at the time of their last meeting in Spain—this must have been one of the reasons which finally led him away from communism.

As Rubashov reminisces about the past in his Moscow prison, we see him as his old self—the party officer—unconcerned about the individual, and serving the "cause" unquestioningly. The "cause," of course, had little to do with any ideas in particular: it was consideration of party interests that could justify supporting the Spanish Communists and, at the same time, fighting against the Trotskyist and the anarchist left-wing; signing a pact with Hitler and then, after his unexpected attack, going to war with him. The events which inform Rubashov's flashbacks are based on true events of which, in spite of the enormous propaganda apparatus disguising them, many of the "old-guard" communists in Russia and abroad were fully aware.

Koestler's early and late works alike are products of ideology. To suggest that Koestler, disappointed by the mendacious Stalinist ideology, converted to a "truthful" Western liberal Weltanschauung would itself be a naïve, two-dimensional statement. We are all tied to ideology and it is only through ideology—which always distorts to varying degrees—that we can formulate accounts of the world. Fully objective accounts are, therefore, not available. The truthfulness of the text is a matter of the ideological—even biological—components of its authors. The best we can have, perhaps, is the kind of writing which is informed by an awareness of the workings of ideology. Good examples of this are provided by some of Koestler's works which ultimately reject communism, but do so from a position of deep familiarity with it.

NOTES

1. Michel Foucault, "What Is an Author," Trans. Kari Hanet, *Screen* 20, n.1(1979): 19: ". . . the author's name characterizes a particular manner of discourse . . . [the discourse's] status and its manner of reception are regulated by the culture in which it circulates . . . the function of an author is to characterize the existence, circulation, and operation of certain discourses within a society."

2. See Foucault's discussion on the author-function in "What Is an Author?" p. 23.

3. Ilya Ehrenburg, *Memoirs: 1921–1941,* trans. Tatiana Shebunina, (New York: The Universal Library, Grosset and Dunlap, 1966), p. 385.

4. David Mitchell, *The Spanish Civil War,* (London: Granada, 1982), 75, discusses the general spymania and the harshly enforced discipline that characterized the International Brigades. He also talks about the GPU "heresy-hunters" whose aim was to hunt down the Trotskyists.

5. See Mitchell, pp. 63–67. Ehrenburg *(Memoirs,* 410) describes how many Spaniards were "surprised" and "disturbed" at the Writers' Congress in Madrid, 1937, when Soviet writers announced that "the enemies of the people" were being liquidated in the Soviet Union.

6. See Vera Zalka, "Mate az ember," *Vallomasok Zalka Materol,* ed. Natalia Zalka, trans. Julia Simandi, (Budapest: Kossuth Kiado, 1981), pp. 15, 31, and O. Rossiianov, *Mate Zalka,* (Moskva: Chudozhestvennaya literatura, 1964), p. 221.

7. S. Golovanivskii, "Visszatert a dicsoseg . . .," in *Vallomasok Zalka Materol,* p. 170, (my translation).

8. "Mate Zalka" was also a pseudonym. Zalka was called Bela Frankl and took the Hungarian sounding name "Mate Zalka" after the name of the town Mateszalka in Eastern Hungary, where he attended a secondary school between 1907 and 1911 (Rossiianov, 70–71). Neither Rossiianov nor the twenty-seven memoir writers, including Zalka's wife and daughter in *Vallomasok Zalka Materol,* mention the fact (which is common knowledge in Hungary) that Zalka was Jewish. They keep emphasizing that Zalka was a hero and that he was endowed with strongly recognizable Hungarian national features. The latter is peculiar because in the Soviet Union Jewish people represent a nationality; if somebody is Jewish, he or she would not be considered Russian or Ukrainian. Thus, in Soviet terms, a Jewish person's nationality cannot be Hungarian, even if he is a citizen of Hungary. It is unlikely that none of the writers should have known about Zalka's background. It is more likely, however, that they did not wish to emphasize the Jewish background of a person they were to present as a loyal communist and a hero of the people.

9. Koestler first traveled to Spain as a correspondent for the British *News Chronicle.* He also carried the press card of the Hungarian *Pester Lloyd.* When he was arrested on his second visit, it was thanks to the intervention of the British authorities that he was freed in June 1937. See Stanley Weintraub, "The Adopted Englishman," *The Last Great Cause* (New York: Weybright and Talley, 1968), pp. 122, 127.

10. Although George Orwell suggests in his review of the Spanish Testament (*The Collected Essays, Journalism and Letters of George Orwell,* vol. 1, ed. Sonia Orwell and Ian Angus, [London: Secker and Warburg, 1968], p. 295) that "the earlier part . . . even looks as though it had been 'edited' for the benefit of the Left Book Club," he also argues that Koestler's book is "probably one of the most honest and unusual documents that have been produced by the Spanish Civil War." Koltsov, in turn, also received praise. Ehrenburg wrote (*Memoirs,* 378): "The history of Soviet journalism knows no greater name, and his fame was well deserved."

11. Arthur Koestler, *Spanish Testament* (London: Victor Gollancz Ltd, 1937), p. 119. Orwell writes ("Looking Back on the Spanish Civil War," *The Collected Essays, Journalism and Letters of George Orwell*, vol. 2, p. 256–57): "Early in life I had noticed that no event is ever correctly reported in a newspaper, but in Spain, for the first time, I saw newspaper reports which did not bear any relation to the facts, not even the relationship which is implied in an ordinary lie. I saw great battles reported where there had been no fighting, and complete silence where hundreds of men had been killed. I saw troops who had fought bravely denounced as cowards and traitors, and others who had never seen a shot fired hailed as the heroes of imaginary victories."

12. The Soviet writers who were delegated to the West were, on the whole, reliable mouthpieces of Stalin. Conquest (666) provides an account of the International Congress of Writers for the Defense of Culture which was held in Paris in June 1935. When the fate of Victor Serge was brought up, all of the Soviet delegates (Tikhonov, Ehrenburg, Koltsov, and Kirshon) with the exception of Pasternak accused Serge of involvement in the assassination of Kirov, notwithstanding the fact that Kirov was killed two years after Serge's arrest had taken place in 1932.

13. Benson (126) suggests that General Lukacs was actually Hemingway's closest friend in the Twelfth International Brigade.

14. This was suggested to me by Maurice Friedberg.

15. Koltsov, *Ispanskii dnevnik,* quoted from *Vallomasok,* p. 195 (my translation).

16. Alexander Orlov argues, in *The Secret History of Stalin's Crimes* (New York: Random House, 1953), p. 99, that the "Special Department" of the NKVD accused Koltsov of supplying Lord Beaverbrook with secret information about the Soviet Union and of spreading rumors about the liquidation of Sergei Orzhonokidze, Commissar of Heavy Industry. The Soviet news agency reported that Orzhonokidze died of a heart attack.

17. Koltsov's remarks (quoted from Ehrenburg, 378) remind one of Orwell's comments to Koestler about the Spanish Civil War (*The Collected Essays*, vol. 2, p. 257): "I saw, in fact, history being written not in terms of what happened but of what ought to have happened according to various 'party lines.'"

18. *The Invisible Writing: The Second Volume of an Autobiography: 1932–1940* (London: Hutchinson and Co., 1969), p. 441. Arthur Koestler wrote: "In all foreign editions, including the American, *Dialogue with Death* appeared as a self-contained book. In the original English edition [Gollancz and Left Book Club, 1937], however, it formed the second part of *Spanish Testament,* the first part of which consisted of the earlier propaganda book on Spain that I had written for Muenzenberg (*L'Espagne ensanglantee*). *Spanish Testament* is (and shall remain) out of print; *Dialogue with Death* has been reissued in England under that title, in the form in which it was originally written."

WORKS CITED

Benson, Frederick R. *Writers in Arms.* New York: New York University Press, 1967.

Conquest, Robert. *The Great Terror.* Harmondsworth: Penguin, 1968.

Ehrenburg, Ilya. *Memoirs: 1921–1941.* Trans. Tatiana Shebunina. New York: The University Library, Grosset and Dunlap, 1974.

Foucault, Michel. "What Is an Author?" Trans. Kari Hanet. *Screen* 20, n.31(1979): 14–32.

Koestler, Arthur. *The Invisible Writing: An Autobiography.* London: Collins with Hamish Hamilton, 1954.

——. *The Invisible Writing: The Second Volume of an Autobiography: 1932–40.* London: Hutchinson and Co, 1969.

——. *The Spanish Testament.* London: Victor Gollancz Ltd, 1937.

Lang, Hans Joachim. "Der Spanische Bürgerkrieg als Wendepunkt: Die Fälle Koestler und Orwell." In *Englische Literatur und Politik im 20. Jahrhundert.* Ed. Paul Goetsch and Heinz Joachim Mullenbrock. Wiesbaden: Verlagsgessellschaft Athenaion, 1981.

Levene, Mark. *Arthur Koestler.* New York: Frederick Ungar Publishing Company, 1984.

Mitchell, David. *The Spanish Civil War.* London: Granada, 1982.

Orlov, Alexander. *The Secret History of Stalin's Crimes.* New York: Random House, 1953.

Orwell, George. *The Collected Essays, Journalism and Letters of George Orwell.* Ed. Sonia Orwell and Ian Angus. New York: Harcourt, Brace and World, 1968.

———. *Homage to Catalonia.* Chatham: W & J MacKay Limited, 1975.

Rossianov, O. *Mate Zalka.* Moskva: Khudozhestvennaya literatura, 1964.

Weintraub, Stanley. "The Adopted Englishman." In *The Last Great Cause.* New York: Weybright and Talley, 1968.

Zalka, Natalya, ed. *Vallomasok Zalka Materol.* Trans. Julia Simandi. Budapest: Kossuth Konyvkiado, 1981.

Zelinsky, K. "Koltsov v Ispanii." *Literaturnaya gazeta,* 11 November 1936.

For Whom the Bell Tolls
as Contemporary History

Jeffrey Meyers

> *I think that we are born into a*
> *time of great difficulty. . . . I*
> *think any other time was probably*
> *easier. One suffers little because*
> *all of us have been formed to*
> *resist suffering.*
>
> For Whom the Bell Tolls

I

Hemingway's unique talent, experience, and knowledge made him particularly well suited to write about the Spanish Civil War. He had seen action and been seriously wounded in World War I while serving with the American Red Cross on the Italian front. He had made many visits to Spain since his first trip in 1923. He knew the language, had many Spanish friends, and identified with the country and the culture. He had converted to the Roman Church in 1927 and was still a nominal Catholic. He had set two of his books—*The Sun Also Rises* and *Death in the Afternoon*—as well as many of his finest stories, in Spain, and had created the image of that country for English and American readers. He was in love with Martha Gellhorn, a politically committed writer whom he later married, and was inspired by her beauty and her devotion to the Loyalist cause. He was the most famous author and reporter in Spain, and became a leading propagandist for the Left.

In addition to his film *The Spanish Earth*, his play *The Fifth Column*, and his four stories on the Spanish War, he wrote many syndicated dispatches for the North American Newspaper Alliance, and in New York and Hollywood made speeches to raise money for ambulances and medical supplies. He felt there was a clear distinction between his journalism and his fiction. In his war reports, he emphasized the Loyalist victories and disguised their defeats. As he wrote in his preface to Gustav Regler's *The Last Crusade* (1940), "The Spanish civil war was really lost, of course, when the Fascists took Irún [sealing the unfriendly frontier with France] in the late summer of 1936. But in a war you can never admit, even to yourself, that it is lost."[1]

In *For Whom the Bell Tolls* (1940), however, Hemingway not only suggests that the war is lost, but also explains the reasons for the defeat. Released from the obligation to write propaganda, he was now free to criticize the country he loved and the side he had supported, to express his disillusionment with the Spanish character and with the Spanish Left. Like *A Farewell to Arms*, the Spanish novel expresses Hemingway's idealism while it confirms his scepticism about the possibilities of heroism in battle.

Hemingway spent eight months in Spain during four trips in 1937 and 1938. His first journey, in March through May 1937, took place just after the Loyalists' defensive victory in the battle of Jarama in February 1937, and coincided with their successful resistance to the siege of Madrid and their great triumph over the Italians in the battle of Guadalajara. In March 1937, the Fascists held the southwestern, western, northwestern, and northern parts of the country (except for the Basque provinces around Bilbao and Santander); the Loyalists controlled the southeastern, eastern, and northeastern parts, including Madrid, Alicante, Valencia and Barcelona. By October 1937, the north central Basque provinces, a major industrial base, had fallen to the Fascists, but the north-south boundary remained stable. In the fall of 1937 when Hemingway toured the Aragon front after the victory at Belchite and saw the Loyalists take Teruel, the war was going badly, but was not definitely lost. By the spring of 1938, when Hemingway reported the defeats in the Ebro Delta and the events leading to the fall of Barcelona, it was painfully clear that the Fascists would win.

Like *War and Peace*, a conscious model, *For Whom the Bell Tolls* combines fictional and historical characters. Maria is based on Martha Gellhorn, Robert Jordan on Hemingway, Karkov on the Russian correspondent Mikhail Koltzov, and General Golz on the Polish soldier Karol Swierczewski, and many other figures appear under their real names to give a sense of historical immediacy. The name, but not the character of Hemingway's Russian translator, Ivan Kashkeen, is given to Kashkin, Jordan's predecessor, who is killed while fighting with the guerrillas.

Hemingway not only modeled his characters on people who were actually involved in the war, but also used a Parisian friend for one of the most important figures in the book. No one has noticed that Gertrude Stein, a forceful and dominant lesbian who first introduced Hemingway to Spain, is a model for Pilar. Hemingway alludes playfully to the most famous phrase of Stein (whose name means "stone" in German) when Jordan thinks, "A rose is a rose is an onion. . . . A stone is a stein is a rock is a boulder is a pebble" (289). Though Pilar denies she is a lesbian ("I am no *tortillera* but a woman made for men," 155) and does not "make perversions," she is physically attracted to Maria and jealous of her love affair with Jordan. Most significantly, Hemingway's physical description of Pilar, who is ugly in an attractive sort of way, is very close to his description of Stein in *A Moveable Feast*.

In *For Whom the Bell Tolls*, Jordan

> saw a woman of about fifty [Stein was 48 when Hemingway met her in 1922] almost as big as Pablo, almost as wide as she was tall, in a black peasant skirt and waist, with heavy wool socks on heavy legs, black rope-soled shoes and a brown face like a model for a granite monument. She had big but nice looking hands and her thick curly black hair was twisted into a knot on her neck. (30)

Pilar's clothes resemble Stein's practical "steerage-gear" (which she recommended to Hadley Hemingway); and Hemingway emphasized that he had liked Stein until she exaggerated her lesbianism by cutting her hair.[2] Pilar's great girth, thick legs, olive skin, peasant hair tied in a knot, and monumental form—which Picasso depicted in his great portrait of 1906 (a painting that Hemingway had seen frequently in Stein's flat)[3]—recur in Hemingway's late portrait of Stein:

> Miss Stein was very big but not tall and was heavily built like a peasant woman. . . .
> She reminded me of a northern Italian peasant woman with her clothes, her mobile face and her lovely, thick, alive immigrant hair which she wore put up.[4]

Hemingway's knowledge of two previous civil wars also influenced the novel. As he composed the book, he was reading W. P. F. Napier's standard *History of the War in the Peninsula (1828–40)*, which described the guerrillas who fought against the Napoleonic invaders in the early nineteenth century.[5] And the guerrilla warfare of the Confederate soldier John Mosby[6] may also have affected his portrayal of Pablo's band.[7]

II

The vitally important and carefully portrayed geographical, military, and political situation in the novel has been virtually ignored by literary critics, who have concentrated on the romantic, aesthetic, and ideological aspects. But an understanding of the thirty Fascist, Loyalist and foreign politicians and soldiers to whom Hemingway refers illuminates both the historical meaning and the significance of two crucial political chapters: chapter 18 on Karkov at Gaylord's Hotel and chapter 42 on the confrontation between Karkov and André Marty.[8]

The action of the novel takes place in the Sierra de Guadarrama, northwest of Madrid between El Escorial and Segovia (the nearest town is La Granja) during three days in late May 1937—just after Hemingway had left the country. The fictional attack was directly inspired by the Loyalist offensive on May 30, led by the Polish General "Walter" (Karol Swierczewski), designed to capture Segovia and to relieve the mounting pressure on Bilbao by diverting Fascist forces from the north. On the night of May 29, a sergeant with plans of the attack deserted to the Fascists, who had spotted the headlights of the Loyalist convoys as they moved into position. The Loyalists

> were steadily pushed back, and after suffering 1,500 casualties, suspended the operation on June 3. Poor preparation, the repeated use of troops in frontal attacks on easily defensible positions, and ineffective tank and aerial support in conjunction with the Nationalists' tenacity and effective air power, assured its failure.[9]

In the novel, the Loyalist headquarters is at Navacerrada (Karkov drives there from Madrid via Colmenar and Cercada) and the army must cross the Navacerrada Pass (1,860 meters high) before descending to La Granja and attempting to capture Segovia, the provincial capital. The guerrillas, who help Jordan blow up the bridge, hope to elude the Carlist troops from Navarre and escape to the Sierra de Gredos, west of Madrid, between Avila and Talavera de la Reina.

Hemingway also gives a precise account of the military and political background. The Fascists have taken Valladolid and Avila (July 1936). The Alcázar in Toledo, besieged by the Loyalists, has been captured by the Fascists (September 1936). Madrid is still under siege, and the cowardly government has fled east to Valencia (November 1936) and "settled happily into the sloth and bureaucracy of governing" (246). But the Italian troops have been defeated at Guadalajara (March 1937). The Loyalists are fighting defensively, and Jordan believes they can win the war and stop the spread of Fascism if they receive political and military support from France and America:

> As long as we can hold them here we keep the fascists tied up. They can't attack any other country until they finish with us and they can never finish with us. If the French help at all, if only they leave the frontier open and if we get planes from America they can never finish with us. Never, if we get anything at all. These people will fight forever if they're well armed. (432)

Jordan's guerrillas are anti-Catholic (Hemingway also broke with the Church, which supported the Fascists). But they have a residual longing for religion and sometimes resort to prayer during moments of danger. Speaking to Jordan about the personal ethics of killing, Anselmo (the most sympathetic Spaniard) denies the existence of God and affirms an existential belief:

> "Since we do not have God here any more, neither His son nor the Holy Ghost, who forgives? I do not know."
> "You have not God any more?"
> "No. Man. Certainly not. If there were God, never would he have permitted what I have seen with my own eyes. Let them have God."
> "They claimed Him."
> "Clearly I miss Him, having been brought up in religion. But now a man must be responsible to himself." (41)

Jordan, like all the American volunteers in Spain, is tremendously idealistic. He believes he is taking part in a crusade that has replaced religion and feels, "in spite of all bureaucracy and inefficiency and party strife, something that was like the feeling you expected to have and did not have when you made your first communion. . . . The fighting in the Sierras had been that way. They had fought there with the true comradeship of the revolution" (235).

Jordan is an anti-Fascist, not a Marxist or a Communist—an important distinction that was forgotten in America after the war. But he thinks that "in Spain the Communists offered the best discipline and the soundest and sanest for the prosecution of the war" (163). Yet Jordan's naïve belief is shattered by the accounts in the novel of the Communists' savage execution of their own men, of their attacks on all the other factions of the Spanish Left (the internecine war within the Civil War), and of the disastrous interference of political commissars like André Marty in the conduct of the war.

The Russians gave the military aid that Jordan hoped to get from America. But "it was of the greatest importance that there should be no evidence of any Russian interference to justify an open intervention by the fascists" (237). (If Madrid falls, Karkov must poison the three wounded Russian soldiers in his care and destroy all evidence of their identity.) As the doomed attack starts, after Andrés has been prevented from delivering the crucial message from Jordan to Golz, Golz is moved by watching the flight of Loyalist planes, which "had come, crated on ships, from the Black Sea through the straits of Marmara, through the Dardanelles, through the Mediterranean and to here, unloaded lovingly at Alicante, assembled ably, tested and found perfect and now flown in lovely hammering precision" (429).

Yet Hemingway makes it absolutely clear that the Russians hurt the cause far more than they helped it. Karkov—whose model, Koltzov, would be purged and liquidated in a Russian prison camp in 1941— venomously defends the Soviet Purge Trials of 1936–37, which corresponded with the opening years of the Spanish war: "We detest with horror the duplicity and villainy of the murderous hyenas of Bukharinite wreckers and such dregs of humanity as Zinoviev, Kamenov, Rykov and their henchmen. We hate and loathe these veritable fiends" (245).

The paranoid suspicion that incited the Purge Trials had a direct impact on the Civil War. In early May 1937, they led to a murderous *putsch* against the radical Marxist Partido Obrero Unificación Marxista (POUM), with whom Orwell fought on the Aragon front.[10] Karkov, in another burst of dogmatic ranting, lies about the Fascist support of POUM and condemns it maliciously as "a heresy of crackpots and wild men and it was really just an infantilism. There were some honest misguided people. There was one fairly good brain [Andrés Nin] and there was a little fascist money" (247). Karkov (whose actual model would suffer the same fate as Nin) adds that Nin—the Trotskyite leader of POUM, who broke with Stalin and was arrested and executed in June 1937—"was their only man. We had him but he escaped from our hands" (247). And the guerrilla Agustín who like Karkov hates all the other factions on the Left, expresses a characteristic view by exclaiming that when the war is won they will "shoot the anarchists and the Communists and all this *canalla* except the Republicans" (285).

Hemingway is also severely critical of the Loyalist leaders—most of whom he knew personally and had seen in action—for their divisiveness and incompetence, which drove the pragmatists of the Left into the hands of the Communist disciplinarians. Agustín tells Jordan that the government has abandoned its principles, has resumed the use of formal titles, and "moves further to the right each day. In the Republic they no longer say Comrade but Señor and Señora" (285). When the battalion commander Gómez, who accompanies Andrés, is obstructed at brigade headquarters, he accuses the officer of reading the Seville newspaper, *ABC,* which supported the Fascists (the *ABC* of

Madrid, of course, supported the Loyalists), and threatens to liquidate him after the war: "The Army is still rotten with such as thee. With professionals such as thee. But it will not always be. We are caught between the ignorant and the cynical. But we will educate the one and eliminate the other" (398).

The most extreme expression of Hemingway's rage, scorn, and contempt occurs just after Pablo has stolen the detonators that were meant to blow the bridge and has deserted the guerrilla band. Jordan, lying beside the sleeping María, thinks Pablo's betrayal is entirely characteristic of the "treachery ridden country." In a densely allusive and crucially important political passage (which requires considerable explication), he euphemistically condemns the Loyalist leaders.

> Muck them all to hell together, Largo, Prieto, Asensio, Miaja, Rojo, all of them. . . . Muck their egotism and their selfishness and their selfishness and their egotism and their conceit and their treachery. . . . One good man, Pablo Iglesias, in two thousand years and everybody else mucking them. How do we know how he would have stood up in the war? I remember when I thought Largo was O.K. Durruti was good and his own people shot him there at the Puente de los Franceses. Shot him because he wanted them to attack. Shot him in the glorious discipline of indiscipline. . . . They always muck you instead, from Cortez and Menéndez de Avila[11] down to Miaja. Look what Miaja did to Kleber. The bald egotistical swine. The stupid egg-headed bastard. Muck all the insane, egotistical, treacherous swine that have always governed Spain and ruled her armies. (369–70)

Largo, Prieto, Asensio, Miaja and Rojo—whom Americans in 1940, when the novel was published, had been reading about for the last three years—were well known and closely connected, but they have now been forgotten and must be identified in order to understand the meaning of this passage. Francisco Largo Caballero, whom Jordan once admired, was the revolutionary leader of the UGT trade union who became the Republican Prime Minister and Minister of War during 1936 and 1937. He was defeated by the Communists and driven from office after refusing to suppress the POUM during the riots in Barcelona in early May 1937. Indalecio Prieto, a leader of the Spanish Socialist Party, was an ineffective naval and air minister in Largo Caballero's government and supported the Communist drive to defeat the Prime Minister. While serving in the government of Juan Negrín, who succeeded Largo Caballero, Prieto became increasingly defeatist and pessimistic about the possibility of winning the war (Jordan feels he had no "faith in the ultimate victory"), and was finally removed from office in March 1938.

José Asensio Torrado was promoted to general by Largo Caballero and appointed commander of the central theater of operations. When his counterattack at Illescas failed, he was replaced. Largo

Caballero soon named him Undersecretary of War, but he was held responsible for the fall of Málaga in February 1937 and dismissed from office. José Miaja, Republican general and legendary defender of Madrid in November 1936, actually knew very little about operational details and followed the orders of his Soviet advisers. He later commanded all the military forces in central and southern Spain, but was considered dull-witted. Karkov tells Jordan that when the government abandoned Madrid and took all the cars from the Ministry of War, "old Miaja had to ride down to inspect his defensive positions on a bicycle" (237). Jordan also explains that "the old bald, spectacled, conceited, stupid-as-an-owl, unintelligent-in-conversation, brave-and-as-dumb-as-a-bull, propaganda-built-up defender of Madrid, Miaja, had been so jealous of the publicity [the popular and able Rumanian-Jewish commander of the Eleventh International Brigade, Emilio] Kleber received that he had forced the Russians to relieve Kleber of his command and send him to Valencia. Kleber was a good soldier, but limited and he *did* talk too much for the job he had" (233). Miaja also feared that Kleber might use his position to stage a Communist coup against the government. Vicente Rojo, Miaja's chief of staff, developed the plan for the victory at Guadalajara. But Rojo, like Prieto, was pessimistic about winning the war, and in the winter of 1938, after the Fascists invaded Catalonia, he failed to plan an effective defense of the north.

Pablo Iglesias, the venerable and incorruptible Spanish Socialist leader—the one good man in two millennia—founded the UGT as an organization of Madrid printers in 1882, died in 1925, and was succeeded by Largo Caballero. Buenaventura Durruti, the most famous Spanish anarchist during the war, was assassinated while commanding militia on the Madrid front on November 20, 1936. Hugh Thomas confirms that he was killed by his own men.[12] His death was an important cause of the Barcelona riots of May 1937 and he "remains a symbol of the 'pure' political revolutionary, the archetypal Spanish rebel."[13] Hemingway's attack on the five Republican leaders, though influenced by the Loyalist defeat in the war, is essentially just, and it is balanced by his praise for Kleber, Iglesias and Durruti.

Hemingway does not even bother to condemn the Fascist leaders, who are manifestly despicable. Juan March, whom Hemingway calls a criminal, was the richest man in Spain before the war. He encouraged the Fascist rebellion and the Italian intervention, and financed from Rome the purchase of ten percent of the Fascist war materiel. March's motives were neither patriotic nor political, but merely materialistic: "March was neither a friend nor a foe of anyone.

'March was for March.'"[14] Karkov is writing a book on the true Spanish Fascist, José Calvo Sotelo, and says that "he was very intelligent and it was very intelligent that he was killed" (244). Calvo Sotelo, a leader of the militant Right whose attacks on the Republic intensified the deterioration of political conditions in Spain, was killed by Assault Guards on July 13, 1936. His death helped provoke the Fascist rising, and he became one of their principal martyrs and ideological prophets.

Hemingway also mentions the volatile broadcasts of Queipo de Llano, one of the three most important Nationalist generals (the others were Franco and Mola), who plotted the military rising and boldly seized Seville. The "Radio General," an extremely effective propagandist, was famous for his caustic taunts at the "Reds" and his gloating over Fascist victories.

III

Durruti and "La Pasionaria" ("The Passion Flower," Dolores Ibarruri) were the martyr and orator of the Loyalists (as Calvo Sotelo and Queipo de Llano were the martyr and orator of the Fascists). Hemingway enraged the Communists by attacking their sacred heroine. He also criticized the Spanish Communist commanders as well as the foreign soldiers (many of them trained in Russia after combat in World War I), who led the volunteers of the International Brigades.

Just before El Sordo's doomed band is wiped out by the Fascists, a young Communist with an idealistic belief in La Pasionaria quotes her words in order to inspire his comrades: "Pasionaria says it is better to die on your feet than to live on your knees." But he is immediately deflated by another guerrilla who asks bitterly: "Do you know your Pasionaria has a son thy age in Russia since the start of the movement?" He then adds, alluding to the loss of religious belief: "If thou believest so much in thy Pasionaria, get her to get us off this hill" (309).

In a brief ironic chapter that cuts from the fighting in the mountains to the Communists in Madrid—and stresses the difference between the suffering combatants and the ignorant civilians—an unattractive, unidentified Russian, the *Izvestia* correspondent in Spain (based on Ilya Ehrenburg), citing Pasionaria as his source of information, radically misinterprets the meaning of the massacre of El Sordo's band and tells Karkov: "It is wonderful. All day the fascists have been fighting among themselves near Segovia. They have been forced to quell the mutinies with automatic rifle fire and machine gun fire. In the afternoon they were bombing their own troops with planes. . . . That is true. . . . Dolores brought the news herself. . . . Goodness and truth shine from her as from a true saint of the people. Not for nothing is she called La Pasionaria" (357–58).

Dolores Ibarruri, La Pasionaria, the impoverished but attractive daughter of a Galician miner, was elected Communist deputy and vice-president of the Cortes in February 1936. When the Fascists rebelled on July 18, she roused the defenders of Madrid with the "die on your feet" speech that ended with "No pasarán!" ("They shall not pass!") and gave the Loyalists their battle cry. She was influential in all aspects of the government during the war. After the defeat, she flew to Russia and became president of the Spanish Communist Party in exile. Hemingway's statement (probably inspired by Fascist propaganda) is false, for Hugh Thomas writes that in October 1937 "her miner husband was all the time at the front with her son."[15] Only two of her six children survived to adulthood, and her son Rubén died during the siege of Leningrad in World War II. Hemingway's dislike of her blind adherence to the Party line led him to repeat the malicious rumor about her son in Russia. He later told friends that "Dolores always made me vomit always."[16]

The most important Spanish-Communist commanders were Modesto, El Campesino, and Lister. Hemingway gives qualified praise to the first two and condemns the latter. In chapter 18 Jordan recalls what he learned about the leaders at Gaylord's Hotel. The Andalusian cabinetmaker Juan Modesto, "had just been given an Army Corps. He never learned his Russian in Puerto de Santa María although he might have if they had a Berlitz School there that the cabinet makers went to. He was the most trusted of the young soldiers by the Russians because he was a true party man" (230), and was much more intelligent than the other two commanders.

At Gaylord's, Jordan also learned that Valentín González, El Campesino, "had never been a peasant but was an ex-sergeant in the Spanish Foreign Legion who had deserted and fought with Abd el Krim" (229), the chief of the Riffian tribes in Morocco. He criticizes Campesino's appearance, personality, egoism, and loose tongue (a fault he shared with Kléber), but praises his courage in adversity.

> From what he had seen of Campesino, with his black beard, his thick negroid lips, and his feverish, staring eyes, he thought he might give almost as much trouble as a real peasant leader. The last time he had seen him he seemed to have gotten to believe his own publicity and think he was a peasant. He was a brave, tough man; no braver in the world. But God, how he talked too much. And when he was excited he would say anything no matter what the consequences of his indiscretion. And those consequences had been many already. He was a wonderful Brigade Commander

> though in a situation where it looked as though everything was lost. He never knew
> when everything was lost and if it was, he would fight out of it. (230)

Anselmo taints by association the Russian-speaking stonemason, Lister, by recalling that he comes from El Ferrol in Galicia, "the same town as Franco" (193). Though Jordan realizes that discipline makes good troops, he thinks Lister is savagely severe: "Lister was murderous in discipline. He was a true fanatic and he had the complete Spanish lack of respect for life. In few armies since the Tartars' first invasion of the West were men executed summarily for as little reason as they were under his command. But he knew how to forge a division into a fighting unit" (234).

Hemingway's criticism of all three men, reliable soldiers and good disciplinarians who had fought well at Guadalajara, was that they, like Miaja, "had been told many of the moves they should make by their Russian military advisers. They were like students flying a machine with dual controls which the pilot could take over whenever they made a mistake. . . . After a while there would not be dual controls and then we would see how well they handled divisions and army corps alone" (234). Though Hemingway admired the bravery of these soldiers, he stressed Modesto's dogmatism, Campesino's indiscretion, and Lister's savagery.

All three commanders actually had distinguished records in combat. Juan Modesto, formerly a woodcutter, who had served as a noncommissioned officer in Morocco and then led a Communist paramilitary group, commanded the 5th Army Corps in the defense of Madrid; he fought in the battle of Jarama (February 1937), which blunted the Fascist offensive, and participated in the battle of the Ebro in the summer and fall of 1938. James Cortada calls this brilliant but despotic officer "a realistic and effective commander with no political ambitions."[17]

The brutal and bearded Campesino had a reputation as a successful soldier. He fought in all the major battles around Madrid, at Boadilla and Corunna Road, Guadalajara, Brunete, Aragon, and Teruel (February 1938), where he was surrounded by Fascist forces but fought his way out of the encirclement. In retaliation for a Fascist massacre at Brunete, he executed an entire Moroccan battalion.

Enrique Lister was a field commander in most of the major battles of the war: "A resourceful, skilled, and energetic officer, he often commanded troops that were poorly disciplined and hardly provisioned; yet, he proved successful in launching offensives against the Nationalist armies on several occasions."[18]

These generals bitterly resented Hemingway's distrust of their allegiance to the Communists and his cynical suggestion, which disparaged their very considerable achievements, that their dependence on Russian advisers made them incapable of independent command. In *Nuestra Guerra* (1966) and in a BBC-TV documentary on Hemingway (September 30, 1987), Lister stated that Hemingway had only a superficial understanding of the war, that he was retaliating for the restrictions that Lister had imposed on him in Spain, and that the novel betrayed both the Loyalists and his own profoundest beliefs.

> When I read *For Whom the Bell Tolls,* several years after the end of the war, I was furious, but not greatly surprised. . . . In spite of his talent he was not able to understand it in all its depth. Hemingway, like many others, looked only at the external, the anecdotal, the superficials of our struggle, without really going into it deeply. . . . That was his way of getting even, for I knew, and he had told me many times, that he would never forgive me for not letting him see everything he wanted to see. . . . If it is true that the book as a whole is an insult to the struggle of the Spanish people, it is also treason to the opinions that Hemingway himself had expressed of that struggle.[19]

Lister, like all the Communists, felt Hemingway should write propaganda to support the cause. Hemingway, who had supported the Loyalists in his reporting, believed he was free to write honestly in his fiction once the war was over. In a letter of October 14, 1952, to Bernard Berenson, he indirectly answered the accusations made by Lister and many other Communists, and defended his journalism as well as his loyalty to the movement: "I did not start the book until after the Republic had lost the war and it was over because I would not write anything in the war which could hurt the Republic which I believed in and tried to serve as well as I could."[20]

Though Hemingway criticized the hard line Communists, he praised the handsome, cultured, and humane artist Gustavo Durán, who was his personal friend and came from a very different background than the rough worker-generals. The confident and charismatic Durán was the fighting commander of a battalion in August 1936, a brigade in January 1937, a division in July and (as a colonel) of the Twentieth Army Corps in November: "Wounded twice, he fought in Madrid, the retreat from Toledo, the front at Casa del Campo, the counter-offensive at Jarama" as well as in Brunete, Teruel and Valencia.[21] He quarreled with the popular but violent El Campesino and hated the political control of the Soviet commissars. Toward the end of the war, he sided with the moderate Socialist General Miaja against the Communist commanders, Modesto and Lister, who wanted to prolong the hopeless conflict. In *For Whom the Bell Tolls*, Durán, who fights under Golz, is praised—as no other contemporary was ever praised by Hemingway—when Jordan (on the night before the attack) is inspired by thoughts of Durán's achievement: "Just remember Durán, who never had any military training and who was a composer and a lad about town before the movement and is now a damned good general commanding a brigade. It was all as simple and easy to learn and understand to Durán as chess to a child chess prodigy" (335).[22]

IV

Hemingway also evaluated the leaders of all five of the International Brigades (which were numbered eleven through fifteen), criticizing Gómez, Gal, and Čopić, and praising (in addition to Kléber) Lukacz, Hans, and Golz.[23] After sleeping with Maria for the second time (Jordan's lovemaking often sparks recent memories of the war), he thinks: "He had seen enough of commanders to whom all orders were impossible. That swine Gomez in Estremadura" (162)—where Franco's Moors developed a reputation for extreme brutality. In the chapter on politics in Madrid, Jordan recalls, "there was Gal, the Hungarian, who ought to be shot if you could believe half you heard at Gaylord's" (233). And at the end of the novel, the political commissar, André Marty, remembers that "Golz has always hated Gal" and that he had heard Golz exclaim "Čopić's a fool" (421). Gal and Čopić, "who were men of politics and of ambition" (422), allowed Marty to interfere in military matters, though it often led to the death of many men.

"Gómez" was the *nom de guerre* of Wilhelm Zeisser, a German Communist who commanded the Thirteenth Brigade in the campaigns around Madrid in 1937. In 1938, he took charge of the International Brigades' headquarters at the military base in Albacete and increased disillusionment in the ranks at a time when the Brigades were having difficulty recruiting volunteers. After fighting in World War II, Zeisser served as Minister of State Security in East Germany.

"Gal" was the pseudonym of Janos Galicz, a Hungarian Communist who commanded the Fifteenth Brigade in the battle of Jarama (February 1937). "Most of his men considered him incompetent and unpopular," writes James Cortada. "He suffered many casualties while failing to inflict heavy losses on the Nationalists. . . . He also proved unable to maintain good relations among the various nationalities within his command, [but] he continued to lead troops."[24] Vladimir Čopić, a Croatian Communist deputy in Yugoslavia, succeeded Gal, commanded the Fifteenth Brigade as a shock force, and was wounded in the battle of Brunete (July 1937). Hemingway's assessment of these men seems more balanced and convincing than his harsh criticism of the Spanish generals.

In the Gaylord chapter, Jordan also evaluates Hans and Lukacz and concludes that they "had done a fine job in their share of the defense of Madrid" (233). Hans had explained the battle of Guadalajara to Jordan, showing him all the maps and marveling at the miracle of it. He told Jordan that the troops of Modesto, El Campesino, and Lister had fought well in that battle, but that the generals had been directed by their Russian advisers.

In the novel, André Marty remembers that "Golz had captured the gold train that winter with Lucasz in Siberia" (421), while commanding cavalry in the Red Army during the Civil War that followed the Bolshevik Revolution. And in the flashback to Karkov in Madrid (chapter 32), immediately after the *Izvestia* correspondent reveals ironically that Pasionaria had misinterpreted the fighting in the mountains, Karkov converses with an unidentified general, who is Lukacz, "a man of about forty-eight, who was short, chunky, jovial-looking with pale blue eyes, thinning blond hair and a gay mouth under a bristly yellow moustache. He was a divisional commander and he was a Hungarian" (358). This general doubts Pasionaria's naïve belief that the Fascists are fighting among themselves, insists on the need for secrecy, and suggests that all journalists and scandal mongers should be executed, especially "the intriguing German unmentionable of a Richard. Whoever gave that Sunday *függler* [fucker] command of a brigade should [also] be shot" (358).

In the Spanish war, "Hans" was Hans Kahle, a Prussian-born Communist, who had been a career officer in the German army. He led the Eleventh Brigade, served with distinction in the early battles around Madrid, and commanded Loyalist forces until late 1937. After World War II, he became a police chief in East Germany.

General Lukacz was the Hungarian writer, Mata Zalka, "who had served in the Austrian Army in the First World War, had been captured by the Russians and had joined the Red Army. . . . He was a man full of what the casual traveller supposes to be typical Hungarian gaiety."[25] Lukacz (the correct spelling of his name) commanded the Twelfth Brigade in the defense of Madrid and the battle of Guadalajara. Gustav Regler, Lukacz's political commissar, says Hemingway's visit to Lukacz's troops in March 1937 was a great occasion and that all the girls in the nearby village were invited to attend the dinner. Two months later, during the Huesca offensive, Lukacz was killed when a shell struck his car: He "was lying with his grey head against the upholstery; his brains were exposed."[26]

Golz, the most important historical figure in *For Whom the Bell Tolls*, appears in important scenes at the beginning and end of the novel. Jordan remembers "his strange white face that never tanned, his hawk eyes, the big nose and thin lips and the shaven head crossed with wrinkles and with scars" (8). In the first chapter, he describes his plan of attack carefully and orders Jordan to blow up the bridge. Golz anticipates the fatal meddling of André Marty ("always some one will interfere"), the unexpected appearance of Maria ("do you have many girls on the other side of the lines?"), and even the hair fetish that occupies Jordan and Maria during their lovemaking. Golz's allusion to girls unites the major Tolstoyan themes of love and war, suggests the compensations of irregular service, and emphasizes Jordan's need to concentrate his entire life in the precious few nights that are left to him. Golz like Lukacz, also displays an impressive gaiety before the impending attack.

"I never think at all. Why should I? I am General Sovietique. I never think. Do not try to trap me into thinking. . . . I joke if I want. I am so serious is why I can joke. . . .."(8)

Golz was gay and had wanted him to be gay too before he left, but he hadn't been. (17)

Jordan, who thinks of Golz many times throughout the novel, considers him "a good general. The best [he'd] ever served under" (162). At Gaylord's, Golz is the touchstone for all the other commanders, and Jordan thinks he is "a fine soldier but they always kept him in a subordinate position and never gave him a free hand" (233). In the penultimate chapter 42, when Marty intercepts Andrés who is carrying Jordan's message to Golz, Marty (like La Pasionaria) misinterprets the true meaning and becomes irrationally convinced that Golz is using Andrés to communicate with the Fascists: "Golz, he thought, in a mixture of horror and exultation" (420). At the end of that chapter Golz realizes that it is too late to call off the ill-fated attack and stoically tells his chief of staff Duval (based on the French colonel, Jules Dumont) that they must accept the situation and do their best in adversity.

Unlike the politically ambitious Gal and Čopíc, Golz is not afraid to oppose Marty and (despite his claim that he never thinks) thinks: "I should shoot you, André Marty, before I let you put that gray rotten finger on a contour map of mine. Damn you to hell for all the men you've killed by interfering in matters you know nothing of. Damn the day they named tractor factories and villages and co-operatives for you so that you are a symbol that I cannot touch." Instead of

expressing these thoughts, Golz patiently but courageously contradicts his dangerous superior: "Yes, Comrade Marty. I see your
point. It is not well taken, however, and I do not agree. You can try
to go over my head if you like. Yes. You can make it a party matter as
you say. But I do not agree" (423).

Jerzy Krzyzanowski provides a useful summary of Golz's model,
Karol Swierczewski, who was known in Spain as "General Walter":

> He was born in 1897 in Warsaw but spent his youth in Russia. During the revolution
> he fought in the Red Army. After graduating from the Frunze Military Academy in
> 1927, he rose to the rank of general and was appointed to a professorship in the
> Military Academy. . . . In November, 1936, when the International Brigades went
> into action, Swierczewski . . . took command of the XIV International Brigade. Later
> he led the 35th International Division and remained in Spain almost until the end of
> the war.[27]

After a distinguished career in World War II, he became the Polish
Vice-Minister of National Defense. On March 28, 1947, while inspect-
ing Polish troops, he was killed by anti-Communist Ukrainian guerrillas.

Golz's confrontation with Marty in the novel is based on an actual
incident. Hugh Thomas writes that in late December 1937, after
Walter's abortive attack on the Córdoba front, "André Marty appeared at General Walter's headquarters, and Major Lasalle, commander of the Marseillaise Battalion, was accused of spying for the
Nationalists [as Golz is accused by Marty in the novel], tried and shot."[28]

In a letter to Edmund Wilson of November 8, 1952, Hemingway
emphasized Walter's coolness and gaiety in adversity, associated him
with a blown bridge and recalled, "I saw Walter at a bridge with nothing to blow it and the fascists' tanks on the other side thinking it was
mined and four of us watching them. Under these circumstances
Walter could make jokes."[29] In conversation with Bronislaw
Zielinski, his Polish translator and friend, Hemingway confirmed his
profound admiration for Walter and emphasized the historical accuracy of his fictional portrait. Zielinski "asked him why historical
figures appear in 'The Bell' under their real names, and Swierczewski
is neither Swierczewski nor [General] Walter? He replied: 'He was
such a splendid man and splendid soldier that I wouldn't dare to present
him in fictitious situations, and put in his mouth fictitious words.'"[30]

The flashback confrontation of Golz and Marty is repeated and
fully rendered in Hemingway's description of the confrontation between Karkov and Marty. When Andrés, escorted by Captain Gómez
(not to be confused with Wilhelm Zeisser, who adopted the name of
"Gómez"), reaches the top of the Navacerrada pass, they stop to ask
directions to Golz's headquarters. Marty—the Commander of all the

International Brigades, who had come from the Central Committee of the French Communist Party—arrives in a staff car at the same time. Hemingway gives a detailed description of Marty's appearance, background and character, and (drawing on his experience in Africa) ends with a brilliant simile:

> A large man, old and heavy, in an oversized khaki beret, such as *chasseurs à pied* [light infantry] wear in the French army, wearing an overcoat, carrying a map case and wearing a pistol strapped around his greatcoat, got out of the back of the car. . . . [Gómez] recognized his bushy eyebrows, his watery gray eyes, his chin and his double chin under it, and he knew him for one of France's great modern revolutionary figures who had led the mutiny of the French Navy in the Black Sea [in 1919. . . . But] he did not know what this man had become with time, disappointment, bitterness both domestic and political, and thwarted ambition and that to question him was one of the most dangerous things that any man could do. . . . His face looked as though it were modeled from the waste material of his victims that you find under the claws of a very old lion. (416–17)

Hugh Thomas, who confirms Hemingway's judgment of the French Catalan, writes that Marty lacked both ability and humanity.

> He was the son of a worker condemned to death in his absence for his part in the Paris Commune. He had first come to prominence in 1919 when as a seaman-machinist he had led the mutiny of the French Black Sea fleet in protest against orders received to support the White Russian armies. . . . He owed his appointment at Albacete [headquarters of the International Brigades] to his alleged military knowledge and to his favour with Stalin. . . . By 1936 he had become obsessed with an imaginary fear of Fascist or other spies. . . . He was also arrogant, incompetent and cruel. . . . Even Stalin had a less suspicious nature than André Marty.[31]

James Cortada agrees that he was both suspicious and malicious, and that he ruled with an iron hand and never hesitated to execute his own men if he doubted their Communism or their courage.

In the novel, Marty, true to character, immediately suspects and arrests both men. While they are being searched, the sympathetic guard explains that Marty, like Lister, "has a mania for shooting people. . . . That old one kills more than the bubonic plague. . . . But he doesn't kill fascists like we do. . . . He kills rare things. Trotzkyites. Divagationers" (418). As Marty fantasizes about all the generals involved in Golz's "Fascist plot," Karkov—on his way from Madrid to Golz—suddenly appears.

Karkov, though not a brilliant soldier like Durán or Golz, is the *Pravda* correspondent "in direct communication with Stalin" and "one of the three most important men in Spain" (424). He had initiated Jordan into the mysteries of Communist politics in Spain, and also instructed him about how to take poison. Jordan admires

Karkov's intelligence as well as his wife and mistress. He describes Karkov's ludicrous appearance and relates how their friendship developed:

> Karkov was the most intelligent man he had ever met. Wearing black riding boots, gray breeches, and a gray tunic, with tiny hands and feet, puffily fragile of face and body, with a spitting way of talking through his bad teeth, he looked comic when Jordan first saw him. . . . Kashkin had made him out to be a hell of a fellow and Karkov had at first been insultingly polite and then, when Robert Jordan had not played at being a hero but had told a story that was really funny and obscenely discreditable to himself, Karkov had shifted from the politeness to a relieved rudeness and then to insolence and they had become friends. (231)

Karkov asserts his authority, takes Jordan's dispatch from Marty, and gives it back to Andrés and threatens to find out exactly how untouchable Marty really is. Karkov, though cynical, has an idealistic "belief in the good which could come from his own accessibility and the humanizing possibility of benevolent intervention" (426).

In his letter, Hemingway explained that he admired Koltzov for letting him see everything he had wanted to see (just as he disliked Lister for preventing him from seeing things), and for his faith in Hemingway's work: "He knew I was not a Communist and never would be one. But because he believed in me as a writer he tried to show me how everything was run so that I'd give a true account of it."[32]

Hemingway's judgment of all the Spanish and foreign politicians and commanders was influenced inevitably by his knowledge of their final fate. Calvo Sotelo and Durruti were assassinated, Lukacz was killed at the front, Nin was executed. Kléber, Copíc, Gal, and Koltzov were recalled, purged, and liquidated, partly because they objected to Stalin's policy toward the Spaniards for whom—like Robert Jordan—they had fought. Robert Merriman has been accepted as the historical model for Robert Jordan ever since the publication of Cecil Eby's influential but speculative article in 1966. Eby gives the essential facts of Merriman's career:

> A native of Eureka, California, he had worked at various manual jobs, the last of which had been logging, before going to the University of Nevada in 1929, where he had been an end on the football team, house manager of his fraternity, and an officer of the ROTC. Following graduation three years later, he received a fellowship in economics at Berkeley. When the war broke out in Spain, he was studying in the Soviet Union on a traveling fellowship and was gathering materials for a book about collective farming. In January, 1937, he was among the first Americans to reach Spain, and because of his ROTC experience and his political rapport with the Communist leaders of the International Brigades, he was appointed adjutant of the original Abraham Lincoln Battalion. When the Lincolns first went into action at Jarama a month later, Merriman was acting commander until wounded in the twelfth day of fighting. When he returned to duty after the Brunete offensive in July, he was promoted to chief of staff. [Merriman was killed in action in April 1938.][33]

Hemingway expressed his admiration for—and got the maximum propagandistic value from—Merriman when reporting from Belchite on the Aragon Front on September 14, 1937.

> Robert Merriman, a former California University professor [sic], and now chief of staff of the fifteenth brigade [under Čopíc], was leader in the final assault. Unshaven, his face smoke-blackened, his men tell how he bombed his way forward, wounded six times slightly by hand-grenade splinters in the hands and face, but refusing to have his wounds dressed until the cathedral was taken.[34]

But, apart from their first name, nationality, and the fact that both fought and died in Spain, Merriman and Jordan have nothing in common. Merriman, born in California, was heavy, dark-haired, balding and bespectacled. He was shy and stiff and had studied economics at Nevada and Berkeley. Jordan, born in Montana, is thin, blond, long-haired, and without glasses. He is bold with Maria and on easy terms with the guerrillas, and had studied Spanish at the University of Montana. ("Montana" alludes not only to the fighting in the Sierras, but also to the Montana army barracks in Madrid, which was seized in July 1936 by the workers, who captured 50,000 rifles and used the buildings until the end of the war.) Merriman was married, had studied in Russia, had never been to Spain before the war, knew only a little Spanish, and had not written anything about the country. Jordan, by contrast, is single, has never been to Russia, had traveled widely in Spain for twelve years before the war, has an expert knowledge of the language, and has described his Spanish experiences in a book that Karkov has read and praised.

Most importantly, their military experience is entirely different. Merriman reached Spain in January 1937; Jordan, who has been in the country for nearly a year, arrived soon after the war broke out in July 1936. Merriman fought the Italians at Guadalajara, and then the Nationalists in Aragon and on the Ebro Delta—in the north and northeast. Jordan fought at Carabanchal and Usera, near Madrid, and then in Córdoba and Extremadura—in the south and west. Merriman was a military commander who led the American volunteers of the Lincoln Brigade. Jordan is a demolitions expert who has no contact with Americans and fights an irregular war behind enemy lines with a band of Spanish guerrillas. Eby concedes that "the finished portrait of Robert Jordan, killed in the Guadarrama Mountains, retains only a few resemblances to Hemingway's model, who was killed along the Ebro." But he concludes that "in spite of transpositions and transmutations, the outlines may still be traced."[35] Yet Eby offers neither convincing evidence to prove that Jordan is based on Merriman nor an explanation of the radical differences in

the backgrounds, appearances, characters, educations, interests, experiences and military careers of these two men.[36] Robert Jordan is a
fictional character in a historical context.

For Whom the Bell Tolls is an allegory, as well as an explanation, of
the Loyalist defeat in the Spanish war. Pablo's theft of Jordan's
detonators symbolizes the difficulty of fighting without adequate war
materiel. Andrés' journey through enemy lines—he is "impeded by
the ignorance of the anarchists. Then by the sloth of a bureaucratic
fascist. Now by thy oversuspicion of a Communist" (420)—is
obstructed by the factionalism of the Left and by the dominance of
political commissars over military commanders, and symbolizes the
betrayal of Spain by the foreigners. Andrés' inability to convince his
allies to call off the attack represents the Loyalists' failure to persuade
France and England to stop the German and Italian invasion.
Hemingway's allegory explains the three main reasons for the Loyalist
defeat: the factionalism of the Left, the interference (at the time of the
Russian Purge Trials) of political commissars, and the successful intervention of Hitler's and Mussolini's armies while the democratic
countries remained passive and indifferent.

Kenneth Lynn's distorted account of Hemingway's politics in the
Spanish war—his sneering at Hemingway's "lack of political sophistication" and "service for Stalin"[37]—blindly ignores the fact that
Hemingway was more critical of the Communists than almost
anyone else on the Left. His fictional rather than propagandistic account of the Communist role in the war did not advance the cause of
the Revolution. The Spanish Communist Party condemned the book
as soon as it appeared, and it was not translated into Russian until
1968 (and then only in an expurgated edition, with heavy cuts in the
Gaylord's chapter).[38] But Hemingway's insight about the complexity
of the Spanish tragedy, written immediately after the events it
records, makes *For Whom the Bell Tolls* the greatest political novel in
American literature.[39]

NOTES

1. Ernest Hemingway, Preface to Gustav Regler, *The Last Crusade* (New York: Longman Green, and Company, 1940), p. vii.

2. See Ernest Hemingway, *Selected Letters, 1917–1961*, ed. Carlos Baker (New York: Scribner's 1971), p. 650: "I liked her better before she cut her hair and that was a sort of turning point in all sorts of things."

3. When critics complained about the painting, Picasso replied: "everyone thinks she is not at all like her portrait but never mind, in the end she will manage to look just like it"—and she did. Quoted in Roland Penrose, *Picasso: His Life and Work* (New York: Harper & Row, 1973), p. 122.

4. Ernest Hemingway, *A Moveable Feast* (1964; Reprint, New York: Bantam, 1965), p. 14.

5. Interview with Martha Gellhorn, London, November 28, 1982. On Radio Madrid, La Pasionaria frequently evoked memories of the Spanish rising against Napoleon in 1808.

6. In a clear parallel to his discussion of the Spanish leaders, Hemingway mentions Mosby and Quantrill as well as Grant, Sherman, Jackson, Stuart, Sheridan, and McClellan in *For Whom the Bell Tolls* (1940; Reprint, New York: Scribner's, 1968), p. 233. Fitzgerald also refers to the heroic Mosby in *Tender Is the Night* (1934; Reprint, New York: Scribner's 1962), p. 101. Hemingway's critical comments on the leaders in the Spanish War is similar to his condemnation of the generals in World War II—Eisenhower, Patton, Bradley, Bedell Smith, and especially Montgomery and Leclerc—in *Across the River and into the Trees* (1950).

7. Guerrilla bands actually existed but played an insignificant part in the Spanish war. See Franciso Pérez Lopez, *A Guerrilla Diary of the Spanish Civil War*, ed. Victor Guerrier, trans. Joseph Harris (London: André Deutsch, 1972).

8. For the use of historical background to explain the meaning of a novel, see Jeffrey Meyers, "The Politics of *A Passage to India,*" *Journal of Modern Literature* 1(March 1971): 329–38; "*The Plumed Serpent* and the Mexican Revolution," *Journal of Modern Literature* 4(September 1974): 55–72; and "Chink Dorman-Smith and *Across the River and into the Trees,*" *Journal of Modern Literature* 11(July 1984): 314–22.

9. Verle Johnston, "La Granja Offensive," *Historical Dictionary of the Spanish Civil War, 1936–1939,* ed. James Cortada (Westport, Conn.: Greenwood, 1982), pp. 286–87. I have relied heavily on this book for all the historical information in this essay.

10. For an account of Orwell in Spain, see Jeffrey Meyers, "'An Affirming Flame': *Homage to Catalonia,*" *A Reader's Guide to George Orwell* (London: Thames and Hudson, 1975), pp. 113–29.

11. Pedro Menéndez de Avilés (1519–74) was a Spanish naval officer, conquistador and colonizer of St. Augustine, Florida. It is worth noting that most of the accents are missing from the Spanish words in *For Whom the Bell Tolls.*

12. See Hugh Thomas, *The Spanish Civil War* (New York: Harper & Row, 1961), p. 328.

13. Robert Kern, "Durruti, Buenaventura," *Historical Dictionary,* p. 175.

14. Robert Whealey, "March Ordinas, Juan," *Historical Dictionary,* p. 319.

15. Thomas, *The Spanish Civil War,* p. 492.

16. Quoted in Carlos Baker, *Ernest Hemingway: A Life Story* (New York: Scribner's, 1969), p. 347. By contrast, Ilya Ehrenburg wrote in his propagandistic *Memoirs: 1912–1941,* trans. Tatania Shebunina (Cleveland: World, 1963), p. 333: "She had all the traits of the Spanish character: gravity, kindness, dignity, courage and, most endearing of all, humaneness."

17. James Cortada, "Modesto Guilloto, Juan," *Historical Dictionary,* p. 339.

18. James Cortada, "Lister Forjan, Enrique," *Historical Dictionary,* p. 300.

19. Enrique Lister, *Nuestra Guerra* (Paris: Globe, 1966), quoted in Norberto Fuentes, *Hemingway in Cuba,* trans. Consuelo Corwin (Secaucus, N. J.: Lyle Stuart, 1984), p. 171.

20. Hemingway, *Selected Letters,* p. 789.

21. José Martín-Artajo, Introducción a *Una enseñanza de la Guerra Española* (Madrid: Júcar, 1980), p. 12. My translation.

22. Durán's appearance, mannerisms, speech, and actions also inspired the character of Manuel in Malraux's *Man's Hope* (1938). See André Malraux, *Man's Hope,* trans. Stuart Gilbert and Alastair Macdonald (New York: Random House, 1938), pp. 10, 57. For Durán's relations with Hemingway in Cuba and his postwar career, see Jeffrey Meyers, *Hemingway: A Biography* (New York: Harper & Row, 1985), pp. 369–73, 376–78, 383–84, 606–9.

23. Kléber and then Hans (Kahle) commanded the Eleventh Brigade, Lukacz the Twelfth, "Gómez" (Zeisser) the Thirteenth, Golz and then the Alsatian Colonel Putz the Fourteenth, Gal and then Čopíc the Fifteenth. Hemingway was most closely attached to the Twelfth Brigade.

24. James Cortada, "Galicz ('Gal'), Janos," *Historical Dictionary*, p. 230.

25. Thomas, *The Spanish Civil War*, p. 326.

26. Gustav Regler, *The Owl of Minerva*, trans. Norman Denny (London: Rupert Hart-Davis, 1959), p. 312.

27. Jerzy Krzyzanowski, "*For Whom the Bell Tolls:* The Origin of General Golz," *Polish Review,* 7(1962): 72. Karkov (whose name is taken from an industrial city in the Ukraine) refers to Walter—not Golz—on p. 247. Golz's 35th Division is mentioned on p. 376.

28. Thomas, *The Spanish Civil War,* p. 348.

29. Hemingway, *Selected Letters,* p. 794. Hemingway repeats Walter's joke about being a nonthinking Soviet general in *Selected Letters,* pp. 538 and 634.

30. Letter from Bronislaw Zielinski to Jeffrey Meyers, January 3, 1983, quoted in Meyers, *Hemingway: A Biography,* p. 605, n. 16.

31. Thomas, *The Spanish Civil War,* pp. 300–301.

32. Hemingway, *Selected Letters,* p. 789. In *The Spanish Civil War,* p. 262n, Hugh Thomas calls the chapter on Gaylord's "perhaps the best piece of *rapportage* Hemingway has yet written." Koltzov probably arranged the publication of Hemingway's attack on the Fascists, "Humanity will not Forgive This!" which appeared in *Pravda* in July 1938. See "Hemingway on War: An Essay Discovered," *Miami Herald,* November 29, 1982, pp. C1–C2.

33. Cecil Eby, "The Real Robert Jordan," *American Literature,* 38(November 1966): 382–83. See also Marion Merriman and Warren Lerude, *American Commander in Spain: Robert Hale Merriman and the Abraham Lincoln Brigade* (Reno: University of Nevada Press, 1986).

34. Ernest Hemingway, *The Spanish War* (London: Fact, 1938), p. 35.

35. Eby, "The Real Robert Jordan," p. 386.

36. In Denis Brian, *The True Gen* (New York: Grove, 1987), p. 120, Milton Wolff, who succeeded Merriman as commander of the Lincoln Brigade, suggests two other farfetched models for Hemingway's fictional hero: "Robert Jordan, the character in the novel, is really a Jewish boy from the Bronx, Alex Kunslich, a communist who was the inspirational leader of the American group of guerrillas who operated behind the lines. Physically, the description of Jordan is like Philip Detro, a battalion commander who was seriously wounded at Teruel and died of wounds." Three American guerrillas, including Alex Kuntzlich, are discussed in Edwin Rolfe, "The Secret Fighters," *New Masses* 33(November 14, 1939): 12–14, which appeared too late to provide material for Hemingway's novel.

37. Kenneth Lynn, *Hemingway* (New York: Simon & Schuster, 1987), pp. 444, 450.

38. See Audre Hanneman, *Supplement to Ernest Hemingway: A Comprehensive Bibliography* (Princeton: Princeton University Press, 1975), p. 75.

39. For the critical reception of the book, see Jeffrey Meyers, *Hemingway: The Critical Heritage* (London: Routledge & Kegan Paul, 1982), pp. 35–39, 314–67.

Works Cited

Baker, Carlos. *Ernest Hemingway: A Life Story.* New York: Scribner's, 1969.

Brian, Denis. *The True Gen.* New York: Grove, 1987.

Cortada, James. "Galicz ('Gal'), Janos." In *Historical Dictionary of the Spanish Civil War, 1936–1939,* 230. Ed. James Cortada. Westport, Conn.: Greenwood, 1982.

———. "Modesto Guilloto, Juan." In *Historical Dictionary of the Spanish Civil War, 1936–1939,* 339. See Cortada, "Galicz ('Gal'), Janos."

———. "Lister Forjan, Enrique." In *Historical Dictionary of the Spanish Civil War, 1936–1939*, 300. See Cortada, "Galicz ('Gal'), Janos."

Ehrenburg, Ilya. *Memoirs: 1921–1941*. Trans. Tatania Shebunina. Cleveland: World, 1963.

Eby, Cecil. "The Real Robert Jordan." *American Literature* 38 (1966): 382–83.

Fitzgerald, F. Scott. *Tender is the Night*. New York: Scribner's, 1962.

Fuentes, Norberto. *Hemingway in Cuba*. Trans. Consuelo Corwin. Secaucus, N.J.: Lyle Stuart, 1984.

Gellhorn, Martha. Interview. 28 November 1982.

Hanneman, Audre. *Supplement to Ernest Hemingway: A Comprehensive Bibliography*. Princeton: Princeton University Press, 1975.

Hemingway, Ernest. *For Whom the Bell Tolls*. New York: Scribner's, 1968.

———. *A Moveable Feast*. 1964. Reprint New York: Bantam, 1965.

———. "Hemingway on War: An Essay Discovered." *Miami Herald*, 29 November 1982, C1–C2.

———. Preface to *The Last Crusade*, by Gustav Regler. New York: Longman Green, and Company, 1940.

———. *Selected Letters, 1917–1961*. Ed. Carlos Baker. New York: Scribner's, 1971.

———. *The Spanish War*. London: Fact, 1938.

Johnston, Verle. "La Granja Offensive." In *Historical Dictionary of the Spanish Civil War, 1936–1939*, 286–87. See Cortada, "Galicz ('Gal'), Janos."

Kern, Robert. "Durruti, Buenaventura." In *Historical Dictionary of the Spanish Civil War, 1936–1939*, 175. See Cortada, "Galicz ('Gal'), Janos."

Krzyzanowski, Jerzy. "*For Whom the Bell Tolls:* The Origin of General Golz." *Polish Review* 7(1962): 69–74.

Lynn, Kenneth. *Hemingway*. New York: Simon & Schuster, 1987.

Lister, Enrique. *Nuestra Guerra*. Paris: Globe, 1966.

Merriman, Marion, and Warren Lerude. *American Commander in Spain: Robert Hale Merriman and the Abraham Lincoln Brigade*. Reno: University of Nevada Press, 1986.

Meyers, Jeffrey. "'An Affirming Flame': *Homage to Catalonia*." *A Reader's Guide to George Orwell*. London: Thames & Hudson, 1975.

———. "Chink Dorman-Smith and *Across the River and Into the Trees*." *Journal of Modern Literature* 11(1984): 314–22.

———. *Hemingway: A Biography*. New York: Harper & Row, 1985.

———. *Hemingway: The Critical Heritage*. London: Routledge & Kegan Paul, 1982.

———. "The Politics of *A Passage to India*." *Journal of Modern Literature* 1(1971): 329–38.

———. "The Plumed Serpent and the Mexican Revolution." *Journal of Modern Literature* 4(1974): 55–72.

Malraux, André. *Man's Hope*. Trans. Stuart Gilbert and Alastair Macdonald. New York: Random House, 1938.

Martín-Artajo, José. Introducción a *Una enseñanza de la Guerra Española*. Madrid: Júcar, 1980.

Penrose, Roland. *Picasso: His Life and Work*. New York: Harper & Row, 1973.

Pérez Lopez, Francisco. *A Guerrilla Diary of the Spanish Civil War*. Ed. Victor Guerrier. Trans. Joseph Harris. London: André Deutsch, 1972.

Regler, Gustav. *The Owl of Minerva*. Trans. Norman Denny. London: Rupert Hart-Davis, 1959.

Rolfe, Edwin. "The Secret Fighters." *New Masses* 33(1939): 12–14.

Thomas, Hugh. *The Spanish Civil War*. New York: Harper & Row, 1961.

Whealey, Robert. "March Ordinas, Juan." In *Historical Dictionary of the Spanish Civil War, 1936–1939*, 319. See Cortada, "Galicz ('Gal'), Janos."

Ramón Sender's Civil War

Charles L. King

When the Spanish Civil War broke out, Ramón Sender was thirty-five years old. Social ferment had long been strong in the air that the young Aragonese journalist and novelist breathed. Attracted from early youth to the anarchists who not only shared his fierce opposition to the existing order of things but also were willing to engage in violent, at times heroic, action against the regime, the Monarchy, and later the Republic itself, Sender joined the powerful Confederación Nacional de Trabajo (National Labor Federation), whose membership of one-and-a-half million by 1931 consisted of both anarchists and more moderate Anarcho-Syndicalists.[1] Furthermore, from about 1928 until 1933 he was also a member of the most radical of the anarchist groups, the Iberian Anarchist Federation (Federación Anarquista Ibérica).[2]

At the same time, despite his affinity for anarchism, Sender was also attracted to communism, an attraction that apparently was mutual, for his first book, *El problema religioso en Méjico* (The Religious Problem in Mexico),[3] was published by a Communist press in Spain as were almost all of the fourteen books, seven journalistic works, and seven novels he had published by the time he fled Spain in December of 1938.[4] In 1933, having become disillusioned with the political ineffectiveness of the methods employed by the anarchists, and doubtless concerned about the rising tide of fascism in Europe, Sender moved away from the anarchists, the National Labor Federation, and closer to the Communists, spending four months that year in Russia as a guest of the Union of Soviet Writers.[5] Upon returning to Spain, he published *Madrid-Moscú* (Madrid-Moscow), an uncritical book of praise for the Soviet experiment. As Nonoyama commented, Sender went to the Soviet Union "with the prior desire of being able to find everything good." Apparently he did indeed find things good, so good in fact that "were Communism as Sender described it," Nonoyama adds, "it would have contented the anarchists also."[6]

The hybrid term libertarian-communist, not in spite of its inherent contradictions but precisely because of them, seems best to describe the writer's lasting political philosophy, an ambivalent one embracing both libertarianism or anarchism with its reverence for the individual, and communism with its theoretically just organization of society. Francisco Carrasquer stated in 1982 that "Sender expressed himself fundamentally more in Bakuninian than in Communistic terms."[7] Carrasquer is correct, although Sender, ever fond of Hegelian dialecticalism, never ceased trying to harmonize or synthesize the demands of the two antithetical positions of the oxymoron libertarian-communist. In 1978 he wrote, "I had anarchistic and communistoid experiences . . . and I continue being a man of the people. . . ."[8] Here in Senderian terms, in poetic terms, we have the two contradictory isms, anarchism and communism, both experienced by Sender's persona, that is, by his social man, but neither one nor the other radically altering his inner man or hombria. Both thesis and antithesis are resolved not on an abstract or ideological level, an impossible task if words are to have any meaning, but on a personal, human one, synthesized in Sender himself, "a man of the people."

When one compares Sender's journalistic book about the Civil War, *Contraataque*, 1938 (*Counter-Attack in Spain*, Boston 1937; *The War in Spain*, London, 1937; French trans. published in France, 1937), with histories of the Civil War, it is evident that Sender's text is simply propaganda designed primarily to arouse sympathy in the United States, England, and France for the Republican cause. In its English translation, for example, it reports that the Nationalists had executed "more than seven hundred and fifty thousand" people, a figure mysteriously reduced to 700,000 in the Spanish edition.[9] In his excellent history *The Spanish Civil War*, Hugh Thomas, whom Sender called in 1962 "the most veracious of the historians" of the Spanish conflict,[10] concluded that the number of executions by the Nationalists during the entire War did not exceed 40,000.[11] On the other hand, executions by the Loyalists far exceeded that number and were often carried out under the most monstrous of conditions, yet Sender, knowingly or unknowingly, glossed them over in his book.[12] Though well written, the book is neither history nor literature.

It is difficult, therefore, to see any substantial reason for reprinting it in Salamanca in 1978, other than as a symbol of the completion of Don Ramón's restoration to Spanish society three years after Franco's death. It does, however, have a degree of testimonial value and interest for literary historians of the future, especially since much of its content forms the basis for the author's autobiographical novel of his experiences in working with the Communists during the Civil War, *Los cinco libros de Ariadna* (The five books of Ariadne).[13] This novel is not so much about the Civil War as it is about the author's personal entanglements during the War and is, at best, second-rate literature.

In his book *Novela española de nuestro tiempo* (the Spanish novel of our time), Gonzalo Sobejano divides the novelists who have treated the Spanish Civil War as a theme, rather than as mere background or occasion, into three groups: observers, militants, and interpreters.[14] He places Sender in the last group, the interpreters, because of Sander's novel, *El rey y la reina* (The king and the queen)(1948). Sobejano devotes a paragraph to it, calling it a parable (73–74). Another Senderian novel with the Civil War as its theme is *Réquiem por un campesino español* (Requiem for a Spanish peasant)(1953). These two works are the author's best-constructed novels and combine historical accuracy and literary excellence; both were written after years in exile and long meditations upon the meaning of the war.[15]

The King and the Queen was Sender's first book in six years, an unusual hiatus for such a prolific author, who produced over a hundred books during his lifetime. The six years, 1942–1948, correspond to his first six in the United States, obviously a period of adjustment for him to a new cultural environment, and yet one in which he reflected deeply about the war, the major shaking event of his life. The novel was long in incubation; Sender, uncharacteristically, must have written and rewritten much over time. The result was a restrained, sober, personal interpretation of the moral meaning of the war, an allegorical yet realistic narrative, which has aroused surprisingly little critical acclaim, either for its English translation in 1948 or for its Spanish version, published first in Buenos Aires in 1949 and again in Barcelona in 1970.

As the war breaks out, Republican militiamen occupy the palace and the grounds of the Duchess in Madrid, using it for military purposes, while retaining Rómulo, the middle-aged gardener, as custodian since he has recently by chance joined the National Labor Federation and is regarded by the militiamen, therefore, as one of their own. In the confusion, the Duchess, who thinks that the war will be over in a few days, hides, with the connivance of Rómulo, in a remote room on the fifth floor of the palace tower. The day before, in a strange encounter at the palace swimming pool, Rómulo looked at the Duchess in the nude, though so bedazzled by the experience that he really didn't see her. The swimming-pool incident has left his head spinning, having on him the effect of a revelation of absolute reality. Thenceforth the Duchess is to Rómulo his own private, passionate ideal, and protecting her from the brutal excesses of both Loyalists and Nationalists has become his primary concern. The gardener is both an individual and the incarnation or symbol of the pueblo, the people; his individual drama parallels the collective drama of the Republican militiamen.

The militiamen on the ducal grounds are the people who, like Romulo, have been awakened to a dream, the dream of possessing their own country, and they are fighting for that ideal. The Nationalists are fighting to preserve the Duchess, Spain, for themselves. Just as the gardener, having glimpsed the dream, the secret reality of the Duchess represented by her nakedness, and feeling a return of his lost youth, becomes expansive and heroic in his efforts to protect Her Grace at all costs, so the militiamen fight to regain their lost past lives of servile submission. The War has awakened them to their full manhood and to the performance of heroic actions, though in the heat of the struggle they commit brutal atrocities and would, Rómulo fears, kill the Duchess herself were they to find her. Rómulo excuses them, imagining that they are fighting "to get back their past, their lost lives, and in such a great getting back there's bound to be blood."[16] In these last words there is perhaps a hint of the author's wish to excuse the inhuman atrocities committed by certain uncontrolled elements among the Loyalist forces. A dissolute marquis, Esteban, representing the other side in the conflict, also is stirred to heroic action, risking his life almost nightly to maintain his illicit liaison with the Duchess, that is, with Spain, in the tower. But he, unlike Rómulo, does not really love the Duchess; subordinating her to his own selfish partisan interests he risks destroying her in a bombardment of the palace in which she narrowly escapes death.

Rómulo represents the best of liberal Spain, the Duchess the best of traditionalist Spain. The militiamen are fighting to take possession of their own country but in the process, in the horrible atrocities that both they and their opponents the Nationalists are committing, the Spain that they both dream of may itself (herself) be destroyed. Rómulo suffers great anguish for the safety of his idealized Spain, his ideal ambition, the Duchess, whose life is in jeopardy from both sides, just as the author himself must have suffered from the disillusioning experiences of the War, especially from events in the chaotic early days of the War. For Sender, as for Rómulo, the ideal Spain must be placed above all partisan interests. "'Nothing in the world matters so much as My Lady's safety,'" the quixotic gardener worriedly tells the Duchess after she has turned on a tower light that has guided Nationalist bombers to the palace, thus endangering her own life and resulting in the death of many militiamen. "'If suspicions gather round what the sentry said about "a stream of light," Her Grace is lost,'" he tells her. "'They [the Republicans] 'll kill her. And, if they kill her, the whole world—do you hear, My Lady?—the whole world'll be lost, too.'"[17] Without the ideal, the dream of a Utopian Spain, Spanish society will be lost. If there is no dream there will be no dreamers, and the whole world will perish in a human, moral sense; that is, it will be left without transcendent human values, which alone make a society or a nation worth living or dying for. As Rómulo needed the Duchess so she needs Rómulo. Without idealists there is no ideal, in Sender's view; Spain needs the pueblo for its very existence as a worthwhile nation.

In the end Rómulo, brutally surprised, finds that his dream can be realized only in death. As the Duchess expires in his arms, she recognizes him as the only real man she has ever known. In pursuing his illusion, Rómulo has recovered his youthful idealism and has grown in stature as a natural man. He has become a king and the Duchess his queen, the two of them meeting on the level of their common humanity as the destruction of war closes in on them. His adventure parallels that of the Spanish masses whom he sees fighting to possess their own dream of Spain. Esteban the marquis from Traditionalist Spain who almost nightly (at least until the devastation of war becomes extreme) visits the Duchess in her tower hideaway at great risk, is nicknamed the "diable" (devil). In his moral outlook on life he is just the opposite of Rómulo; he is cynical whereas the gardener is a man of faith and full of innocent wonder at life. The author's intention is clear: the Spanish Civil War was for him a struggle between two opposing views of man, one artificial and cynical, the other natural and reverential.

Réquiem por un campesino español, originally published in 1953 as *Mosén Millán,* is a very short, compact novel that masterfully interprets the moral causes and effects of the Civil War. Certainly Sander's most published, most read novel, it is also the one that has received by far the most critical attention.

A highly realistic narrative, it embodies an implicit interpretation of the origins and the end of the war, the *why* (el *por qué*)and the *for what* (el para qué) it was fought. As the village priest Mosén Millán sits (late in 1937, the reader infers) in the sacristy awaiting the arrival of parishioners to attend the requiem mass that he is offering gratuitously for an executed villager, Paco el del Molino, on the first anniversary of the execution, he remembers high points from Paco's entire life, from baptism to marriage to death by a fascist firing squad. As a young village councilman, Paco had led efforts at land reform, efforts made legal by the new Republican Government but regarded with dismay by the local traditionalists. The wait for the mass to begin, about twenty minutes, is the novel's primary plane of action. During it nothing happens except for the arrrival, ironically, of the three men most responsible for Paco's death, the three most affluent and powerful men in the village; the comings and goings of a young altar boy who remembers, as does the priest, snatches of a ballad composed anonymously by the villagers on the life and death of Paco; the mysterious entrance of Paco's colt into the sanctuary and its subsequent expulsion by the three men aided by the acolyte and sexton; and finally, the priest's moving into the chancel and beginning the mass. Present and past are woven together through the priest's periodic surfacing to the present from his world of memories, the secondary plane of action. A third plane, as Marcelino Peñuelas has pointed out, an atemporal and mythical projection to the future, is achieved in the ballad. Through it Paco enters the popular mind as legend.

Old Spain and New Spain, as Sender conceived them, are here locked in mortal combat. Mosén Millán with his inertia, his indifference to social injustice, his tendency to kowtow to the propertied classes, his isolation from much of the vital life of his rural parishioners (e.g., that represented in the village witch doctor or healer, La Jerónima), and his fatalistic attitude is clearly the Church itself, firmly entrenched in Old Spain. On a collision course with the priest is his young parishioner Paco, who has maintained his innate sense of justice and whose social conscience was awakened at an early age, ironically while serving the Church as an acolyte. Disillusioned with the Church's backward-looking posture, Paco becomes an activist, believing that what man has done man can undo. The coming of the Second Spanish Republic has encouraged him in his revolutionary hopes and imbued him with a new sense of self-assurance. In turn the three leading pillars of the Old Order (one of whom administers the Duke's landed estate and thus represents the Monarchy, which, along with the Church and the Falange, constitute the three major bulwarks of Nationalist Spain) feel themselves threatened by the new turn of events. In time they strike back to reassert their threatened authority, and Paco, betrayed by the priest's close collaboration with fascistic outsiders, is summarily executed. In symbolic terms, the brutal shooting of Paco by strangers giving the fascist salute means that elements foreign to Spanish life, aided and abetted by the Church, have crushed the Spanish pueblo, the common people, in order to affirm the threatened status quo.

Yet, the novel tells us that the spirit of revolution, the spirit of the people, can never be finally crushed; symbolically it survives in the ballad and in the dead hero's colt that is still running wild through the streets and that bolts into the empty church sanctuary in a dumb, brute protest against injustice. Paco's widow, though half insane from the cruel repression, is pregnant, so that hope remains for the next generation. Meanwhile the Church is empty except for its priest and the three guardians of the Spanish status quo; having taken sides in a war between brothers, the Church is left impotent to heal the wounds of division. Having deserted the people it is now deserted by them. It is obvious that Mosén Millán and the three chief enemies of Paco constitute victorious Spain and that they all are suffering from a troubled conscience and even further isolation from the *pueblo* than before the war.

The Church made Paco into the revolutionary that he became. Neither an anarchist nor a communist, he was a liberal whose parents were small landholders as were Sender's and who, also like Don Ramón, desired that changes be effected in an orderly and legal manner. Attracted to the Church as a young boy, he soon learned that it, as he experienced it in the priest Mosén Millán, was not only indifferent to economic injustice, but had no viable program for achieving what he regarded as a more just society. Finding the Church unresponsive and even antagonistic to measures designed to eradicate economic injustice and misery in the village, Paco quietly turned his back upon it as an institution just as did millions of Spaniards of his generation, many of whom in time became, as Sender, openly hostile to it. Their hostility resulted in the total destruction of 150 church buildings and the partial destruction of thousands more during the Civil War, in barbarous acts suggested in the novel by Paco's colt running loose in the church sanctuary.[18]

As it produced the rebel Paco, the Church helped to create the conditions in Spain that issued finally in the spring of 1936, in the Popular Front, a veritable revolution that led to the counterattack by the conservative traditionalist elements in July of that year. In the novel, the movements of history are paralleled. Just as Paco is at the point of succeeding in his reforms, his two chief opponents Don Gumersindo and Don Valeriano, who have left the village, a microcosm of Spain, return suddenly. They are soon followed "one day in July" by a group of señoritos (dandies) with whips and pistols, who teach the villagers the fascist salute and begin a bloody reign of terror, culminating in the execution of Paco. Not once in the novel is the Civil War mentioned; it is only implied.

The absolute center of the narrative is the priest; his memory flash-backs relate the story of Paco, effectively uniting past with present, and his own life with that of his parishioner. The novel is not only of Paco's tragedy but of the priest's as well; nothing could be more tragic than his isolation and troubled conscience as the story ends. Though Republican Spain lies vanquished and the Old Order has been rees-tablished, the Francoists are obviously uneasy about their victory.

The liberal reforms contemplated by the Republican Government or by radical elements within that Government, especially in 1936, alarmed elements of conservative or traditionalist Spain, including the Church. Old Spain responded by resorting to arms and, aided by outsiders, won a bloody victory over the so-called New Spain, and reestablished itself. This is the war as Sender interprets it in *Requiem*. It was indeed his civil war; Malcolm Compitello has written: "*Réquiem por un campesino español* is the ballad of Ramón Sender."[19] In the prologue to *The Five Books of Ariadne* (*Los cinco libros de Ariadna*), Sender's misguided novelistic apology for his collaboration with the Communists in the war, he wrote: "We are all guilty of what happened in Spain. Some through stupidity and others through wicked-ness. The fact that the stupidity is on our part (on the part of the better ones) does not save us either in the eyes of history or in our own eyes" (xii–xiii). Though he achieved a remarkable objectivity in the two novels chosen for special comment here, he never lost his convic-tion of the justice or rightness of the Republican cause and his belief that if the Republic had had stronger leadership and had Stalin not really wished its defeat even while supporting it, it would have won the war.

The impact of the war on the novelist can be measured in part by the fact that it inspired not only the writing of the two works dis-cussed here but also his most ambitious philosophical novel, *La esfera* (*The Sphere*), originally published under the title *Proverbio de la muerte* (Proverb of Death) in 1939.[20] Shaken profoundly by the holocaust, he sought to formulate a personal philosophical-religious answer to the human dilemma posed by the war. The book's defini-tive edition, published in 1969, was thirty years in the making. In-directly the war enters several other Senderian novels including *Crónica del alba* (*Chronicle of Dawn*), *La antesala* (The Ante-Chamber), *El Superviviente* (The Survivor) and *La efemérides* (The Ephemeris).

Though the war is not present in *El lugar de un hombre* (*A Man's Place)*, the novel was being written during the war and was published in 1939. It constitutes an eloquent statement of Sender's faith in the transcendent value of the individual member of society, no matter how insignificant he may seem.[21] The lack of true political and economic democratization of Spanish society, portrayed vividly in *A Man's Place*, was quite likely in Sender's mind the main issue over which the war was fought.

In prefatory remarks to his book of four Civil War stories, *La cabeza del cordero* (The Lamb's Head), Francisco Ayala, Sender's fellow exile, wrote that the narratives present the theme of the Civil War "under the permanent aspect of the passions that nourish it; it could be called: the Civil War in the heart of men" (33). Also in his novels, especially in the two works discussed in this paper, *The King and the Queen* and *Réquiem for a Spanish Peasant*, Sender has dealt with the permanent aspect of the the passions of the Spanish Civil War, the war "in the heart of man." "We were the evil," wrote Sender in 1977, "those on one side and on the other."[22]

NOTES

1. Hugh Thomas, *The Spanish Civil War* (New York: Harper & Brothers, 1961), p. 40.

2. Marcelino C. Peñuelas, *Conversaciones con R.J. Sender* (Conversations with R.J. Sender)(Madrid: Magisterio Español, 1969), p. 94. Sender says, in reply to a question by Peñuelas, that he was "about twenty-seven years" old when he joined the "Espartaco" group of the Federación Anarquista Ibérica, i.e., in 1928. Michiko Nonoyama, to whom I am indebted here, has documented the author's close collaboration with the National Labor Federation during the late twenties and early thirties, especially from 1930 until 1932, in her excellent study, *El anarquismo en las obras de R.J. Sender* (Anarchism in the Works of R.J. Sender)(Madrid: Playor, 1979), pp. 14–32. Titles of books not translated into English are not italicized here except when referred to in English in the text of this paper.

3. Prologue by Ramón del Valle-Inclán (Madrid: Cenit, 1928).

4. In his introduction to the reprinting of *Contraataque* (Salamanca: Almar, 1978), p. 11, Sender wrote: "In that time [1937] the Russians had published ten or twelve of my books retouching them wherever the texts did not serve the purpose of their propaganda." The publishers of all of Sender's pre-exile books in Spain except the two novels, *Siete domingos rojos*, 1932 (*Seven Red Sundays*, 1934), and *Mr. Witt en el cantón*, 1936 (*Mr. Witt Among the Rebels*, 1936) were, I believe, considered Communist: Cenit, Zeus, Pueyo, and Nuestro Pueblo.

5. Nonoyama documents Sender's growing disagreement with the National Labor Federation and closer adherence to the Communist official line during the period, 1934–1936, pp. 32–46.

6. Nonoyama, pp. 90–91.

7. "El raro impacto de Sender en la crítica literaria española," in *Homenaje a Ramón J. Sender* (Homage to Ramón J. Sender), edited by Mary S. Vásquez (Newark, Del.: Juan de la Cuesta Hispanic Monographs, 1987), 179. ("Sender se expresaba fundamentalmente más en términos bakunianos que marxianos.") In the prologue to *Los cinco libros de Ariadna* (The Five Books of Ariadne) (New York: Ibérica, 1957), p. xi, Sender professes: "Anarchists are those who individually seem closest to me. . . . One can get along only with men of faith (Los

anarquistas son los que individualmente me parecen más cerca de mí. . . . Uno sólo se entiende con los hombres de fe)."

8. *Contraataque,* p. 16: "Yo tuve experiencias anarquistas y comunistoides [. . .] y sigo siendo un hombre del pueblo . . . ."

9. See *Contraataque,* p. 137, and/or Ramón Sender, *Counter-Attack in Spain* (Boston: Houghton Mifflin, 1937), p. 89. At that time (mid-1937) Sender wrote: "Let us keep in our minds the fact that by now there have been more than seven hundred and fifty thousand executions in the rebel camp, and that they have had the horrifying virtuosity of exterminating whole families because in them there has been a single prominent Republican."

10. In his syndicated newspaper column, "Los libros y los días," released June 4, 1962, Sender, commenting on Hugh Thomas's *The Spanish Civil War,* calls Thomas "el más veraz de todos los historiadores [of the Civil War]" ("the most veracious of all historians").

11. Hugh Thomas (note 1 above, p. 169): "A careful examination of the meagre evidence suggests that a very approximate figure of 40,000 Nationalist executions during the whole war is likely" (p. 169). Later in the book he repeats this figure, stating that it is his "considered belief that the total number of Nationalist 'atrocities'—by which I understand any shooting outside the battle line—is unlikely to have been greater than 40,000" (p. 631).

12. Thomas (pp. 172–73) notes that the "Nationalists since the war have named a figure of 85,940 for all reputed murdered or executed in Republican Spain during the war," and concludes that "about 75,000 persons may be supposed to have been executed or murdered [by Republicans] between July 18 and September 1, 1936—for nearly all the illegal killings in the Republic occurred at the start of the war" (pp. 172–73). Furthermore, many were monstrously arbitrary with victims often being people from "the rank and file of the Right" (p. 177), while other executions were accompanied "by a partly frivolous, partly sadistic cruelty" (p. 173). Many of the Republican killers "were butchers of the sort that all revolutions spawn; many actually enjoyed killing and even gained from it a near-sexual pleasure" (p. 179).

13. *Los cinco libros de ariadna* (New York: Ibérica, 1957). It was reprinted by Destino (Barcelona, 1977).

14. (Madrid: Prensa Española, 1975), p. 54. Chapter ll, "La guerra española, objeto de novelas," pp. 53–85, is of special interest.

15. *El rey y la reina* (Buenos Aires: Jackson, l949); (Barcelona: Destino, l970 [Ancora y Delfín, 341], 1972, 1979 [Destinolibro, 5]); the edition from which I quote is *The King and the Queen,* trans. Mary Low (New York: Vanguard Press, 1948). The second novel, *Réquiem por un campesino español* (Barcelona: Destino, 1974), was first printed as *Mosén Millán* (Mexico: Aquelarre, 1953). A bilingual edition of *Réquiem* with translation into English by Elinor Randall is the only one published in English (N.Y.: Las Américas, 1960).

16. *The King and the Queen,* pp. 166, 153–54 (in the Spanish Destinolibro edition, pp. 121, 120).

17. *The King and the Queen,* pp. 155, 153–54 (in the Spanish Destinolibro editions [l972, 1979], pp. 121, 120).

18. Thomas writes: "150 churches were totally destroyed and 4,850 damaged, of which l,850 were more than half destroyed" (p. 606). Ironically—at least in Sender's view—most Spanish peasants were, mainly perhaps because of their adherence to Catholicism and traditional Spanish values, more inclined to follow the Nationalists than the Republicans. Paco, therefore, does not reflect the typical political-social attitudes of the rural populations of Spain.

19. "*Réquiem por un campesino español* and the Problematics of Exile," in Mary S. Vásquez, ed., *Homenaje a Ramón J. Sender,* p. 99.

20. *La esfera* (Buenos Aires: Siglo Veinte, 1947); *The Sphere,* trans. Felix Giovanelli (N.Y.: Hellman & Williams, 1949); *Proverbio de la muerte* (Mexico: Quetzal, 1939).

21. Sherman H. Eoff has studied the novel (in English, *A Man's Place*, trans. by the North American novelist Oliver La Farge [N.Y.: Duell, Sloan and Pearce, 1940; London: Jonathan Cape, 1941]) for its emphasis on the transcendent meaning of the individual in his outstanding book, *The Modern Spanish Novel* (New York: New York University Press, 1961), pp. 213–54. A shorter study of the same theme—in which I borrow heavily from Eoff—is my own: "The Role of Sabino in Sender's *El lugar de un hombre*," in *Hispania* 50, 1(March 1967): 95–98; and in Spanish in *Ramón J. Sender. In memoriam (Antología crítica)*, edited by José-Carlos Mainer (Zaragoza: Diputacion General de Aragón, et al, 1983), 351–55. Unfortunately the Spanish translation contains serious errors.

22. "¿Evitar lo inevitable?," a column from the author's syndicated column "Los libros y los días," released on May 19, 1977: "... el mal éramos nosotros, los de un lado y del otro." At the time Sender was worried lest civil discord in Spain lead to another national tragedy.

WORKS CITED

Ayala, Francisco. *La Cabeza del cordero.* 2nd Edition. Buenos Aires: Los Libros del Mirasol, 1962.

Carrasquer, Francisco. "El raro impacto de Sender en la crítica literaria española." In *Homenaje a Ramón J. Sender*, ed. Mary S. Vásquez.

Compitello, Malcolm. "*Réquiem por un campesino español* and the Problematics of Exile." In *Homenaje a Ramón J. Sender*, ed. Mary S. Vásquez.

Eoff, Sherman. H. *The Modern Spanish Novel.* New York: New York University Press, 1961.

King, Charles L. "The Role of Sabino in Sender's *El lugar de un hombre*." *Hispania* 50, 1(1967): 95–98.

Mainer, José-Carlos, Ed. *Ramón J. Sender. In memoriam (Antología crítica).* Zaragoza: Diputación General de Aragón, et al, 1983.

Nonoyama, Michiko. *El anarquismo en las obras de R. J. Sender.* Madrid: Playor, 1979.

Peñuelas, Marcelino C. *Conversaciones con R. J. Sender.* Madrid: Magisterio Español, 1969.

Sender, Ramón. *Contraataque*, 2d ed. Salamanca: Almar, 1978.

———. *Counter-Attack in Spain.* Trans. Peter Chalmers Mitchell. Boston: Houghton Mifflin, 1937.

———. *Los cinco libros de Ariadna.* New York: Ibérica, 1957.

———. *La esfera.* Buenos Aires: Siglo Veinte, 1947.

———. *Mosén Millán.* Mexico: Aquelarre, 1953.

———. *Mr. Witt en el cantón.* Madrid: Espasa-Calpe, 1936.

———. *The King and Queen.* Trans. Mary Low. New York: Vanguard Press, 1948.

———. *A Man's Place.* Trans. Oliver La Farge. New York: Duell, Sloan and Pearce, 1970.

———. *El problema religioso en Méjico.* Madrid: Cenit, 1928.

———. *Proverbio de la muerte.* México: Quetzal, 1939.

———. *El rey y la reina.* Buenos Aires: Jackson, 1949.

———. *Réquiem por un campesino español.* Barcelona: Destino, 1974.

———. *Réquiem por un campesino español.* Bilingual Edition. Trans. Elinor Randall. New York: Las Américas, 1960.

———. *Siete domingos rojos.* Barcelona: Colección Balagué, 1932.

———. *The Sphere.* Trans. Felix Giovanelli. New York: Hellman & Williams, 1949.

Sobejano, Gonzalo. *Novela española de nuestro tiempo.* Madrid: Prensa Española, 1975.

Thomas, Hugh. *The Spanish Civil War.* New York: Harper and Brothers, 1961.

Valle-Inclán, Ramón. Prologue to *El problema religioso en Méjico*, by Ramón Sender. Madrid: Cenit, 1928.

Vásquez, Mary S., ed. *Homenaje a Ramón J. Sender.* Newark, Del.: Juan de la Cuesta Hispanic Monographs, 1987.

Icons of War in Alberti:
"Madrid-Otoño"

Salvador J. Fajardo

The battle for Madrid, which began in November 1936, came to a standstill in March 1937. Subsequently, upon the Nationalist conquest of much of Northern Spain, in April through October 1937, the balance of power was definitely tilted in favor of the Franco forces. With the Nationalist conquest of Catalonia, December 1938 through February 1939, the fate of the Republic was effectively sealed. Throughout the war, however, the resistance of the capital had stood as a symbol of hope for the Republicans, and one should read Rafael Alberti's "Capital de la gloria" with this notion in mind.[1]

In her fine book *Rafael Alberti's Poetry of the Thirties* Judith Nantell describes "Capital de la gloria" as "Alberti's intimate diary of the Spanish Civil War" (92). Although only a few poems in the collection deal specifically with Madrid, it is significant that Alberti's title sets forth the importance of the capital as background to his war poetry. The first, and probably the most powerful, piece in the "poemario," "Madrid-Otoño," deals precisely with the besieged city. A mimetic reading of "Madrid-Otoño" clearly features the notion of rebirth as its central theme (Nantell, 92–98). This idea has the added appeal of informing many of Alberti's poems in "Capital de la gloria." But if we read the poem at another level, rhetorically as well as mimetically, we realize that the opposition death-birth generates an intrinsic contention at the very source of the poet's voice.

My interest in reading "Madrid-Otoño" lies at the intersection of rhetoric and semiotics. I am looking for the origins of Alberti's voice of battle, when he becomes the spokesman for the combatants and, considering the devastation of the Civil War, he ponders his instrument, his poet's words, as an inadequate, yet necessary substitute for bullets.

It is apparent from the outset that the poem is an extended apostrophe. One of several interesting components of apostrophe is that, as Jonathan Culler reminds us, "it makes its point by troping not on the meaning of a word but on the circuit or situation of communication itself" (135). It is the very possibility of such communication that Alberti investigates. In fact, the poem becomes a foundational communicative gesture as the need to speak asserts itself gradually from initial self-contradiction ("yo quisiera . . . / arrancarme de cuajo la voz, pero no puedo [I would like . . . / to tear out my voice by the roots, but I cannot]") to final self-assertion ("Ciudad, quiero ayudarte a dar a luz tu día [City, I want to help you bring forth your day], 94).

What can we deduce from the vocative situation embodied in the poem? First, the I-thou axis establishes "ciudad" as a sentient being, as another subject, and will define a series of relations between two subjects: poet-city. At another level of reading, however, the invoked city appears as a mirror image of the poet's spirit, and the poem's apostrophic form reveals another strand in its composition: it serves to establish the poet's identity as singer of the city's plight. The poem then is a parturition, the *seeking to be* of a proper poetic voice. In this light, the events of the poem, the poet's deambulatory description of the city's ruin, are hypostasized as aspects of the birth of the voice. And here we rejoin the mimetic reading of the piece as the tale of a rebirth, though at a level of significance that implicates the poet. The birth of the future city is dependent on the poet's voice, on his song as poem for the future; that is to say, as ideology.

The communicative gesture of apostrophe, while establishing the rhetorical move of interiorization, is not itself sufficient. The poet will be the city's singer only if he marks out its space, if he can plumb its essential being behind the ruins, and if he can merge this essential being with his own responsibility as a poet. Two intertwined developments pursue this end: (1) a series of images, which, as they evoke the city's destruction, serve to intensify the poet's feelings and (2) a parallel series identifying the witness-poet, first as an aspect of the city, then as a presence that gradually merges with it. This double isotopy remains in force throughout the poem; I will focus primarily on the first strophe, where it takes form; thus I hope to make available a direction for future readings.

> Ciudad de los más turbios siniestros provocados,
> de la angustia nocturna que ordena hundirse al miedo
> en los sótanos lívidos con ojos desvelados,
> yo quisiera furiosa, pero impasiblemente

arrancarme de cuajo la voz, pero no puedo,
para pisarte toda tan silenciosamente,
que la sangre tirada
mordiera, sin protesta, mi llanto y mi pisada.

(City of darkest provoked disasters,
of nightly anguish that orders fear to sink
into livid cellars with watchful eyes,
would that in fury, yet impassive,
I could tear up my voice by its roots,
but I cannot,
to pace upon you so silently,
that strewn blood
might bite, without protest, my weeping
and my steps.)

In stanza 1, the city is invoked as a blank space—"Ciudad"— upon which dire events are inscribed:
"los más turbios siniestros provocados"
"la angustia nocturna"
"sótanos lívidos"
"ojos desvelados"
These figures are all synecdoches, and as such their ontological function is double: they act as representations of the city of which they are a part or an aspect, and as instances of the essence of the city.[2]

The semantic nucleus "Ciudad" initiates a braided isotopy along a space-time axis, as announced in the title of the poem "Madrid-Otoño": a space and the events that befall that space. "[T]urbios siniestros provocados" and "angustia nocturna" particularize the city's latency as vulnerable space. It should be noted that "provocados," as second degree synecdoche, identifies the city as victim and anticipates the role of the poet as its defender through language, midwife of its future new day. The syntactical linkages in the phrase also have their role to play. The first synecdoche is introduced by a *de*, genitive of attribution. In general, the genitive produces a shift from species to genus (as, for instance, "a man of the people"), so that we have a counter movement in which grammar contradicts semantics. The trope isolates an aspect of "ciudad," then the syntax reverses the circuit and transforms "ciudad" into an aspect of "turbios siniestros." Likewise, in the case of "de la angustia nocturna," a particularizing synecdoche is articulated by a generalizing genitive. The contradiction of one level of discourse by another also anticipates an attribute of the poet's emergence in self-contestation.

The initial isotopy, as we isolated it, portrays man's destruction of the city—"turbios siniestros provocados" encompassing the space above, "angustia nocturna," and space below, "que ordena hundirse el miedo." The genitives of attribution that articulate the syntagmatic chain turn the city into the birthed entity: ciudad—siniestros—angustia. Thus, the city is born out of catastrophe and contradiction. In terms of the prevalent space-time isotopy, these last two tropes constitute as well the scene of a semantic intersection:

> angustia—human component
> nocturna—space (above)—city
> hundirse—destruction + descent = city + man
> miedo—human component

The cataclysm is a human event, the city is a human space. The reciprocity is confirmed below ground where fear finds its refuge, "en los sótanos lívidos con ojos desvelados." Here the attributive *con* introduces the determination of *ojos desvelados* to the *sótanos*. An important semic intersection occurs at this point and encompasses all aspects of the signifying chain. (1) graphemic: as the recurrence of "o's," the graphic representation of the line's isotopy, (2) phonemic: as alliteration and internal rhyme, (3) prosodic: in the two balanced hemistychs separated by *con*: "sótanos lívidos /con/ ojos desvelados," (4) figural: the two figures (synecdoches) abstracting the notion of representation and relating it to vision—representation as a form of vision, (5) finally, semantic decomposition revealing the isotopy to be:

> cavity + light = darkness + light
> (sótanos-ojos)(lívidos-desvelados)

The determinative *con* reveals an oxymoron centered on the sense of sight, that is to say, on the notion of space. It serves precisely to introduce the poet who now rises out of this inner space of fear as reluctant voice and vision. His voice inaugurates itself through oxymoron:

> yo quisiera furiosa, pero impasiblemente
> arrancarme de cuajo la voz, pero no puedo.

We have noted already that oxymoron is figured in various ways in the stanza as self-contradicting levels of discourse (trope versus grammar, trope versus content). The city's being, both figuratively, as we saw, and syntactically, emerges out of contradiction, out of its own destruction. The poet's own emerging presence is self-contradictory and is born in the depths of the city, in its chaotic center of fear, out of this very contradiction: destruction is birth. It is the city that gives birth to the poet as it gives birth to its own new being.

As a child clings to his mother's womb and yet is impelled forth by her, his cries announcing both the refusal and the necessity to enter the world, so the poet, whose essence is voice, assumes this refusal and

this necessity together: "yo quisiera . . . / arrancarme la voz."
"[A]rrancarme la voz" is the very emblem of the poet's birth. The
expression also incorporates its own contradiction, since "arranca la
voz" means "the voice rises." In fact, all the terms in these two lines
are in antiphrastic relation around "arrancarme la voz," creating at
the heart of the stanza a striking moment of knotted violence:

yo quisiera   no puedo
arrancarme la voz
furiosa   impasiblemente

The lines that follow reiterate the reason for such self-muting.

> para pisarte toda tan silenciosamente,
> que la sangre tirada
> mordiera, sin protesta, mi llanto y mi pisada.

"Toda" is a generalizing synecdoche for "ciudad"; it becomes the
space of the poet (alliteration—pisar*te toda tan*—impresses the steps
upon our mind). His wished-for state is silence still, but a silence that
voices itself and whose self-contestation is imaged by the last line,
"mordiera. . . ." The line is a double oxymoron in that the action it
depicts is twice reversed: (1) Blood bites the heel, (2) Blood bites
without protesting. At the same time, its central term, the apposi-
tional "sin protesta," introduces some semantic hesitancy; while syntax indicates that it is in apposition to "mordiera," sense wants to
draw it toward "mi llanto . . ." as its qualifier. Finally, the line is a
concluding intersection for two synecdoches: blood, for the city,
weeping steps for the poet.

In the following five stanzas, which constitute the poem's first part,
the poet's voice is inaugurated through its description of the
destroyed cityscape, which, as the apostrophic stance implies, is mirror of the poet's spirit. The space-time intersection is given full
development, with particular emphasis on space. Vertical and surface
space are encompassed together in each strophe, as the poet's gaze
identifies, incorporates the multiple wounds of war. The exploration
follows concentric circles from the city's outer limits (stanza 2), to
streets and neighborhoods (stanza 3), to vacant homes (stanza 4), and
then outwardly, as vulnerable body on the plain, extended for death
or for birthgiving (stanza 5). The final strophe hypostasizes the
recovered space as scene of the future birth ("el germen más hermoso
de tu vida futura"), an echo of the poet's voiced silence in stanza 1.

The voice traces and assumes the space of the city; it finds its reason
to be in this very act, as it defines the site of its representation. And
in each self-generating circuit of the city's space—each stanza—there

remains a trace of unassumed space, available blanks, images that elicit or represent the gaze.

```
ojos desvelados          st. 1
ojos fijos espían        st. 2
museos (as site of
unspecified represented
spaces)         st. 3
la menguada luna de los
pobres roperos
(luna as mirror and moon)     st. 4
más que nunca mirada/
. . . ciudad          st. 5
Ciudad, ciudad presente      st. 6
```

In this latter instance, "presente" means both present *and* dead, as in "cuerpo presente," but also laid out for viewing. This very meaning is a reiteration of "más que nunca mirada/. . . ciudad" of the previous stanza.

The poem could end here, but it would be truncated. The poet's voice has not yet found the register proper to construction. So far it has defined itself, and the city, as the scene of catastrophe and of a hoped-for future, but it lacks the ideological component that will make this future possible and will fully enable the voice's constructive potential. While stanza 6 proposes a response to stanza 1 as to the city, the second part of the poem, which consists of one stanza, echoes the poet's self-instituting voiced silence, turns it into voiced affirmation, and makes of the poet the midwife of the city's future. Now the poet's fury finds its full voice:

> . . . este furor que ahora
> me arranca lo que tienes para mí de elegía
> son pedazos de sangre de tu terrible aurora.
> Ciudad, quiero ayudarte a dar a luz tu día.

> [. . . this fury which now
> tears from me what there is in you that is elegy
> are chunks of blood from your terrifying dawn.
> City, I want to help you to bring forth your day].

The poet's voice rises to erase and replace those signs of the past (Palacios, retratos, jaeces militares, cuadros, libros). "[A]rrancarme la voz de cuajo" has become "este furor que ahora/ me arranca lo que tienes para mí de elegía," actualizing the potential of the first "arrancar" as rising voice. Palaces, portraits, are the signs of the enemy, those who would reestablish a dead past. They are being replaced by the poet's song, his signs, born in the ruins of battle.

The poet's vision/voice can now proceed to construct on those spaces newly available to the gaze and the word the signs of the future. Through the internalization of the city, the poet has availed himself of the space of his writing. In other words, the poem has enabled the poet to speak about war, to see the cataclysm and not be silenced by despair, to realize that words may not be bullets, but they can serve. And if the poet must inaugurate his speech in this manner, it is because of the intrinsic incompatibility of poetry and violence.

Alberti has transformed Madrid into a hyper-icon, or, to paraphrase W. J. T. Mitchell, an image that is itself the scene of sign production (5–6). The poem is a powerful instantiation of the birth of a poetic voice as representation. To its overall apostrophic disposition, which establishes the self-generating communicative gesture, corresponds the internal play of oxymoron. To the generative activity of the gaze corresponds the distribution of imagery along a synecdochic path that defines the space of representation.

I can only mention in these concluding lines the poems that follow in "Capital de la gloria." I think that they acquire their full meaning when seen against the background of "Madrid-Otoño" as their enabling hyper-sign. They are the signs that the poet inscribed in the space of the capital as he took up the song for those who could not sing. Alberti has become the poet of the city at war, of the people besieged, or, as he himself said, "pulmón de todo un pueblo [the lungs of a whole people].[3] His voice must serve as weapon and elegy, incitement and celebration. Such high energy verse, when recited to the assembled soldiers and volunteers, must have lifted their spirit. The poetry has an epic ring: it echoes with the naming of heroes, the almost ritual repetition of gestures, the labeling of events. The poet assumes a variety of voices: salutatory ("Soy del quinto regimiento"); hortatory in a folk vein, in several traditional ballads ("Defensa de Madrid/Defensa de Cataluña," for example); elegiac ("Al general Kleber"); propagandistic ("A Hans Beimler, Defensor de Madrid"), lyrical ("Los soldados se duermen"), meditative ("Nocturno"), and vituperative ("Balada de los cuatro cerdos y la paz"). This is the iconography of Alberti's Civil War.

NOTES

1. Rafael Alberti, "Capital de la gloria," section 4 of *De un momento a otro*, in *El poeta en la calle* (Madrid: Aguilar, 1978), pp. 92–119. The poem "Madrid-Otoño" opens the collection, pp. 92–94.

2. Kenneth Burke, *A Grammar of Motives* (Berkeley and Los Angeles: University of California Press, 1969), pp. 506–9. My rhetorical analysis is also based on the work of the "Groupe μ." It appears in *Rhétorique générale* (Paris: Larousse, 1970), and *Rhétorique de la poésie* (Paris: Presses Universitaires de France, 1977).

3. In "Aniversario" ("Capital de la gloria"), *El poeta en la calle,* p. 111.

WORKS CITED

Alberti, Rafael. "Capital de la gloria." *El poeta en la calle.* Madrid: Aguilar, 1978.

Burke, Kenneth. *A Grammar of Motives.* Berkeley and Los Angeles: University of California Press, 1969.

Culler, Jonathan. *The Pursuit of Signs.* Ithaca, N.Y.: Cornell University Press, 1981.

Groupe μ, *Rhétorique générale.* Paris: Larousse, 1970.

———. *Rhétorique de la poésie.* Paris: Presses universitaires de France, 1977.

Mitchell, W. J. T. *Iconology.* Chicago: University of Chicago Press, 1986.

Nantell, Judith. *Rafael Alberti's Poetry of the Thirties.* Athens: The University of Georgia Press, 1986.

From Page to Screen: Contemporary Spanish Narratives of the Spanish Civil War

Thomas Deveny

During the past two decades, many Spanish movie directors have turned to novels as a source for their film narratives, and this is the case with several of the most significant Spanish movies about the Civil War.[1] I view the war here in a broad sense; although the fighting officially ended in February of 1939, the aftermath of the war is difficult to separate from the conflict itself. In 1976, director Carlos Saura stated, "La guerra española ha estado y está todavía gravitando sobre nosotros, pertenece a un pasado inmediato que dificilmente puede separarse de nuestro presente" (Campos 34–37). Indeed, Ignacio Sotelo has declared that "la guerra terminó con la muerte de Franco" (11).

Some films emphasize the turbulent years immediately prior to the war itself. In *Pascual Duarte*, the cinematic version of Nobel Prize winner Camilo José Cela's *La familia de Pascual Duarte*, director Ricardo Franco emphasizes the sociopolitical element throughout. A close-up of Pascual's letter regarding unemployment precedes a scene where two men are fighting over a job. Pascual later listens to a radio broadcast of the declaration of the Republic, and as Juan Carlos Rentero points out, "este recalcamiento de fecha concretísima nos delata claramente la intencionalidad de su autor" ("Pascual Duarte," 37). An important deep shot from inside a train car shows graffitti— "CNT" and "Tierra y libertad"—which at once underscores the political emphasis and also manifests the principal source of conflict. The violence of the the literary text sometimes appears in the film with visual imagery that also underscores the social theme. Jorge Urrutia notes that, in the shot in which Pascual kills his dog, the town looms symbolically in the background: "Pascual no ha disparado sobre la perra, sino sobre el pueblo" (91–92). In all, Franco paints an agonizing portrait of both the protagonist and Spanish society.

Mi hija Hildegart, the 1977 film directed by Fernando Fernán Gómez, is based on a work by Eduardo de Guzmán entitled, *Aurora de sangre (Vida y muerte de Hildegart).* In the forward, Guzmán notes, "El relato que sigue no es una novela, sino un reportaje" (5), since it is based on historical events: the murder in 1934 of the precocious Hildegart Rodríguez by her mother Aurora. Director Fernán Gómez provides a framework for the narrative with Eduardo, the elderly narrator, who tells the story at a bar. Unlike Guzmán's work, where the judicial process is a scant epilogue, the trial constitutes a principal narrative vehicle for the film. An important theme is the question of loyalty, especially between Hildegart and her mother. The harsh auditory image when Aurora strikes the keyboard of a piano symbolizes the irreconcilable discord that arises between them. Unfortunately, this film suffers more than others from *destape;* its gratuitous nudity may have been included to achieve greater commerciality of the film, but it ironically contradicts Hildegart's ideals in real life.

Requiem por un campesino español is a film from 1985 directed by Francisco Betriu, and based on the novel by Ramón Sender. In some cases, Betriu is able to intensify certain poetic symbols of the novel, such as Paco's entrance on his white horse in symbolical contrast with the entrance into the town square of two automobiles from which a band of youths emerge dressed in black military uniforms. The film version loses some of the intensity of the original, however, and is unable to provide the character of Mosén Millán with the tragic dimension which Sender's narrative contains.[2]

Soldados, the 1978 film by Alfonso Ungría, is based on *Las buenas intenciones,* by Max Aub, but Ungría has changed the narrative structure significantly. The novel follows a basically linear temporal progression from 1924 to 1939, and the civil war does not even appear until more than two-thirds into the narrative. Ungría begins in the middle of the war and weaves a complex narrative through the constant use of flashbacks and dream sequences. This important transformation in the narrative structure, together with the radical change in title, serves to foreground the war. Ungría adds narrative information that heightens the sense of disillusionment and loss in each of the protagonists, and he takes considerable liberty with the end of the novel. In the film, Agustín returns to Madrid, and encounters Remedios in a brothel, where, during a lengthy scene, they consummate their relationship. After the Nationalist soldiers burst into the brothel and capture him, they lead him away and shoot him in the back. Both the sexual encounter and the assassination manifest how Ungría visually expands on the terse, connotative prose of Aub.

The novelist's description of the sexual act is simply "Cumplieron, ella sabía su oficio" (273); after Agustín's arrest, he was to be taken to prison, and we learn of his assassination only through the comment, "No llegaron" (280). In the film, while both scenes are visually more explicit, they also are highly connotative within the contexts of the narrative that Ungría has created.

Many narratives concentrate on the rearguard, on the lives of civilians and the repercussions that the war had on them. *El otro árbol de Guernica*, a film by Pedro Lazaga after a novel by Luis de Castresana, narrates the story of Republican children who were evacuated from Spain and taken to Belgium. The film version is a faithful illustration of the novel. It maintains the fundamental narrative events of the original in the same chronological order: the trip to Belgium, life with a Belgian family and in a boarding school, and return home. The final shot of the film in which the jubilant children enter into the harbor at Bilbao upon their return to Spain contrasts with the end of the novel in which the protagonists return by train; the film narrative thus provides a more circular and complete sense of resolution.

In *Retrato de familia*, a film by Giménez Rico based on Delibes' *Mi idolatrado hijo Sisí*, the director emphasizes the years of the war in his tragic portrait of a bourgeois Spanish family. The emphasis on the historical period from 1936 to 1938 is evident in the chronology of the narrative, as Giménez Rico radically departs from the mainly linear depiction of events that Delibes utilizes in the novel, whose opening line places the action in 1917. In the film, all events prior to 1936 are subordinated to that historical present through seven major flashbacks, going back to the moment of Ceci's conception, and including the boy's rebellious youth, signs of social unrest, and Ceci's death in the war. The bourgeois merchant cannot comprehend his tragedy, and his combination of rage, depression, and lack of understanding lead to his final act: suicide, throwing himself from the window of Lina's apartment, an act for which the film provides adequate motivation, but which is even more strongly underscored in the novel.[3]

La Plaza del Diamante is a film by Francesc Betriu based on the novel by Mercè Rodoreda; it focuses on the life of a young woman from Barcelona who loses her husband in the war. Perhaps the most important stylistic technique of the film is the constant voice-over of the female protagonist, nicknamed Colometa, a technique which corresponds to the interior monologue in the novel. The movie contains many motifs common to films of this genre, such as Colometa's thinking that the conflict will soon terminate, and a child's asking about the nature of the conflict that caused the death of his mother.

The Nationalist victory brings many changes manifested in the visual images of the change of street signs and stencils of Franco on building walls, and in the rejections when Colometa seeks work. In her most important speech of the film, she looks directly at the camera in a medium shot and speaks about her ability to survive in beautiful metaphors: "Cuando alguna vez había oído que las personas estaban de corcho, no sabía lo que querían decir. Por fin lo entendí. Porque yo era de corcho, tuve que hacerme de corcho con el corazón de nieve." Francisco Marinero praises this scene, saying, "Es un lenguaje claramente literario y un plano que interrumpe la ficción. Es el mejor y más arriesgado momento de la película" (*"La Plaza,"* 34). Colometa represents the lives of many Spaniards, particularly in Catalonia, who survived the difficult years after the war. Unfortunately, the film is impoverished by an apparent lack of resources in the filming of exterior sequences, with pitifully small groups of extras.

The portrait of the postwar years appears in novels such as *La colmena,* by Camilio José Cela, *Tiempo de silencio,* and *Los santos inocentes* by Delibes, all of which critics Fanny Rubio and Javier Goñi characterize as "novelas de la guerra de España" (158–59). Hunger, the black market, political favoritism, underdevelopment, and lost opportunities are elements in these narratives which paint a bleak picture of Spanish society from the 1940s to the 1960s.

Mario Camus directed the cinematographic version of *La colmena.* The screen writers tackled the formidable task of reducing to about sixty the numerous characters of Cela's famous novel, and Camus filled the cast with stars of the Spanish screen. The director went to great lengths to visually recreate La Delicia café of the 1940s. Camus underscores sociopolitical divisions of the time, which are based on the dichotomy of victor and vanquished, in the relationships between Leonardo and Don Mario, Visi and Flora, or Martín and Roberto. Roberto's Spain is clearly connoted in a scene in which he and his wife listen to the radio with its martial music and cries of "Viva Franco," and the camera seeks out a photograph of Roberto in a soldier's uniform. The scene is charged with irony, however, because, after the triumphant cries, the lights go out, and Roberto's comment, "Sí que estamos buenos otra vez," makes it evident that electrical shortages are a common occurrence. Martín's Spain is that of the soup lines, police interrogations, and ideological capitulation in the form of biographical articles on Spanish monarchs for the official press. The final voice-over by a narrator gives the ending of the film a very literary resonance.

In 1983, Camus brought Miguel Delibes' *Los santos inocentes* to the screen. The film's director has commented, "el cine, aunque tiene un lenguaje diferente a la literatura, ha conservado en esta ocasión el lirismo que encerraba la novela" (Inurria, 20). Camus has the film's literary quality by dividing it into four distinct "chapters." This division represents a departure from the novel in both quantity (the novel contains six) and denomination: whereas the novel's chapter headings combine names of characters with titles which give hints of the denouement ("El accidente," "El crimen"), Camus limits the titles to characters' names. A fundamental structural change in the narrative is the dispersion of characters and temporal jump of four years, which serves, according to the director, as the narrative platform of the film (Inurria, 20). Thus, the film's narration consists of a present time frame broken by four flashbacks, each of which Camus overtly marks. Although the film's chapter headings do not foreshadow the illfated ending as do those of the novel, director Camus guides the viewer subtly from the very beginning. A still shot of Paco's family begins as a negative that is overexposed and gradually grows darker, thus foreshadowing the darkness that eventually overcomes the household. The other technique that Camus utilizes to this end is the visual metaphor contained in the close-ups of excrement. Azarías, the innocent, defecates even on the grounds of the big house. The singling out of these remains by the camera lens visually symbolizes a fundamental expression of Spanish billingsgate, "Me cago en . . ." His symbolic curse on those who oppress and exploit turns to reality at the end of the narration as he carries out his vengeance on don Iván.

Like all film adaptations, Vicente Aranda's version of Martín Santos' *Tiempo de silencio* is a personal reading of the original. Of all the novels under consideration here, however, this is the least "cinematographic." As critic Antonio Lara points out, "*Tiempo de silencio* es una novela cuya adaptación al cine resulta imposible, o poco menos, porque sus principales valores no son propiamente narrativos, sino estilísticos e ideológicos" (50). Aranda's version of the absurd world in which Pedro lives does not depend on the subtle ironies of the literary text; instead, many scenes elicit overt laughter from the audience. Aranda also increases the importance of Dorita, played by Victoria Abril, who seems to be ever present in his films. Octavi Martí notes that "la omnipresencia de Dorita, así como el carácter edípico de las relaciones entre Matías y su madre . . . son dos de las vías de escape que el cineasta Vicente Aranda ha encontrado para dotar al filme [sic] que presenta de una dimensión que trascienda la estricta crónica" (47).

La guerra de papá, by Antonio Mercero, based on the Delibes novel, *El príncipe destronado,* often uses visual imagery to shift the psychological emphasis of the novel to the sociopolitical as Mercero portrays a family dominated by the values of a father who fought on the victorious side of the war. In the opening scene, a cannon, "para ir a la guerra de papá," in the hand of the three-year-old Quico contrasts with the image in the novel of a tube of toothpaste that he makes believe is a truck (12). The father's role in the war appears in the images of objects in his study—flags, a photograph of himself as a young soldier, and a pistol in his desk drawer—as well as in a tense dinner conversation concerning the war, with terms such as "buenos," "malos" and "cosa santa" that divide the ideological question into clear-cut areas of black and white. The father tries to impose his ideology on his oldest son, but the film ends on a note of reconciliation. Although much of the movie narrative consists of a series of mischievous acts carried out by Quico and his brother, Mercero emphasizes the repercussions of the war on the family, even twenty-five years after the end of the conflict.

In Adelaida García Morales's short novel, *El sur,* the war is overtly mentioned on only one occasion (p. 8), but its presence dramatically shapes the destinies of Agustín and his family. In the magnificent film version, director Víctor Erice emphasizes this theme with the character of Milagros, who, during a visit, talks to Estrella about her father's past, and explains that when Franco triumphed, Agustín was a "devil" who went to jail. In the film script, Erice changed all of the characters' names. The most significant of these is the change of name of the female protagonist from Adriana to Estrella, which seems to underscore the the important aesthetic handling of light in the film. The effective use of the voice-over by Estrella captures admirably the tone of the novelistic narrative, which is an epistle or confession to her father who has committed suicide. The most radical narrative change from the novel to the film is the fact that the cinematographic narrative terminates when Estrella is about to go to Sevilla to search out her father's past, whereas, in the novel, she makes the trip. The presentation of a so-called "unfinished" film caused considerable controversy. Nevertheless, the ending of the film imbues the work with an even greater poetic quality and cannot be considered a defect. Indeed, it captures perfectly the sentiment expressed by Adriana in the novel: "siempre era mejor lo que se queda en el espacio de lo posible, lo que no llega a existir" (41).

Another important theme of contemporary Spanish narratives, that of memory and the attempt to retrace the past, appears in the 1979 film *La muchacha de las bragas de oro,* directed by Vicente Aranda, based on the novel by Juan Marsé. The aging Falangist Luys Forest decides to write his autobiography in order to understand himself. The film begins with the voice-over of Luys's memoirs as he walks along the beach: "Los trágicos sucesos de aquellos años que me conviertieron en nómada." The change from the original text ("avatares" [40] becomes "trágicos sucesos") underscores Luys' hypocrisy. Although Luys was "cronista oficial de la victoria," he would have us believe that he began to doubt his ideological stance. It slowly becomes apparent, however, that Luys falsifies and glorifies his past. A series of flashbacks constitute Luys's memories, and the visual imagery of the film often creates a greater sense of irony in the process of negation of Luys's false narrative. Thus, although an early scene shows a close-up of the young Luys shaving his "bigotito cursi y simbólico," a physical attribute that linked him to the fascist ideology, his neice Mariana later calls this memory into question, saying "Sin embargo, yo de niña te acuerdo con bigote, y no hace tanto tiempo." All of the subsequent flashbacks show the young Luis with the moustache, belying his claims. At the end of the narrative, Luys must finally face the truth that Mariana is not his niece, but his daughter. In the film version, when Forest learns of his incest, he goes to his bedroom to get his pistol. Accompanying an exterior shot of his window, we hear a gunshot, and can only guess that he has committed suicide. Forest, however, has merely shot himself in the hand. In the novel, the old pistol does not go off, and Mariana and her mother find Luys crying on the floor; this transformation of the ending contains a greater sense of irony and a heightened sense of poetic justice for his repugnant shooting in the hand in the 1930s of a young man who was urinating while leaning against an exterior wall of his house where the symbol of the Falangist party was displayed.[4]

    Although contemporary Spanish directors use novels as the basis of their films on the Civil War, the two narratives are often quite disparate. The question of what Dudley Andrew calls the fidelity of transformation is a complex one, due to the basic differences in the two signifying systems (101). If, as Robert Scholes points out, "our primary effort in attending to a narration is to construct a satisfying order of events . . . [and] to do this we must locate or provide two features: temporality and causality" (422–23), then the changes in the plots of the novelistic narratives are is indeed significant. Most often, there is a distinct shift on the part of the film makers to emphasize certain sociopolitical aspects of the narrative: the war and its aftermath acquires an even greater importance in the film narratives.

André Bazin points out that cinematographic adaptation of novels has its inherent values, since "publishers' statistics show a rise in the sale of literary works after they have been adapted to the screen" and "culture in general and literature in particular have nothing to lose from such an enterprise" (65). In Spain, photographs of screen stars that appear on the latest editions of the novels demonstrate this relationship between film and novels. Both types of narratives, films and novels, constitute an important manifestation of how Spaniards come to grips with their conflict of fifty years ago.

NOTES

I would like to express my appreciation to the National Endowment for the Humanities for a Travel to Collections Grant, which helped make it possible for me to carry out the research for this paper.

1. My study comprises film adaptations done after 1965, the year in which the New Spanish Cinema movement comes of age. See Rodero, *Aquel nuevo cine español.*

2. Angel Fernández Santos gives this opinion of the film: "Transcurre sobre los datos argumentales de la tragedia, pero no logra representarlos como tales y se limita a enunciarlos" (34).

3. In the novel, Cecilio's death is foreshadowed by—or at least reflects—that of his grandfather, as the narrator informs us in Chapter 3: "Cecilio Rubes sabía que su abuelo materno tuvo el extraño capricho de arrojarse desde un cuarto piso por el hueco de la escalera. Eso fue muchos años atrás" (512).

4. In the novel, it is ironic that a shower head installed by the young man falls on Luys's head (250).

WORKS CITED

Aranda, Vicente. *La muchacha de las bragas de oro.* Script: Vicente Aranda, Santiago San Miguel, and Mauricio Walerstein. Photography: José Luis Alcaine. Music: Manuel Campos. Starring Victoria Abril, Lautaro Murúa, Hilda Vera, Perla Vonasek. Morgana Films, S.A., 1980.

———. *Tiempo de silencio.* Script: Vicente Aranda and Antonio Rabinat. Photography: Juan Amorós. Starring Imanol Arias, Francisco Rabal, Victoria Abril, Joaquín Hinojosa, Juan Echanove, Charo López. Lola Films-Morgana Films, 1986.

Andrew, Dudley. *Concepts in Film Theory.* New York: Oxford University Press, 1984.

Aub, Max. *Las buenas intenciones.* Madrid: Editorial Andorra, 1968.

Bazin, André. *What is Cinema?* Trans. Hugh Gray. Berkeley: University of California Press, 1967.

Betriu, Francesc. *La Plaza del Diamante.* Script: Francesc Betriu, Benet Rosell, Gustau Hernández. Photography: Raúl Artigot. Music: Ramón Muntaner. Starring Silvia Munt and Lluís Homar. Figaró Films, S.A., 1982.

———. *Requiem por un campesino español.* Script: Raúl Artigot, Francisco Betriu, and Gustav Hernández. Photography: Raúl Artigot. Music: Antón García Abril. Starring Antonio Ferrandis, Antonio Banderas, Fernando Fernán Gómez, Simón Andréu, Emilio Gutiérrez Caba, María Luisa San José, Terele Pávez, Antonio Iranzo. Nemo Films, 1985.

Campos, Vicente. "Un individualista al habla: Carlos Saura." *Cinema 2002,* 14 April 1976, 34–37.

Camus, Mario. *La colmena*. Script: José Luis Dibildos. Photography: Hans Burman. Music: Antón García Abril. Starring José Sacristán, Francisco Rabal, Agustín González, Ana Belén, Francisco Algora, Victoria Abril, Concha Velasco, Imanol Arias, Fiorella Faltoyano, Mary Carrillo, José Luis López Vázquez, José Bódalo, José Sazatornil, Emilio Gutiérrez Caba, Antonio Resines. Agata Films, S.A., 1982.

——. *Los santos inocentes*. Script: Antonio Larreta, Manuel Matji, Mario Camus. Photography: Hans Burmann. Music: Antón García Abril. Starring Alfredo Landa, Francisco Rabal, Terele Pávez, Juan Diego, Maribel Martín, Agustín González, Agata Lys, Mary Carrillo, Belén Ballesteros, Juan Sánchez, Susana Sánchez. Ganesh S.A., 1984.

Castresana, Luis de. *El otro árbol de Guernica*. Madrid: Prensa Española, 1968.

Cela, Camilo José. *La colmena*, 7th ed. Barcelona, 1966.

——. *La Familia de Pascual Duarte*, 3rd ed. Buenos Aires: Austral, 1969.

Delibes, Miguel. *Mi idolatrado hijo Sisí*, 3rd ed. *La Obra completa de Miguel Delibes*. Barcelona: Destino, 1964.

——. *El Príncipe destronado*. Barcelona: Destino, 1973.

——. *Los santos inocentes*. Barcelona: Planeta, 1981.

Erice, Victor. *El sur*. Script: Víctor Erice. Photography: José Luis Alcaine. Music: Ravel, Schubert, Granados. Starring Omero Antonutti, Sonsoles Aranguren, Iciar Bollain, Lola Cardona, Rafaela Aparicio. Elías Querejeta, P.C., 1983.

Fernán Gómez, Fernando. *Mi hija Hildegart*. Script: Rafael Azcona and Fernando Fernán Gómez. Photography: Cecilio Paniaqua Starring Amparo Soler Leal, Carmen Roldán. Cámara P. C.—Jet Films 1977.

Franco, Ricardo. *Pascual Duarte*. Script: Emilio Martínez Lázaro. Photography: Luis Cuadrado. Music: Luis de Pablo. Starring José Luis Gómez, Paca Ojea, Héctor Alterio, Diana Pérez de Guzmán, Eduardo Calvo, José Hinojosa. Elías Querejeta, P. C., 1975.

García Morales, Adelaida. *El sur*. Barcelona: Anagrama, 1985.

Giménez Rico, Antonio. *Retrato de familia*. Script: José Samano and Antonio Giménez Rico. Photography: José Luis Alcaine. Music: Carmelo Bernaola. Starring Antonio Ferrandis, Amparo Soler Leal, Mónica Randall, Miguel Bosé, Gabriel Llopart, Encarna Pasó, Alberto Fernández, Mirta Miller, Carmen Lozano, Josefina Díaz. Sabre Films, S.A., 1975.

Guzmán, Eduardo de. *Aurora de sangre. (Vida y muerte de Hildegart)*. Madrid: G. del Toro, 1972.

Inurria, Angel Luis. "La literatura como inspiración: entrevista con Mario Camus." *Fotogramas,* Segunda época, 1698 (Junio 1984), 20–22.

Lara, Antonio. "La generación de los años cincuenta: *Tiempo de silencio* de Vicente Aranda." *Ya,* 16 March 1986, 50.

Marinero, Francisco. "La Plaza del Diamante." *Diario 16,* 6 April 1982, 34.

Martí, Octavi. "El libro mítico de Martín Santos llega al cine." *El país,* 13 March 86, 47.

Marsé, Juan. *La muchacha de las bragas de oro*. Barcelona: Planeta, 1978.

Martín Santos, Luis. *Tiempo de silencio*, 11th ed. Barcelona: Seix Barral, 1976.

Mercero, Antonio. *La guerra de papá*. Script: Antonio Mercero and Horacio Valcárcel. Starring Lolo García, Teresa Gimpera, Héctor Alterio, Verónica Forqué, Queta Claver, Rosario García Ortega, Vicente Parra. J F Films, 1977.

Rentero, Juan Carlos. "Pascual Duarte." *Dirigido por 33* (May, 1976), 37–38.

Rodero, José Angel. *Aquel nuevo cine español de los años 60. Espíritu, estética, obra y generación de un movimiento*. Valladolid: 26 Semana Internacional de cine de Valladolid, 1981.

Rodoreda, Mercé. *La Plaza del Diamante*. Trans. Enrique Sordo. Barcelona: Edhasa, 1982.

Rubio, Fanny, and Javier Goñi. "Un millón de títulos: las novelas de la guerra de España." In *La guerra civil española. Una reflexión moral 50 años después*. Ed. Ramón Tamames. Barcelona: Planeta, 1986: 153–69.

Scholes, Robert. "Narration and Narrativity in Film." In *Film Theory and Criticism*, 2nd ed. Ed. Gerald Mast and Marshall Cohen. New York: Oxford University Press, 1979: 417–33.

Sender, Ramón J. *Requiem por un campesino español.* Buenos Aires: Proyección, 1966

Sotelo, Ignacio. "Fascismo y memoria histórica." *El país,* 12 February 1986, 11.

Ungría, Alfonso. *Soldados.* Script: Antonio Gregori and Alfonso Ungría. Photography: José Luis Alcaine. Music: Schubert. Starring Marilina Ross, Ovidi Montllor, Francisco Algora, Claudia Gravy, José Calvo, Julieta Serrano, José María Muñoz, Lautaro Murúa. Antonio Gregori, P.C., 1978.

Urrutia, Jorge. *Imago litterae: Cine, literatura.* Sevilla: Alfar, 1983.

The Failed Ideal in León Felipe's Poetry of the Spanish Civil War

Luis F. Costa

The negative impact of the Spanish Civil War on Spanish intellectual life is, sadly, a fact of history that has been extremely well documented.[1] The deaths of such extraordinary literary figures as Miguel de Unamuno, Antonio Machado, Ramiro de Maeztu, Federico García Lorca, and Miguel Hernández, to name only the most recognizable, were directly or indirectly attributed to the war itself. Just as serious was the loss through political exile of the most brilliant generation of poets in Spain since the golden years of the seventeenth century. Lorca was killed early, but Juan Ramón Jiménez, Pedro Salinas, Jorge Guillén, Luis Cernuda, Manuel Altolaguirre, Rafael Alberti, Juan Larrea, Juan José Domenchina, and, not to prolong unnecessarily this extraordinarily long list, our own León Felipe, all left Spain about the same time, and most of them never returned.[2]

Since the years of the war, the one poet who, above all others, has become identified as the poet of the Spanish Civil War in the minds of his exiled compatriots is León Felipe.[3] It would be fair to reflect that from September of 1936 until his death in 1968, León Felipe did not write a single work that in some fairly obvious and direct manner did not recapitulate what for him were the key human issues decided in that conflict. Because he is practically unknown to English readers and in the Spanish mind is linked so firmly to the conflict, it seems quite appropriate to reintroduce him. I shall attempt to trace in these pages his own doctrine of commitment as developed in the poetry. Although his doctrine is perhaps more direct and extreme than that of some of his contemporaries, I believe, nevertheless, that his attitude accurately portrays the general sentiments of his fellow writers, and that it contributes to our understanding of their collective response.

León Felipe's birth in 1884 made him about the oldest poet of his generation. Like practically every one of his peers, he was hardly a committed political figure before the war, although he became an ardent Republican. Unlike his peers, he was anything but a member of the young intellectual elite; in fact, except for a brief encounter with the poet Gerardo Diego in Santander and a few weeks spent with García Lorca during the younger poet's stay at Columbia University, he hardly had any contact at all with new poets, nor, more significantly, did he share in their poetic vision (Ríus, 94 ff.).

He had hardly lived in Spain at all after 1920, and three of the years he did live there were spent in jail (1913–1916), not as a result of some romantic political adventure under Alfonso XIII, but as a common criminal, for embezzlement. He was far from being a sterling citizen, and someone who, upon taking a moral high road in his poetry, might well have drawn skeptical frowns from his readers. (Many of his fellow expatriates did just that.) But his tone is so sustained over the years, his ideas so clear, his sincerity so overwhelming (once he finds his poetic path), that only the most ardent of cynics can question his motives for very long.

Not atypically for a Spaniard, he wrote of Justice (with a capital "J"), of human dignity, of spiritual values above material values, of union and brotherhood, and of selfless sacrifice for the common good. In his poetry, these ideals were embodied in three mythical figures: Prometheus, Christ, and Don Quijote. All of them are variations of the same sacrificial man. He spoke of women only in relation to motherhood. Enviable as it may be in some ways, his manly world was totally utopian; it was as rigid as it was unobtainable. Nevertheless, his beliefs were very much in tune with the ideologies that eventually brought about the Spanish Republic. They also hid the kind of intransigence that would bring about its demise.

We shall begin by retracing some of these concepts to his first books, so as better to understand their development and place in León Felipe's poetic world at the time of the war. He had begun writing poems while in jail, and after several false starts, he published a modest volume of poetry in 1920, *Versos y oraciones de caminante*. In Spain, as in most of Europe, these were the years of wild artistic experimentation that would lead the public and the connoisseur to question the values of the new but dehumanized art, borrowing the adjective from the Spanish philosopher José Ortega y Gasset. León Felipe began his career as a poet officially by reading from his book of poems before they were published. He did so at a meeting of the "Ultra" group, organized by Gerardo Diego. In the poetic spectrum of the time, the members of this group were caught in the fervor of the new creed and were far and away the most radical of the avantgarde. Their books had titles like *Propellers*, and *A Manual for Foam*[4]; their poems were full of images involving airplanes, cubes, and winged cigarettes.

We can only speculate on the sort of impact that León Felipe's prayers had among them. We know that he was not asked back. In his verses he admonished the writers to speak "quietly, poets, quietly," lest their anguish be mistaken for the mercenary wailings of paid criers. But there was little anguish in the poetry of 1920. The world was new; in fact it was being reinvented almost daily. The future was limitless and the anguish of the Great War far behind them by then. The poets were caught in the inventive spirit of the times, and they wanted to create new and wondrous things. But León Felipe was telling them something else; poetry had to become again straightforward, direct, uncomplicated; poetry had to be for the poor, the downtrodden, poetry of hope and caring:

> No quiero el verbo raro
> ni la palabra extraña;
> quiero que todas,
> todas mis palabras
> —fáciles siempre
> a los que aman—,
> vayan ungidas
> con mi alma.
> (*Versos...*, 16)

For León Felipe, poetry made sense only if both "prince and pariah" (Versos, I, 15) could read it and learn from it. His was a poetry that spoke of social concerns, of poverty and death, and of caring for one's fellow travelers as Christ would. It was clearly a poetry out of step with its time, and while the book enjoyed moderate success when it appeared, León Felipe must have sensed that his voice did not blend well with those of his contemporaries. He left Spain for Mexico and the U.S., did not publish another book for ten years, and returned only in 1931 for a brief visit.

This first book might be taken as the inescapable result of his jail house experience and the subsequent couple of years, highlighted by real poverty and disease, when he was an actor in a third-rate itinerant theatrical troupe. His second book leads one, in fact, to believe that the social focus of his first poems was a temporary facet of his work, without lasting consequences. In his 1930 *Versos y Oraciones de Caminante, II,* the poet looks upon life with a great deal of optimism. He has begun to understand the new age, and writes happily of the noise of machinery as the "zumbido familiar y antiguo / que viene de los sueños / de todos los poetas" and, less convincingly, he concludes that "son *ellos* . . . *ellos:* / los motores, las ruedas / y los émbolos / los que marchan al ritmo / de mi verso" (*Versos,* II, 67).

He had encountered prosperity and love in the new continent. He had married a Mexican woman and moved to New York, where she taught Spanish and he found work as an instructor at Cornell University. He was relatively secure in financial terms; he had a vast library at his disposal; he had made friends with whom to discuss his work; the world seemed to him quite benign. While there were echoes of his past concerns in the poems, they were much more narrowly focused, on the plight of the physically impaired, for instance. But the book is definitely upbeat and full of faith in man's ability to conquer his baser nature and to work cohesively for a better world.

The economic realities of 1929 and its aftermath brought him quickly back to his senses. By the end of 1930 he completed another book of poems, written in Spanish but titled in English *Drop a Star,* in which he lamented the loss of ideals in contemporary society. Having succumbed for a time to the euphoria that economic well-being provides, he was convinced quickly by the harsh reality of the crash that if his own world had become better, the larger world continued to be as bitter a place as he had known. With the backdrop of a Chinese beggar asking for alms at the door of a crowded restaurant and a legless man propelling himself on a cart along a deserted Wall Street, *Drop a Star* condemns the loss of spiritual values in a materialist world. The financial upheaval is seen as the consequence of too much reliance on the dollar value of things and too little on their essential value. In the midst of the darkness he senses in New York, the poet sees himself, perhaps immodestly, as a Promethean being. He is here to bring light upon the darkness, to cry for justice, to demand an equal share of bread for all.

Putting words into action, he left the U.S. for Mexico later that year. After witnessing from afar the happy arrival of a new government at home, he returned to Spain for a brief visit. Then, after seeing to the publication of *Drop a Star* in 1933, he made the trip back once more, but this time (1934) in order to offer his services to the new Republic. He was sent to Panama late in 1935 as cultural attaché, where his duties included teaching classes in Spanish literature to Panamanian children. He was there at the outbreak of the war. The Spanish ambassador showed himself to be sympathetic to the Nationalist cause, so he was removed from office, and León Felipe was named ambassador instead. The Panamanian government refused to recognize him, because their sympathies were also with the Nationalist cause. Realizing that he was needed elsewhere, León

Felipe left Panama after writing a powerful and uncomplimentary speech that he was never allowed to read.

If until the moment of the war, León Felipe's rhetoric had been undoubtedly well meaning and relatively on target (at least in his decrying of the modern age), it was also somewhat empty. His less than sterling antecedents made much of what he said suspect, a do-as-I-say-and-not-as-I-do attitude, that, at least from the perspective of his second book, one could question with authority. The crimes of the war, the treasonous nature of the uprising, and the enormity of stakes made all of León Felipe's civil digressions seem unimportant. While still in Panama, his vigorous Republican voice targeted with unerring accuracy the emerging opposition only a few weeks after the initial uprising. Panama's military strongmen, the Church hierarchy, and the monied upperclasses become the target, of his wrath. In his speech, written originally in response to a Panamanian newscaster who glorified the Nationalist cause on his daily radio programs, León Felipe, who had been accused unfairly and inaccurately of being a communist, wrote:

> Me voy porque quiero saber la verdad sobre la tragedia de mi Patria y nadie me la dice . . . Quiero encontrarme frente a frente con la realidid exacta e inmediata porque la otra, la verdad de mañana, ésa ya la sé. Mañana o el mundo se organiza sobre unas bases de justicia y de dignidad humanas o el mundo no se organiza de ninguna manera. Señor Arzobispo: ¿Es esto comunismo, es comunismo lo que yo he explicado en mis últimas conferencias? Pues bien, señores, si esto es comunismo: o mañana somos todos comunistas por la gracia de Dios o el mundo se va al garete. ("Good-bye," 39)

This direct, accusatory and polemical tone was to characterize all of his writings thereafter.

During the war years, poetry was the prevalent art form in Spain.[5] From the right and the left, the schooled and unschooled soldiers wrote poems and songs from the trenches. The more famous of the poets like Rafael Alberti and León Felipe wrote patriotic works designed to inspire the Republican troops in their defense of democracy. Unlike Alberti who was extremely successful as a war poet, the polemical tone of León Felipe and the lofty and unyielding form of his ideals, had on occasion the opposite effect from that which he most desired.

It is important to state from the onset, that in a fundamental sense, León Felipe failed at what he attempted to do with his poetry of the war, even while his works reflect today, perhaps better than anyone else's, the spirit and the problems of Republican Spain during those fateful years of 1936 through 1939.

He had left Panama expecting to find a utopian Spain, a Spain where personal and collective sacrifice, political and otherwise, was the order of the day, where the common great cause had welded all political factions into one coherent body. To his dismay, the truth he found was antithetical to everything he had hoped for. He arrived at a badly divided front, with anarchists and socialists at each other's throats and the Communists awaiting eagerly the outcome of the internal struggle among the leading parties. He found the Republican left, while more to his liking in ideas, to be ineffective, unable to provide the much-needed leadership. He expected unity, but found discord; he expected energetic leadership and found political chaos; he expected unbridled idealism and found petty squabbles over material and political trophies.

He joined the Alliance of Antifascist Intellectuals and hoped to rally the common people around his verses. The angry tone of Panama was not replaced by a new poetic fervor, but simply continued. Only the targets of his anger were changed; they became those upon whom he had placed all his hopes. In "The Symbol," his first major poem after arriving in Spain, he wrote:

> El botín se hace derecho legítimo cuando está sellado
> [por una victoria última y heroica.
> Se va de lo doméstico a los histórico,
> y de lo histórico a lo épico.
> Esta ha sido siempre el orden que ha llevado la
> [conducta del español en la Historia,
> en el ágora
> y hasta en sus transacciones,
> que por eso se ha dicho siempre que el español no
> [aprende nunca bien el oficio de mercader.
> Pero ahora,
> en esta revolución,
> el orden se ha invertido.
> Habéis empezado por lo épico,
> habéis pasado por lo histórico
> y ahora aquí,
> en la retaguardia de Valencia
> frente a todas las derrotas,
> os habéis parado en la domesticidad.
> Y aquí estáis anclados,
> Sindicalistas,
> Comunistas,
> Anarquistas,
> Socialistas,
> Trotskistas,
> Republicanos de Izquierda ...
> Aquí estáis anclados,

custodiando la rapiña
para que no se la lleve vuestro hermano.
La curva histórica del aristócrata, desde su origen [popular
y heroico, hasta su última degeneración actual, cubre
[en España más de tres siglos.
La del burgués, setenta años.
Y la vuestra, tres semanas.

(*La insignia*, 54–55)

Just as he was wrong about what he expected to find in Republican Spain, he was also wrong about the effect that his poem would have among the divided factions. It was published simultaneously in newspapers in Catalonia and Valencia and everywhere it was read with equal disgust. Anarchists, Communists, Socialists, all were looking for him and not to praise his efforts. He had to leave Valencia in secret for Barcelona, where he stayed with Antonio Machado, and left quickly afterwards for Paris. He remained in the French capital long enough for tempers to cool, and for the serious affairs of the war to focus everyone's attention once more on the real business at hand.

He simply had expected too much of his country and its people. Knowing well their virtues and their vices, for they were all deeply etched in his own character, he ignored the fact that absolute idealism would lead to intransigence, though he had available dozens of examples in the records of Spanish history. He spoke as an Old Testament prophet, and could not firmly grasp the extent of the commitment that he was demanding from fellow Republicans.

Ya no hay más que un emblema.
Ya no hay más que una estrella,
una sola, SOLA, y ROJA, sí,
pero de sangre y en la frente,
que todo español revolucionario ha de hacérsela
hoy mismo
ahora mismo
y con sus propias manos.
Preparad los cuchillos
. . . .
Madres,
madres revolucionaries,
estampad este grito indeleble de justicia
en la frente de vuestro hijos.
Allí donde habéis puesto siempre vuestros besos más [limpios.
(Esto no es una imagen retórica.
Yo no soy el poeta de la retórica
Ya no hay retórica.
La revolución ha quemado
todas las retóricas.)

(*La insignia*, 60–61)

But indeed, it was all rhetoric; it could be nothing but. And years later, he would confess with embarrassment that after writing the poem he had thought of carving for himself the first star, but that he had lacked the courage to do it. It is perhaps worth pointing out that the red star had nothing to do with Communism. In León Felipe's poetic symbolism, the stars represent transcendental goals toward which one must aspire: Red blood represents the necessary suffering, as in Biblical terms, demanded by the toil to achieve those goals. All this is terribly chilling, even unpleasant, but perhaps its great sense of immediacy portrays better than any other passage the desperate state of the Spanish Republic in those early months of the war. As we now know, had General Yagüe's forces turned toward Madrid after taking Badajoz, linking up with General Mora's northern army, the war would have been over for all practical purposes in the last months of 1936. Few people could have predicted that more than two long years still lay ahead.

After his return from Paris, León Felipe continued to publish. He sensed ever more clearly, however, that the cause of Republican Spain was inevitably lost, and his poems became ever more bitter and shifted in focus from the present to the future. They lost some immediacy, but they gained poetic quality. His attacks were then more directed to the external enemy, not only Nationalists, whom he viewed generally as misguided Spaniards, but to other nations, England in particular, who in this hour of need had abandoned Spain. The tone became ever more prophetic, and at times the poems were uncannily accurate in their predictions. To Lord Duff Cooper, chief of the British Admiralty, who had said in the British Parliament, "Whatever the fight is about in Spain today, it is not worth the life of a single British sailor," León Felipe replied by calling him a merchant and a "go-getter," this last word in English, interested only in profits and possessions. Lord Cooper's attitude was attributed more generally to England as a whole, and in a bitterly resentful passage repeated by the poet in several books, he accused England's leaders of using Spanish blood to protect themselves:

> . . . has dejado meterse en mi solar
> a los raposos y a los lobos confabulados del mundo
> para que se sacien en me sangre
> y no pidan en seguida la tuya.
> Pero ya la pedirán las estrellas..
>
> (*La insignia*, 69)

By 1939, the war not yet finished but most certainly lost, León Felipe left Spain for what would become his permanent exile in Mexico. Although he had not been a soldier in the front lines, he was permanently scarred by the fighting, particularly that which had taken place within the ranks of Republican Spain. Having seen his most cherished ideals trampled by the inertia of pragmatic and historical realities, León Felipe arrived in his adopted country determined not to give up the fight and to continue to work for his ideals and his lost Spain. He worked very actively in the creation of certain institutions in Mexico with other exiled figures, most notably Juan Larrea. In a short time, the Spanish exiles brought about the Spanish House in Mexico City, with the journal *Cuadernos Americanos*, and León Felipe himself became an active participant in theater and film projects cooperating with Luis Buñuel, and writing or translating a number of plays.

But his poetic activities became foremost in his mind. A last debt had to be paid to Spain. He set out, therefore, to write over the following years, until the death of his wife in 1956, a series of books in which he highlighted what were for him the essential values of the Spaniard, clearly not those brandished by the Nationalist cause. He hoped to ensure that they should not perish under the yoke of Franco's dictatorship. They are a sort of personal biography in which he highlights the most relevant steps in his personal trajectory toward knowledge of self and knowledge of the world.

The most significant of these books is *Ganarás la luz,* of 1943. The Biblical allusion of the title already makes clear some of the work's principal tenets that recall much of what he said during the War. One must strive on earth for a better world, but we must not set the sights too close to the ground. Bread is not enough; we must look beyond the satisfaction of our material needs to find the needed nourishment for the spirit. The poet clarifies the meaning of his book:

> Salimos de aventura en la madrugada por el mundo, con un nombre que nos prenden en la solapa como una concha en la esclavina, y creemos que por este nombre van a llamarnos los pájaros. ¡No nos llama nadie! Y cuando ya estamos rendidos de caminar y el día va a quebrase, gritamos enloquecidos y angustiados, para no perdernos en la sombra: ¿Quién soy yo?
>
> ¡Y nadie nos responde!
>
> Entonces miramos hacia atrás para ver lo que dicen nuestros pasos. Creemos que algo deben de haber dejado escrito en la arena nuestros pies vagabundos. Y comenzamos a descifrar y a organizar las huellas que aún no ha borrado el Viento. (*Ganarás,* 13)

After recapitulating his own personal trajectory in life, the poet arrives at a key section of this book by announcing that he is about to "define Hispanism," but he finds that he has lost the concrete referent to it. Hispanism has become the vague idea of Don Quijote's defiant madness, a thirst for absolute justice and absolute dignity. These are the great qualities of the Spaniard, but are equally his downfall: "Cuando se muera España para siempre, quedará un ademán en la luz y en el aire . . . un gesto . . . Hispanidad será aquel gesto vencido, apasionado y loco del hidalgo manchego" (*Ganarás*, 117). This passage suggests the trajectory of León Felipe himself: always the man gesturing wildly to an audience who is otherwise engaged. He wrote his simple prayers, verses at the "exact level of man" as he wanted, when the poetic realities called for the contorted imagery of a modernist aesthetic in full swing. He demanded supreme sacrifices before a Spain awash in its own blood. If left alone, he would have carved a star of hope on the forehead of every Spanish loyalist, while admitting that he hadn't the courage to do it on his own. He saw a spent and defeated country in need of a rational voice and a new and sane direction in which to move, and all the poet could offer were the desperate gestures of another Quixote tilting at the ancient windmills. This was the voice of the one poet of the war who never seemed able to give up, to understand that the war was lost, and that only time and a new beginning would provide for the Spain he had sought and fought for, a Spain that he did not live long enough to see realized.

NOTES

1. See for example: Gerald Brenan, *The Spanish Labyrinth. An Account of the Social and Political Background of the Civil War* (Cambridge: The University Press, 1943); Hugh Thomas, *The Spanish Civil War* (New York: Harper and Row, 1977); Manuel Tuñón de Lara, *Medio siglo de cultura española* (Madrid: Editorial Tecnos, 1970).

2. See the anthology by Ricardo Morales, *Poetas en el destierro* (Santiago de Chile: Cruz del Sur, 1943).

3. See for example the biography of the poet by Luis Rius, *León Felipe, poeta de barro* (México: Colección Málaga, 1974).

4. Guillermo de Torre, *Hélices* (Madrid, 1922); Gerardo Diego, *Manual de espumas* (Madrid: La Lectura, 1924).

5. Many collections of the poetry of the war have been compiled; among them are the following: J. Alonso Montero, *Cancionero de la guerra* (Madrid: Ediciones Españolas, 1939); I. Pereda Valdés, *Cancionero de la guerra civil española* (Montevideo: C. García Cia., 1937); Emilio Prados y A. R. Rodríguez Moñino, *Romancero general de la guerra de España* (Madrid-Valencia: Ediciones Españolas, 1937); *Romancero de la guerra civil*, Serie I (Madrid: Ministerio de Instrucción Pública y Bellas Artes, 1936); *Romancero de los voluntarios de la libertad* (Madrid: Ediciones del Comisariado de las Brigadas Internacionales, 1937); Jorge Villén, *Antología poética del Alzamiento* (Madrid, 1940).

WORKS CITED

Felipe, León. *Drop a Star*. 1933. Reprint. Mexico: Finisterre Editores, 1974.
———. *Ganarás la luz: Biografía, poesía y destino*. 1943. Reprint. Mexico: Finisterre Editores, 1974.
———. "Good-bye Panamá." In *Drop a Star*, Mexico: Finisterre Editores, 1974.
———. *La insignia: Alocución poemática*. 1937. In *Drop a Star*, Mexico: Finisterre Editores, 1974.
———. *Versos y oraciones de caminante*. 1920. Reprint. Mexico: Finisterre Editores, 1974.
———. *Versos y oraciones de caminante, II*. 1930. Mexico: Finisterre Editores, 1974.
Ríus, Luis. *León Felipe: Poeta de barro*. México: Colección Málaga, S.A., 1974.

Two Spanish Civil War Novels: A Woman's Perspective

Joseph Schraibman

Two women authors, the well-known Ana María Matute[1] of Spain and the more obscure Nivaria Tejera of Cuba, have written novels about the beginning of the Spanish Civil War from the perspectives of adolescent girls. Matute's novel takes place in Mallorca, and Tejera's on Tenerife, Grand Canary Islands. The protagonists of both novels attempt to cope in every way with the loss of father, family bond, home, familiar surroundings and possessions. The descriptive power and the ethical import of both *A School of the Sun* (1960), by Matute and *El barranco* (The Ravine, 1959), by Tejera derive from the juxtaposition, often based on an implied silence, of the child's observations and the reader's ability to fill in between the lines, recognizing the allusions to large historical events from the minimal particularist references to them. In addition, both works create a poetic as well as a real world and, as such, an *Uhr* text. In this sense, the mythological creation is truer than the fragmentary exposition of the "real" episodes of the war itself and its effects on the characters of the novel. Chronologically both novels mark the end of the so-called social realism in Spain, a period in the novel that ended, according to critics, with the publication of *Time of Silence* in 1962. Our works deal, then, with the period before Goytisolo's acid prose and necessary fragmentations broke with the mold of the realistic novel, or before Juan Benet created his mythological *Región*, a Spanish Yoknapatawpha County. In form, therefore, we are dealing with works that include neither the tortured, fragmented figures of Picasso's *Guernica* nor the lucid expanation of the tie between fragmentation and ethics in Erich Kahler's masterful *Fragmentation in Art and Other Forms*.

Of the Spanish Civil War, much has been written, as history, as ideology, and as memoirs, personal and collective; the bibliography is massive. Testimony, rendering witness, is essential to memory. Concentration camp victims wrote on scraps to get their story out. Slaves, too, told their heritage, their happenings, so that they would endure. One of the many such witnesses of the Spanish Civil War, Francisco Bolea, writes from freedom in Mexico in his *Requiem por una generación* (1981): "More than four decades have passed since the events narrated here took place. They are not the product of imagination but of testimony, painful happenings written down in bits about the same time they took place . . ." (10). Gonzalo Sobejano, the most thorough historian and critic of the Spanish Civil War novel, makes a similar point; his book is subtitled *In Search of the Lost People. People, pueblo,* is hard to render. It means folk, population, or a collection of persons. It also means town, townspeople, or the common folk, not the lofty politicians. Matute's and Tejera's novels deal with such "real" people, ideologies, professions, ages, and psychologies. Yet, the more I meditate on these works, the more I think that the key theme in them is the lost father. Matia's father in *A School of the Sun* is fighting on behalf of the Republicans on the peninsula, and her grandmother does not approve. She is a franquista. The "I" narrator in *El barranco* is not given a name in the novel. Her father has been carted off to jail while other, less fortunate ones have been given their final *paseo.* In his case, the family still has hope because he has committed no possible sins. The prevailing mood is silence, mystery. No one can give them information; no one knows anything. All characters behave as automatons. One is faced with existential moments, not reasoned, historical, sensible events. A higher force seems to have taken over, and fear grips everyone. Of course, older members of the family try to protect the children by not telling them the truth, by trying to preserve their childhood. The children know that life is not proceeding normally, but they don't understand why.

Ana María Matute (one of Spain's foremost novelists), along with Carmen Martín Gaite, Carmen Laforet, and Dolores Medio has always been concerned in her writings with children, adolescents, the Spanish Civil War, charity, individual psychology, and, in her later works, myth. Janet Díaz has observed aptly, "The typical Matute character is the solitary, isolated child or adolescent, often handicapped either physically, socially, or mentally (orphans, sick and abnormal children abound)" (146). Matia's Proustian recollections illuminate the war's effect on Mallorca's people, the island's past history, and her own passage into adulthood. Margaret Jones and Janet Díaz have written excellent books in English on Matute as a writer. The focus of the present essay is not the novel as a whole, but rather a curious and ever-present reference to former Mallorcan converted Jews, the chuetas, previously ignored by critics. The question is simply, why *chuetas*? What relation is there between *chuetas,* converted to Christianity in 1391, and the Spanish Civil War?

School of the Sun begins with Matia, the narrator, describing her grandmother. From the beginning, the novel is enriched by the contraposition of two narrative voices. One refers to the summer of 1936 and the few months that follow the uprising by General Franco against the Republican government of Spain on July 18. The other consists of parenthetical reflections that interpret and qualify those same events with a sad and often ironic voice, the result of later experience. Matia had been sent to Palma when she was twelve years old. Her mother had died when she was eight, and she had lived with an old nanny, Mauricia. After Mauricia became ill and could no longer care for Matia, the child's grandmother had taken charge of her. Matia arrived on the island with her black boy rag doll Gorogó (Chimney Sweep), her fears, and her childhood fantasies written in notebooks. She was placed as a boarder in Our Lady of Angels, and expelled from the school a year and a half later when she was fourteen. It was in the middle of that summer that war broke out and her aunt Emilia and her cousin Borja, who was fifteen, were not able to return to mainland Spain, and all had to stay in their grandmother's home. Matia's bittersweet powers of description are beautifully exemplified in the opening words of the novel:

> My grandmother's white hair was set in a bristling wave on her forehead. It gave her a certain angry air. She almost always carried a small gold-headed bamboo cane which she did not need for she was steady as a horse. Looking over old photographs, I think I find in that thick, massive white face, in those gray eyes bordered by smoky circles, a glowing reflection of Borja, and even of me. I suppose Borja inherited her gallantry, her absolute lack of mercy. I, perhaps, my great sadness. (*School of the Sun,* 3)

Of her cousin Borja, Matia singles out his great powers of dissembling. "He was sweet and smooth in her presence, and thoroughly understood the significance of the words *inheritance, money, lands*" (6).

There are faint references in the novel at this point to the fight between Republicans and fascists on the island, a place where tradition weighs heavily on its inhabitants. The grandmother had expected Franco to win quickly, but that was not happening. One learns at this time that Borja is the leader of a gang of ruffians. In a boat, he hides a carbine and some other stolen items: cigarettes, liquor, bullets, and a book that describes the burning of the Jews in ancient times.

Matute introduces two branches of a *chueta* family, the Taronjis, one fascist, the other Republican. Gangs of fascists roam the island, jailing and killing members of the opposition. The children also form gangs and fight one another, often in places where centuries ago others had engaged in killing their fellow Mallorcans. And the grandmother, a symbol of Christian Spain, upon hearing that priests and nuns are being killed on the mainland, exclaims, "They are killing all the decent people; they are filling the country with Martyrs and more martyrs. . ." (33).

Later, one finds that Borja's father belonged to the Carlists, Spain's ultra-conservative Catholic faction that had fought doggedly against religious freedom in the nineteenth century and was then fighting with Franco. Matute obviously chooses to stress the political rift between Carlists and liberals, between the "two Spains," to underscore Spain's history of brother killing brother. Part 1 of the novel ends with the burial of the chueta Taronji, associated with the liberals. This part is entitled "The Descent." One might ask if there shall be an Ascent?

Part 2 deals with the recollection of Matia's growing maturity, her fantasies, her hatreds and likes. She describes the makeup of the two gangs of youths, which upon close examination seem to be organized along class distinctions. One gang, *they* to Matute, is composed of the poor, of tradespeople's children, of the *chuetas*. The other gang, *we*, is composed of Borja, Matia and other children of devout Catholic parents. Matia becomes friendly with Manuel, the son of the dead José Taronji, the enemy. She too cannot comprehend why life on the island is as it is, and she often talks to her puppet Gorogo, just as the child in *El barranco* does with her doll Neca.

In part 3, "The Bonfires," Matia reads from the book about the Jews: "It was something to see how their flesh caught fire, how the flames licked their entrails: how their stomachs were ripped in two from top to bottom with a demoniacal brilliance . . . ." She adds, "It explained how they burned Jews alive. It was the same plaza where those scenes had occurred centuries before" (153–54). Now the youths light bonfires also as they prepare for gang wars by unearthing their black butcher hooks. Matute connects the impending violence between the warring gangs to the "real" war on the mainland: "Sometimes Borja and I would look at the newspapers. Bombed cities, battles lost, battles won. And there, on the island, in the village, a thick and silent vengeance raged. The Taronjis climbed into their black car and scurried about the province" (174).

Part 4, "The White Cock," begins significantly with an "inquisition" conducted by Matia's grandmother. Ironically, Christmas is approaching, but war is raging all over the peninsula and in Mallorca too. Outside, one gang has built bonfires in the Plaza of the Jews, and has burned effigy figures of Borja, Manuel, and Matia. Matute writes of *malsines*, Jews, who, having converted to Catholicism in 1391, denounced other Jews who practiced Judaism in secret. It is obvious that the Taronjis are fascists victimizing the population and, most particularly, the isolated chuetas. A curious parallel is thus established: just as Spaniard is killing Spaniard, one former Jew is killing another former Jew; one Taronji is killing another Taronji. And, one might ask at this point, what in Spanish history makes it possible for one brother to kill another?

It is ironic that Matute at this point chooses to describe that Borja and Matia are wearing medals of the Virgin Mary and Jesus around their necks. Borja is at his most violent. Matia has no choice but to humor his thoughts against "them."

Red is, of course, a color associated with Jews and also with communists. In the house, Borja teases Matia about her father: "Because, on top of everything else, you've a bad past. Your father . . . Your father's a filthy red, who, perhaps at this very moment is shooting at my father. Do you remember what happened to José Taronji?" (229).

Considering that this novel was written at a time of severe official censorship, it appears significant to me that Matute has created a symbolic structure in which "red" associated with chuetas is also "red" meaning the Spanish Republic and liberalism. Of course, Spain debated the issue of religious freedom in the nineteenth century, and, under the Spanish Republic, freedom of religion was declared once again. To add even more poignancy to the sudden growing association between Matia's "blood" and the *chuetas,* Borja insists that she cleanse her sins in the Church of Santa María. What sins one might ask?

The novels last pages are full of symbolic structures based on religious and other images. Borja's betrayal of the *chueta* Manuel recalls Judas's betrayal. The cock is reminiscent of Jesus's words to Peter in Matthew 26:34: "Truly I say to you, this very night, before the cock crows you will deny me three times." And what of the "lost cause"? The Jewish cause? Spain? It is hard to tell for sure. Matute's own views may be close to those of the historical José Taronji, whose book she recommends, a *chueta* who wrote that for reasons of class interests, good Spaniards had been wronged in Mallorca for centuries. Earlier, Spain had lost the Arab and Jewish contributions to its society in becoming "one and Catholic." A more or less tolerant society became a fanatical one, spawning the Inquisition, blood statutes, and an obsession with the honor code. It divided the world into *we* and *they* supposedly in the name of Love and Charity. Matute's opening quotation from Jeremiah 28:15, "The Lord hath not sent thee; but thou makest this people to trust in a lie," seems to me to frame the entire novel, and to suggest that Spain made a grievous error in its history and that it has been paying for it ever since by spilling its own blood.

Such a poetic, complex novel as Matute's suggests its various meanings through polyvalent metaphors. I have tried to suggest an explanation for one of them, the *chueta*/red connection. *School of the Sun* has already attracted much attention from scholars who have studied other of its elements. If complexity is one of the requirements of a great work of literature, however, then this novel is worthy of further study for the ingenious manner in which it weaves individual psychology, the depiction of social interaction, and history into a cohesive work whose universal symbols raise eternal questions of existence and behavior.

El barranco (The Ravine) by Nivaria Tejera was published originally under the title *Le ravin* in Paris in 1958 in a collection of Spanish and Spanish American books sponsored by Maurice Nadeau, publisher of *Les Lettres Nouvelles*. It was translated by Claude Couffon, who also wrote the introduction to the Spanish edition published in the Canary Islands by Edirca in 1982. Robert Sabatier, who later published *Allumettes suedoises*, a novel about children, wrote of *El barranco* in *Les Temps des Hommes*,

> I don't know what fate this marvelous tale will have in France. I think this book is the most subtle, the most delicate, the most truthful which I have read in a long time. It brings me the most terrible of accusations against war: that of a child alone amid the ruins. Inextricably tied to the year 1936 and after, it is a document more real than any history. . . . (11, translation mine)

The plot of the novel is deceptively simple. The child narrator begins her narration on the first day of the Spanish Civil War in La Laguna, Tenerife. "Today the war began. Perhaps some days ago. I don't understand too well when things begin . . . . The war began today in front of Granpa's house"(19). The child's musings encompass a little over a year with the principal focus of them being her feelings at losing her father, first to jail, and eventually to exile and death by assassination. The dedication of the novel points to Tejera's own biographical connection to such a beginning: "To my father in his death: in his name to all Canary Islanders" (17). Tejera has chosen well indeed. Her child narrator is able to express her innermost feelings, to describe objects and events from the ingenuous point of view of someone who just "doesn't understand," who seeks to interpret the adult world and its doings. Her father's place is taken by her grandfather, but he is a simple man who tries to protect her from the negative events that have overtaken Spain. Key themes that appear here are uncertainty, violence, politics, the roles of the Church, the army, "plain folks," who become "the others," good and evil, and physical and mental hardships. All these themes are Kafkaesque elements used in Spanish Civil War novels by such other writers as Juan Goytisolo, Luis Martín-Santos, Juan Benet, Carmen Laforet and others, or by authors who write about war, including Rainer Marie Remarque in *All Quiet on the Western Front,* Jerzy Kosinsky in *The Painted Bird,* and Ann Frank.[2]

The word *war* appears throughout the novel. The noise of war's machines resounding outside is echoed by her aunt's sewing machine turning out undergarments for a local store. "War is war," says the mother as they all huddle in fear of the men who are searching homes. The narrator clutches her doll, asking for her father, adding "Without him I am always lost" (22). This extremely sensitive child reacts to light, to darkness, to birds, to clouds, to presences, to absences, to people's moods, to sounds, to voices, and to song. The writer, who captures her perspective of the moment, writes,

> I listened to broken words: "arms, the Right, the general, the Left, long live, die, bastards, let him live, let him die, the imp, the sly fox, son-of-a bitch, dogs, flag, garbage, moral, road, the whole street, go up, fatherland, come down, shots, search search search, the National Movement, Hooray for the General, there's no light, prison, where are they, search, search." (25)

Furthermore, the child notices that the same people who were friends before are now the ones who point the finger, who are the victimizers. They abuse the grandfather, and the child has a normal child's reaction: "Suddenly I hated papa for not being with us, for not holding me, for not defending Granpa" (27). The child hears the word *prison* and runs to her small dictionary to look it up. She does not understand the concept. Her father is exiled to another island, to an island-prison. She feels her growth stunted; she feels suddenly a grown-up, robbed of the process of growth, her world suddenly having turned into a *we* and *they.* Going to church and praying does not bring her father back, and her visit to a convent does not bring her solace but rather pain and sadness.

In a dreamlike description full of animals, mice, owls, keys, knives, matches, and darkness, the child imagines her father in jail. Her description suggests the mood of Kafka's *Penal Colony* in its horrid details. She cannot understand what is happening, but that does not prevent her using her child's reason to try to give shape to the events around her, to seek at least to explain those events. "Father" and "jail" go together, or, as she writes, "why is it called jail and not father;

does that word mean enclosure, or is the fact that father is enclosed what makes me give it meaning?" (29).

The family cannot keep its home. They must move into the grandfather's house. Thus, another separation, being wrenched from familiar surroundings, affects the child. She loses her room, her toys, her memories. She misses her home, her special space. Her family has now entered into a new routine. She is taken to visit her father in jail. She dreams of freeing him. She feels his presence in her dreams, but she keeps these feelings from her mother. She is aware that she is turning sad and speaking less. She avoids her family more, she muses more, she notices political acts in the streets, and she overhears new words at home: "trial," "consequences," "punishment," "the law." As she plays with the cat, she thinks of what she will say to the Court to defend her father. The sounds and movements of war continue. She says:

> Suddenly one hears a noise like that of a whip striking the air, or of a machine gun or a thunderbolt whose echo ends up in the cat's throat. All that is happening in Los Rodeos where the airbase is, and the tank garage. It all comes from there. The canon snuffs out the lives of platoons of prisoners brought sometimes from the other islands. (86)

The rain, the smoke, the clouds, they cannot erase from her memory the sounds of killing. Her house is searched again. She attends her father's trial. She thinks the men in black robes are priests, priests of some other kind. She hears witnesses accuse her father of being against the Movement. There is testimony that as a child her father read forbidden books. She remembers walks with her father at the sea's edge. She thinks of Christmas, of toys, of years past, of the family together.

Meanwhile, "the war goes on, but each day it becomes more intimate and organized. Granpa says it becomes 'domestic'" (99). They attempt to continue family life. She becomes closer to her grandfather. She dreams of the ravine in a magnificently described surrealist manner. Her mother tells her to accept things, to become resigned. She writes, "But I don't want to know anyone, to think, to hear" (114). She communicates with her cat, which she prefers to the people around her. She would like to stop growing, to stop understanding. She misses her father. She begins to despair of being able to free him, of opening his cell door. She feels shame at school, shopping, everywhere, and feels "I'm not to blame, I'm not to blame"(128).

Her brother dies of diptheria. Her father is now in a concentration camp doing forced labor. Her brother is buried. She remembers a cat she buried. Tejera describes another of the child's nightmares in which she becomes transformed into a lame girl. In the streets she notices Moorish troops. She misses her father more. Once again she hears shots. The family visits the concentration camp. They see her father through the fence. He resembles a crazy man, a shadow of himself. She wants the night to swallow her. Now she is afraid of everyone, of everything. Her nightmares continue. She remembers her father's eyes. She is afraid he will die. At school she is forced to attend patriotic parades. Her only solace is her cat or a stray dog. And she thinks:

> When I was a little girl there were no patriotic parades. Then the homeland existed and one didn't have to invoke its name all the time because each person honored it. Then the war came and it made soldiers who had to find the fatherland and, not finding it, had to invent "Movements" like hammerdrills. (176)

Winter has returned. A circus has come to town, set up near the cemetery where Chicho, her brother, is buried under a pile of earth, no marble stone marking his burial place. A telegram arrives. Her mother refuses to read it. They eventually look at the twisted words on a yellowish piece of paper: "Exiled. 40 years. To the mainland. Signed: The Committee." Her mother repeats "40 years" endlessly. The child feels guilty once more. She dreams of the Generalisimo, of the telegram, of her father, of death. In her dream, it is raining, it is foggy, the bones are wet, the wind is blowing down "covering the tracks of the smelly 'platoon' in the ravine where I would like to think that papa was never buried" (188).

And so, dream and reality become one. The nightmare has turned biographical fact. The unidentified child in the novel is Tejera herself or, at the very least, her narrative voice. The nameless child stands for every child who has lost a father, whose sleep has been disturbed forever, who has felt needlessly guilty, whose innocence was violated, whose childhood has been turned painfully into early adulthood. With the economical strokes of a modern impressionist, Tejera has sketched brilliantly the world seen by a suffering child's eyes, war felt by innocence, right raped by wrong; indeed "the dream of reason producing real monsters" (13). As in Goya's paintings of the *Third of May*, one comes away from Tejera's prose having looked into the eyes and having understood the heart of a victim of war. Words are the vehicle of such magic. May they soon be allowed to spin their web in English.

What, then, sets *El barranco* apart from others; what makes it unique? Its complex simplicity, its effective depiction of child psychology, its magnificent description of the Civil War in a remote island, its poetic truth. In fact, both *School of the Sun* and *El barranco* go against the mode of social realism prevalent in Spain at the time of the publication of both novels. Rather than concentrate on real historic events, describing battles, these novels use an individual's point of view to paint a picture, albeit a real one, one having some correspondence to what actually is happening in history, but filtered here to a more literary mode, in Matute's case poetic and symbolic, in Tejera's more purely poetic and metaphoric.

NOTES

This paper is dedicated to the memory of Bernardo de la Torre, an exiled Canary Islander, whom I met in Mexico. His unpublished *Narraciones de la guerra y el exilio* touches on many of the themes Nivaria Tejera captures in *El barranco*.

1. All references are to Ana María Matute, *A School of the Sun,* trans. Elaine Kerrigan (New York: Random House, 1963); and to Nivaria Tejera, *El barranco* (Las Palmas de Gran Canaria: EDIRCA, 1982). For discussions of Matute's work, see Janet W. Díaz, *Ana María Matute* (N.Y.: Twayne, 1971); Margaret E. W. Jones, *The Literary World of Ana María Matute* (Lexington Ky.: University of Kentucky Press, 1970); Rosa Roma, *Ana María Matute* (Madrid: EPESA, 1971); J. P. Ling, "Time in the Prose of Ana María Matute" (Ph.D. diss., University of Wisconsin, 1972). I have found no critical writings on Tejera other than Claude Couffon's introduction in the edition noted above.

2. See Reinhard Kuhn, *Corruption in Paradise: The Child in Western Literature* (Hanover and London: University Press of New England, 1982), especially chapter 3. See also Robert Con Davis, *The Fictional Father* (Amherst: University of Massachusetts Press, 1981).

WORKS CITED

Amador de los Ríos, José. *Historia social, Política y religiosa de los judíos de España y Portugal.* Madrid: Aguilar, 1973.

Berrettini, Celia. *Algunos aspectos de la obra de Ana María Matute.* Sao Paulo. 1971.

Bolea, Francisco. *Requiem por una generación.* Mexico: n.p., 1981.

Church, Margaret. *Structure and Theme: Don Quijote to James Joyce.* Columbus: Ohio University Press, 1983.

Davis, Robert Con. *The Fictional Father.* Amherst: University of Massachusetts, 1981.

Díaz, Janet W. *Ana María Matute.* New York: Twayne, 1971.

Fortexa, Miquel. *Els descendents dels jueus conversos de Mallorca. Guatre Mots de la veritat.* Mallorca: Grafiques Miramar, 1966.

Jones, Margaret E. W. *The Literary World of Ana María Matute.* Lexington: The University of Kentucky Press, 1970.

Kuhn, Ricard. *Corruption in Paradise: The Child in Western Literature.* Hanover: University Press of New England, 1982.

Ling, J. P. "Time in the Prose of Ana María Matute." Ph.D. diss., University of Wisconsin, 1972.

Martín-Santos, Luis. *Time of Silence.* Trans. George Leeson. New York: Harcourt Brace, 1964.

Matute, Ana María. *School in the Sun.* Trans. Elaine Kerrigan. New York: Pantheon, 1963.

Pérez, Lorenzo. *Anales judáicos de Mallorca.* Palma: Luis Ripoll, 1974.

Porcel, Baltazar. *Los chuetas mallorquines. Siete siglos de racismo.* Barcelona: Bruguera, 1977.

Roma, Rosa. *Ana María Matute.* Madrid: EPESA, 1971.

Sacks, Norman P. "Los chuetas de Mallorca y *Los muertos mandan* de Blasco Ibáñez: un capítulo en la historia de los judíos en España," *Davar* n.120(1969): 96–122.

Selke, Angela. *El santo oficio de la Inquisición.* Proceso de Fr. Francisco Ortiz. Madrid: Guadarrama, 1968.

———. *Los chuetas y la Inquisición. Vida y muerte en el guetto de Mallorca.* Madrid: Taurus, 1972.

Sicroff, Albert A. *Les controverses de status de "Pureté de sang" en Espagne du XVe au XVIIe siècle.* Paris: Didier, 1960.

Smith, Paul C. "Blasco Ibáñez and the Theme of the Jews." *Hispania* 56(1973): 282–94.

Smith, Paul C. "Sobre judios y catalanes." *El urogallo* n.15(mayo–junio 1972): 102–5.

Sobejano, Gonzalo. *Novela española de nuestro tiempo.* Madrid: Prensa española, 1975.

Winecoff Pérez, Janet. *Ana María Matute.* Boston: Twayne, 1971.

Behind the Lines: The Spanish Civil War and Women Writers

Janet Pérez

Women writers in Spain today vary greatly in age, background, and even language, since women are writing in Catalan, Gallego, and Basque, as well as Castilian and a variety of regional dialects. Some six or seven generations or distinct chronological groups of living writers make up the current literary panorama in Spain, and in most of these groupings are women who have written on the Civil War. Among the oldest are the last survivors of the "Generation of 1927," the generation of Lorca, Salinas, Alberti, Guillén, and many others who died in the conflict or suffered exile. Surviving women writers from this group include María Teresa León, wife of Alberti, and long-time exile Rosa Chacel. The great Catalan novelist Mercé Rodoreda, recently deceased, who also belonged to this generation, wrote both novels and short fiction dealing with war, the refugee experience, and exile.

The so-called "Generation of 1936" comprises writers who had barely begun to publish when the war erupted. Theirs is largely a generation of exiles, external and internal, including such well-known women as academician Carmen Conde, poet Concha Zardoya, and philosopher María Zambrano. Following in order of descending age come members of the first postwar generation, most of whom experienced the conflict as university students or teenagers. Among the women writers in this age group is the Catalan novelist and essayist, Teresa Pàmies, one of a scant handful of women who portray frontline or combat scenes. Pàmies draws upon her experience as a militant revolutionary activist, and also finds inspiration in some thirty years of refugee and exile experience. Other women writers of approximately the same age are Carmen Kurtz, María Aurèlia Capmany (who writes in Catalan), Susana March, Mercedes Salisachs, Mercedes Ballesteros, Mercedes Fórmica, and Elena Soriano, to mention only

some of the better known (or in the case of Soriano, the most intellec-
tually significant, although she has remained virtually unknown).
Nearly all of these women narrators have treated the war to some degree in their fiction. More or less coeval with these writers is Dolores
Medio, who at the outbreak of hostilities was a liberal young
Republican educator. Having experienced imprisonment and later
having worked in a war hospital, she recreated these and other aspects
of the war in both her post-Franco memoirs and her earlier novels.

Those who experienced the war as children, the second group of
postwar writers (sometimes called the "Mid-century Generation"),
began as critical or social realists, coming to the fore in the 1950s and
early 1960s. Prominent women in this group include novelists Carmen Laforet, Elena Quiroga, Ana María Matute, Carmen Martín
Gaite, and Concha Alós. For most of these women, the Civil War
ranks as their most significant formative experience, and for most of
them, as for many other writers of both genders who lived through
the war as silent spectators, the conflict with its roots and subsequent
enduring hidden tensions and prolonged rancor forms the obsessive
core or basis for a major portion of their fiction. In the case of
Matute, the war becomes her single most absorbing preoccupation.

The score of names just mentioned is not exhaustive. It comprises
only the better-known women writers who are, save one or two exceptions, authors of fiction who are still living. Many other women have
written on the Civil War, and others who have not portrayed it in
literature were affected by it, such as poet Montserrat Abelló i Soler,
poetcritic Aurora de Albornoz, poet, novelist, and critic María Al-
faro, poet-critic Clementina Arderiú, poet-narrator María Beneyto,
fiction writer Aurora Bertrana, prose writer Rosa María Cajal, outstanding poet Ernestina Champourcín, and many others. Indeed, it
would be less than logical to assume that anyone who lived through
the Civil War was impervious to the experience.

The conflict also left its mark on the work of members of the turn-
of-the-century generation, such as Concha Espina (1869–1955), who
abandoned her between-the-wars social concerns, as expressed in *El
metal de los muertos* (1920), to react against social unrest by taking
refuge with the putative proponents of "law and order" in works such
as *Alas invencibles*. Written during the war years, this propagandistic
novel features a crippled female protagonist who is rescued by a Falangist aviator. *Alas invencibles* may be the first instance of a work by a
woman writer that openly defends Franco and his military uprising,
although Falangist rhetoric is perceptible in Espina's works as early as
Flor de ayer (1934), and is even more pronounced in the wartime

Retaguardia (1937), describing the Republican capture of Santander from a distinctly Nationalist viewpoint. These wartime works were inspired in large part by Espina's personal experience of imprisonment, and Falangist rhetoric visibly diminishes in her postwar works, which move first to a neutral position and then resume the writer's social concerns, now tempered by a nonconflictive stance and purged of ideological content in favor of a more independent, multivalent posture.

To include the remainder of the lesser-known and less significant women who likewise have written on the war would expand the group to forty or fifty and bring the number of novels in which women writers treat the war to one hundred or more. The research reported in this chapter has touched in varying degrees upon perhaps half of these. I should particularly note a number of novels of war and/or exile treated specifically in earlier studies. From the Nationalist (Franco) side, there is Carmen Díaz Garrido's *Los años únicos* (subtitled *Andanzas de una niña en el Madrid rojo*), which features a child-protagonist and examines especially the conflict's effect upon children who witnessed it. Concha Castroviejo (1915–) treats the refugee and exile experience in at least two novels, *Los que se fueron* (1957) and *Víspera del odio* (1959). Likewise, Carmen Mieza devoted a pair of novels to the war's effect upon families, and, specifically, to the way in which separation and/or the exile experience intrudes upon the relationships between parents and children in *La imposible canción* (1962) and *Una mañana cualquiera* (1965). Constancia de la Mora (1906–) wrote upon the years of the Republic and Civil War from a thoroughly unconventional viewpoint in her autobiographical memoir, *Doble esplendor. Autobiografía de una aristócrata española, republicana y comunista* (1938?), translated into English as *In Place of Splendor.*

In *La retirada* (1967), Montserrat Masoliver presents one of the very few "frontline" views of the Civil War by a woman writer, although she does so via focus upon a specific Loyalist soldier, a generic representative of the defenders of the Republic, who is almost suspiciously upright and conscientious. The protagonist's particular activities, leaves, and duty assignments allow the writer to minimize the strategic element and avoid presentation of combat. The work's significance is more historical than aesthetic: it marks an end to the systematic silencing of Republican viewpoints after promulgation of the "Ley de la Prensa" (Press Law), and places Masoliver in the vanguard in striving to offset thirty years' portrayal of the Republic's defenders as beasts and villains. Masoliver continues but moderates her stance in *Hombre de paz* (1969). Isabel de Palencia's *En mi hambre mando yo* (1939) traces the fortunes of an upper-class family embroiled in the prewar political turmoil in Spain, separated ideologically, with members on both of the contending sides. The symbolic marriage between representatives of the opposing factions is a device used by many subsequent novelists (although it should be noted that such marital union does not necessarily signify an end to divisiveness: matrimony does not automatically produce wedded bliss, as Delibes demonstrates graphically with a similar marriage in *Cinco horas con Mario* [1966], where the wedding simply continues the civil conflict on a smaller, more intimate scale).

Other women novelists in Spain who have written of the Civil War include Susana March, *Algo muere cada día* (1955), Carmen Iraizoz, *Belzunegui. El ocaso de una familia* (1969), Cecilia G. de Guilarte, *Cualquiera que os dé muerte* (1969), and *La soledad y sus ríos* (1975), the last combining a view of exile with the theme of economic exploitation in the Third World. Typical in many ways is the case of María del Carmen Rubio y López Guijarro, a Phillipine-born schoolteacher in Spain whose school was burned during the Civil War. Logically enough, therefore, the war is a predominant theme in her literary output, which sketches the war's negative, even devastating effects upon all—even (and, in fact, especially) upon those who win. *El precio del perdón* focuses upon the war's aggravation of marital and familial problems as Rubio studies complications developing in the protagonist's family when her estranged husband abandons her and sends their eldest sons to Russia. While reminiscent of soap-opera plots and the *novela rosa* (pulp romance), the work is characteristic in downplaying partisan issues. In *La rebeldía de los hijos: Historia de una familia* (1933–1966), Rubio utilizes the diary of a woman living in a Madrid refugee center with several other families of women and children, whose men are all fighting or missing. Again, the war's essentially nonideological nature for most Spaniards is paramount: Most are ignorant of political issues, much like Elena (the diarist), whose lack of political comprehension compounds the insecurity and anxiety produced by the conflict and its aftermath. Family difficulties occurring over the next three decades involving Elena's husband and eight children are seen as part of the war's lasting effects, even while such problems may also result from more "universal" factors (e.g., the generation gap).

Quite possibly many Spaniards, including some women writers, indeed did not understand the complex and tangled ideologies in conflict in the war. With few exceptions, those who do not downplay ideological questions tend to oversimplify and misinterpret them. A case in point is María Antonia Salvá (1869–1957), a poet of the Mallorcan school, whose complete works include a section on the Spanish Civil War in which she views the conflict as a struggle between religion and nonreligious forces.[1] Although she was orthodox, Salvá was essentially an apolitical writer, and her somewhat superficial glossing of the ideological clash is not out of character with the rest of her work. What is interesting is the extent to which her treatment coincides with the reluctance of women writers generally to view the conflict from a fixed ideological stance.

Another prose genre in which women have treated the war repeatedly includes the memoir, notably such titles as Felicidad Blanc's *Espejo de sombras* (1977), Mercedes Fórmica's *Visto y vivido 1931–37* (1982), and Federica Montseny's *Cent dies de la vida d'una dona*. Victoria Kent's *Cuatro años en París* (1940–44) is a novelized autobiographical memoir describing the writer's years in hiding, and María Teresa León's *Memoria de la melancolía* also falls within the category of non-fiction prose, although the same writer has published novels and short stories treating the prewar years, the war itself, and the exile experience.

The foregoing sampling is necessarily incomplete (it does not include the more important writers listed first above, whose works I have in many instances also studied elsewhere), but it nonetheless provides some basis for a general introduction to preliminary results of the overall study, a discussion of certain critical problems encountered, and a synthetic presentation of features common to various works.

Of at least two and possibly three younger literary groups or tendencies that are identifiable at present, the members with few exceptions were born during or after the war and have little recollection of it. As a group, they have shown relatively little interest in the war as fiction.

Similarly, writers in the older age groups who spent the war outside Spain—France, England and Portugal were frequent havens for the wealthy—either do not write about the war or do so very obliquely and via characters situated at some remove, as with the work of Mercedes Ballesteros. Another writer who largely escaped the war's trauma in spite of Republican sympathies is Rosa Chacel, who has spent most of her life outside Spain and is one of a very small number who apparently have escaped the need to exorcise the demons of the struggle through writing of it. Quite clearly, writers who did not experience the war directly do not exhibit the obsessions of those who recall the conflict, regardless of the age at which they witnessed it.

Age during the war is a significant factor for subsequent fictional portrayals, however, influencing especially the choice of narrative consciousness and point of view. Of comparable importance is the area of Spain in which the writer spent the war years, inasmuch as the extent, intensity, and nature of the hostilities varied enormously from region to region. Western Spain, occupied by the Franco forces in the first weeks of the war, saw relatively little fighting; and the same applies to Galicia. In the Canaries and most of the Balearic Islands, despite heightened political tensions, the war was a distant echo. Rather typically, Carmen Laforet, who spent the war years in the Canaries as an adolescent, portrays in her first two novels the experiences of girls who spend the war in the islands, going to the Peninsula to study at war's end.

Matute, who spent the war in Barcelona (where some of the longest and bitterest fighting occurred), presents bombardments and civilian deaths in *Las luciérnagas, En esta tierra* and *Los hijos muertos*, as well as portraying the Republic's final days in Barcelona in *Los soldados lloran de noche*. More peripheral and symbolic representations appear in *Primera memoria*, and a study of the conflict's roots is undertaken in *Los Abel* and *Fiesta al noroeste*. By contrast, Carmen Martín Gaite, who was a child in Salamanca at the outbreak of hostilities and spent the war in this relatively sheltered area (occupied almost immediately by the invaders), depicts very little of a conflictive nature, recalling only an occasional officer or soldier seen almost as a curiosity in her novelized memoir *El cuarto de atrás* (1978; *The Back Room*, 1983).

Autobiographical substrata and realistic bias are very significant, even in novels that treat the war allegorically, symbolically, or through fantasy. Time and place of publication likewise influence the tone, content, and other aspects of fictional publication, given the Franco censorship. Writers in exile did not experience the constraints to which those within the Peninsula were subject, but exiles who wrote in the hope of achieving publication in Spain usually wrote accordingly, in restrained fashion. Other exiles may have written with care out of fear of jeopardizing relatives remaining in Spain. In any case, the more violent denunciations and literary exposés come primarily from those expatriates who left no one behind. A slow relaxing of censorship in Spain is perceptible over time, with more freedom of expression existing after the censorship finally came under legal regulation in the late 1960s.

During the Franco era, detractors in Spain of literature inspired by the Civil War would point out that the conflict had not yet given rise to a novel of the stature of Tolstoy's *War and Peace*. Certainly the quality of the vast corpus of warrelated works is uneven. To say that in one sense the criticism continues to be true is not to say that it is valid. To judge the testimonies of hundreds—perhaps thousands—of combatants and civilian victims of the Spanish Civil War exclusively in terms of the impossibility of fitting them into the procrustean bed custom-made for one of the great masterpieces of world literature is unreasonable and unfair. Furthermore, Tolstoy's *bildungsroman* with its interpretation of the 1812 Napoleonic invasion of Russia appeared some fifty-five years after the event, which had occurred well before the author's birth. His work was not written in the heat of battle, in exile, or in a repressive period of difficult postwar recovery and transition.

Understandably, those who have fought and suffered in a conflict do not view it with the same serene objectivity of others who have only read or heard of the battles. The half century since the end of the Spanish Civil War has not sufficed to erase the animosities, and few survivors are prepared to view the remembered atrocities impartially and dispassionately. The outpouring of war-related literature continues, however, with the floodgates opened wider by the dictator's death in 1975, and especially by the abolition of censorship in Spain a decade ago. Half a century is short when reckoning in historical time, and survivors of Spain's civil strife may still publish significant works, although it may require a member of the next generation to view the national struggle with the detachment of a Tolstoy. Unquestionably, the bestselling theme of the last decade in Spain has been the Civil War, as readers restricted to onesided, official versions of events for forty years have rushed to devour anything and everything presenting a pro-Republican or anti-Franco view. If commercial viability is important, the incentive is there.

Like the novel of the Mexican Revolution, the literature of the Spanish Civil War has become something of a genre unto itself, although far more prolific, with titles worldwide numbering in the thousands.[2] Civil war-related titles in all genres (journalism, poetry, diary, essay, autobiography, novel, short story, memoir, drama, study and report) published inside Spain were numbered in five digits already in the past decade. To date, not even all the primary material has been identified and cataloged, nor has most of it been classified. Feasible schemes of classification that might be employed include chronological division (by dates of publication or generations to which the authors belong); subdivision by genre, country, or nationality; or organization according to various ways in which the war is treated (e.g., viewed from the front lines, the rear guard, behind the lines, or simply as the background for other fictional emphases). Additional approaches involve grouping authors by language or dividing them dichotomously: exiles and "insiders," Franco sympathizers and Republican sympathizers, or women and men.

The most significant criticism by Hispanists to date of Civil War-related writing as a whole has involved, almost without exception,

interpretations of a single author or handful of authors. Few observers have attempted such an overview or panoramic synthesis of a
sizeable group such as is the intention of the present study of Spanish
women writing on the Civil War. The numbers of writers and works
involved, and the portion of research still incomplete, as well as constraints of time and space, require something less than complete treatment at this juncture, and few relevant secondary sources exist that
those desirous of further information might consult. Save for three or
four of the most visible postwar women novelists, Spanish women
writers generally have been very much neglected by critics, for reasons
of little relevance to the war per se. This observation, based primarily
on those writing in Castilian, is even more applicable to those writing
in other languages of the Peninsula. A recent exception to the general
pattern of critical forgetfulness is the special double number of *Letras
femeninas* (12:1–2, Spring–Fall 1986) devoted to women writers and
the war, and subtitled *Voces femeninas en la literatura de la guerra civil
española.* Here, too, however, most studies treat a single work or
author. In the extant critical corpus, only two Castilian women
authors of novels on the Civil War have been the objects of several
studies: Dolores Medio and Ana María Matute. The vogue among
critics of Carmen Martín Gaite's *El cuarto de atrás* (1978; *The Back
Room,* 1983), which reconstructs childhood memories of the war and
postwar years, places it among the moststudied works on the Civil
War by a Spanish woman writer, although for the most part, critics
focus on literary and metaliterary aspects, forgetting the war or giving
it short shrift. Quite recently, the late Mercè Rodoreda, who was and
is unquestionably the most important woman writer in Catalan, has
become the object of several critical studies, at least two of which
focus upon her portraits of war and exile.[3] The total phenomenon of
women writers on the Civil War remains essentially unexamined,
however, and indeed, has yet to be identified completely.

   During a conference on literature of the Spanish Civil War, I
presented a study of some dozen fictional treatments of the war by
nine women novelists.[4] That abbreviated survey forms part of the
broader ongoing investigation of which the present considerations are
likewise part. From that overview of nine deliberately chosen lesser or
less-known writers, whose works on the war were examined in the
light of prior analyses of war-related fiction by several better-known
novelists, preliminary conclusions were extracted. Cast in the form of
generalizations, they are the preliminary installment of a poetics of
women's Civil War fiction, or what some critics might term a typology:

1. Support for the Franco regime and its ideology is very much a minority stance, even though the censorship under which nearly all these women wrote threatened those expressing opposition views.

2. Although full objectivity is not achieved, a majority of the women writers appear to strive harder than their male counterparts for a balanced presentation.

3. Ideological elements are subordinated to the focus upon human suffering and other repercussions of the war.

4. Women writers with few exceptions do not attempt to portray actual combat but adopt the narrative perspective of noncombatants.[5]

5. They evince less interest in reconstructing military operations than behindthelines ambients and the war's effects upon women's lives and those of children, adolescents, and families.

6. The vast majority of Spaniards writing on the Civil War prefer to adhere closely to the realm of personal experience in fictional interpretation.

7. The overwhelming majority of war-related writings by Spanish women belongs essentially to the mimetic mode, employing either traditional realistic techniques or some neorealistic variant.

The autobiographical bias has several consequences. Rarely, in fact, does a noncombatant writer, male or female, attempt a novelistic version of a battle, especially in its strategic or strictly military aspects. Battles such as the siege of Madrid, witnessed by many noncombatants unable to escape, are usually described from a civilian perspective. A writer who saw military duty during the war but little action is unlikely to give more than a behind-the-lines description. For example, contemporary novelist Miguel Delibes—who saw little action because he served in the Navy in what was essentially a land war—describes scarcely more than training in the naval academy and shipboard life while the cruisers were on blockade duty.

Similarly, women writers seldom attempt to present more than the civilian perspective, which for certain areas includes bombardments, air raids with civilian casualties, political imprisonment, "fifth column" terrorism or war in the streets, and a lengthy list of lesser war-related hardships and losses, punctuated by occasional moments of respite. Concha Alós, in *El caballo rojo*, depicts the evacuation of civilian refugees before the advancing Franco forces and expansion of the battle zone, relying on autobiographical elements, her own family's wartime experience. Dolores Medio, in *Nosotros los Rivero* and *Diario de una maestra* portrays the war in the North, in Asturias, where she spent most of the war years, but does not attempt to recreate the conflict in Madrid, despite the novelist's many years of residence there both before and after the war.

The autobiographical substratum in women's writing is frequently visible, and many novels prove upon closer examination to be little more than memoirs thinly disguised as fiction. Carolyn Galerstein's study of the numerous points of coincidence between Dolores Medio's memoirs, *Atrapados en la ratonera* (1980), published during the transition to democracy, and her early novels of the war, *Nosotros los Rivero* (1952) and *Diario de una maestra* (1961), confirms the extensive correlation between autobiographical fact and putative fiction.[6] Galerstein's observations are equally applicable to many other Civil War novels by women, as well as to most of those written by men, with the exception of some works in the allegorical or fantastic mode. "Parallels between Medio's own experiences and the narrative. . . are abundant" (Galerstein, 49).

Writers tend to set their portrayals of the war in the precise locations where they experienced it, a practice that not only intensifies the autobiographical content but makes verification easy, given the war's differing character in various regions of the country. The same writer, however, may produce several interpretations of the war, ranging from the realistic or memorialistic (cf. Matute's *En esta tierra*) to the fantastic (*La torre vigía*) to the symbolic (*Primera memoria*) and the allegorical (*Fiesta al noroeste*). Maria Aurèlia Capmany, a similarly multivalent writer, also treats the war realistically (cf. *Lo color més blau* and *Felçiment, jo sóc una dona*) but also fantastically (in *Quim/Quima*, which spans from the year 1,000 to the Civil War), while a surrealistic approach appears in some of Capmany's stories in *Com una ma*. Rodoreda is another case in point. She has depicted the war's frontline ravages realistically in such short stories as "Orleans, 5 quilomètres," in mythic, surreal fashion in *Quanta, quanta guerra*, and with a more detailed psychological study of the war's effects on women and children behind the lines in *La Plaza del Diamant*, for example.

Anyone who attempts to study the novel of the Civil War as genre or the corpus of women writers' contributions soon will encounter technical difficulties concerning inclusions and exclusions. No ready-made criteria exist to aid in discriminations between novels of the war proper—even if narrated by noncombatants—and that allied yet separate group of works delineating the antecedents or causes of the war, which often end with the outbreak of hostilities or some significant date in the summer of 1936, yet stop short of presenting events that transpired between 18 July 1936, and 1 April 1939. The critic must beware, however, of the temptation to include only those works that portray events between Franco's revolt and the unconditional surrender of the Republican government. In many parts of Spain, a de facto state of war existed for more than a year before the rightist uprising. And the hostilities did not end with Franco's military communiqué of 1 April 1939, "la guerra ha terminado." As Ana

María Matute expressed it, "the horrors of war gave way to the horrors of peace": The killing did not stop simply because one side was disarmed. Although the Franco regime was careful to keep no statistics on those who died in purges and political executions and in prison, some Spaniards estimate that the number of Spaniards who died of political causes in the ten years after the war equalled the one million killed in the war.[7]

Events since World War II in Korea, Hungary, Vietnam, Czechoslovakia, and Nicaragua more than suffice to demonstrate the folly of assuming that a state of war exists only when war is declared. For this reason, it may be critically unjustifiable to exclude works that deal with the war's aftermath, especially novels of exodus, or those presenting purges, political execution, imprisonment, or exile, all direct consequences of the war and separable from it only with difficulty. Yet the action of many such novels begins with the capitulation of the Republic. In order for the critic to employ a concept such as Bakhtin's *chronotope* or inseparable space-time,[8] which has a special relevance for historical poetics and the problem of temporal delimitation of the corpus, it becomes necessary to conceive of the war as forming a continuum with its preliminary hostilities and subsequent muted political violence.

The question is further complicated because some novels with at least a portion of the action set from 1936–1939, utilize the war primarily as a background for fictive events. Similarly, a percentage of novels ending with the war's outbreak have as their primary purpose not an examination of the war's roots, but an anguished or nostalgic portrayal of a world or way of life gone forever. This bias suggests strongly the advisability of subcategories, although at present the problem is one of limiting numbers rather than finding bases for subdivisions. Nor do the difficulties of inclusion or exclusion and classification end here. Many portrayals of the war are allegorical or symbolical, mythical, or otherwise not strictly historical. Women writers as well as men have portrayed the war indirectly via intrafamilial or interpersonal conflicts: the "war of the sexes" (e.g., Concha Alós), the Cain-Abel motif (cf. Ana M. Matute), or the symbolic marital conflict between partners whose backgrounds or values situate them on opposing sides, easily identifiable with the opponents in the Civil War (as with Delibes' *Cinco horas con Mario*, but also Tusquets in portions of *Siete miradas en un mismo paisaje*).

Similarly, some novels of exile and return focus upon the children of exiles or refugees, characters who did not really experience the war and who function as vehicles for exploration of the problems of adaptation and assimilation to a new homeland or a debunking of the myth of the exile's return. An additional problem arises when an allegorical work is sufficiently disguised to escape recognition as treating the Civil War, as happened with Torrente Ballester's early novel *El golpe de estado de Guadalupe Limón* that burlesques Franco's rise to power, the myth of the martyred José Antonio, and the new leader's self-mythification. Set in a banana republic to mislead the censors, the work's obfuscation was so successful that practically no one captured its allusions. Ultimately, the critic's decision as to where to establish the parameters delimiting the Civil War novel cannot help but be somewhat arbitrary—as arbitrary, perhaps, as the decision to focus only upon writings by women. Given the difficulties in establishing satisfactory criteria determining which novels should be included, individual judgments must take into account such matters as whether the war is a major issue in the work or merely a background, whether the conflicts portrayed are those which were operative in the war (even if not during the "official" dates), and—in the case of allegorical or fantastic representations—whether there are a sufficient number of details to affirm that clear allusions exist to the Spanish Civil War in particular and not to war in general.

Although coinciding with their male counterparts in adhering closely to empirically observed bases and personal experience for their war narratives, women writers almost never glorify or idealize war. Neither militaristic propaganda nor the romanticized portraits of war presented by some male writers are normal in women writers' work; even those few who may be classed as ideologues usually concentrate upon social and familial concerns. Psychological and spiritual problems, the varied forms of trial and suffering attendant upon the belligerent state, the senselessness of sacrifice, the lives shattered long after the smoke of battle has dissipated—these are the preferred focus of women writers. Nearly all present some variation upon the theme that war is hell, and most prefer the reconstruction of small, seemingly insignificant moments overlooked or forgotten in the larger scheme of things, ignored or scorned by historians and chroniclers of war's "major" events. Their sphere is largely war's "intra-history," as Unamuno would have termed it, the effects upon the daily and future lives of unsung and largely unknown, concrete individuals whose collective human history is more "typical" and authentic than the abstract dates and solitary heroes found in historians' texts. Some writers may argue that these humble data are trivia; for Unamuno they were more "real" than what history heretofore has preserved.

Spain's women writers have chosen by and large to record for future generations this vision of the war.

NOTES

1. *Obres de María Antonia Salvá,* 6 vols. (Palma de Mallorca: Llibres del Moll, 1948–55), vol. 5, *Lluneta del Pagé.*

2. Maryse Bertrand de Muñoz, who has made the novel of the Civil War her life's work, began publishing bibliographical studies in 1968 with "Bibliografía de la novela de la guerra civil española" in *La Torre* 61(1968): 215–42; "Fuentes bibliográficas de la creación literaria de la guerra civil española," *Hispania* 56, 3(1973): 550–56, and "Reflejos de los cambios políticos . . . en las novelas españolas recientes de la guerra civil," *Camp de l'Arpá* 19 (Barcelona, 1975), pp. 16–20. Subsequently she has completed three monographs on the subject.

José Luis Ponce de León, author of *La novela española de la guerra civil (1936–1939)* (Madrid: Insula, 1971) provides an extensive bibliography of novels and studies, as well as attempting an ambitious analysis of a large corpus of works of very uneven quality. Ponce de León also has continued to work as a bibliographer of Civil War literature.

3. See especially José Ortega, "Mujer, guerra y neurosis en dos novelas de Mercè Rodoreda," in *Novelistas femeninas de la postguerra española,* ed. Janet Pérez (Madrid: Porrúa, 1983), pp. 71–84; Geraldine Nichols, "Exile, Gender and Mercè Rodoreda," *Monographic Review/Revista Monográfica* 2(1986): 189–97; and Gene Forrest, "Myth and Anti-myth in Mercè Rodoreda's *Quanta, quanta guerra,*" a paper read at "The Literature of the Spanish Civil War," a conference at Texas A & M University, October 15–18, 1986.

4. "Spanish Women Writers and the Civil War," presented at Texas A & M University conference, "The Literature of the Spanish Civil War," October 15–18, 1986. Forthcoming in selected proceedings, *The Literature of the Spanish Civil War,* ed. Wulf Koepke.

5. Obviously, most women writers did not serve in the army or militia and so did not witness actual combat. Generally they chose not to write of events too unrelated to their own experiences.

6. Carolyn Galerstein, "Dolores Medio's Women in Wartime," *Letras femeninas* 12,1–2 (1986): 45–51.

7. Interview with the late Spanish novelist and long-time political prisoner Angel María de Lera, at Lera's home in Madrid in March 1962. A Republican commissioner, Lera was first condemned to death, later spent more than twenty years in a series of prisons, in all of which political executions took place daily. He made estimates based on the approximate number of prisons and what seemed to be the "average" number of daily executions in several of them. I refer also to further conversations with Lera and contemporary novelist Miguel Delibes at the latter's home in Valladolid in February 1966.

8. Michael Holquist, ed. *The Dialogic Imagination. Four essays by M. M. Bakhtin,* trans. Caryl Emerson and Michael Holquist (Austin: University of Texas Press, 1981; 5th ed., 1987), pp. 84–85.

WORKS CITED

Alós, Concha. *El caballo rojo.* Barcelona: Planeta, 1966.

Blanc, Felicidad. *Espejo de sombras.* Barcelona: Argos Vergara, 1977.

Capmany, María Aurèlia. *Lo color mas blau.* Barcelona: Planeta, 1982.

———. *Com una ma.* Palma de Mallorca: Francesc de B. Moll, 1952.

———. *Feliçment, jo soc una dona.* Barcelona: Nova Terra, 1969.

———. *Quim/Quima.* Barcelona: Estela, 1971; 2 ed., Barcelona: Editorial Laia, 1977.

Castroviejo, Concha. *Los que se fueron.* Barcelona: Planeta, 1957.

———. *Víspera del odio.* Barcelona: Garbo Editorial, 1959.

Delibes, Miguel. *Cinco horas con Mario.* Barcelona: Destino, 1966.

Díaz Garrido, Carmen. *Los años únicos. Andanzas de una niña en el Madrid rojo.* Prólogo de Rafael García Serrano. Madrid: Prensa Española, 1972.

Espina, Concha [Concepción]. *Alas invencibles.* Madrid: Afrodisio Aguado, 1938.

———. *Flor de ayer.* In *Obras completas.* Madrid: FAX, 1972.

———. *El metal de los muertos.* Madrid: Afrodisio Aguado, 1920.

———. *Retaguardia,* 3d ed. Córdoba: Nueva España, 1937.

Formica, Mercedes. *Visto y vivido 1931–1937. Pequeña historia de ayer.* Barcelona: Planeta, 1982.

Guilarte, Cecilia G. de. *Cualquiera que os dé muerte.* Barcelona: Editorial Linosa, 1969.

———. *La soledad y sus ríos.* Madrid: Editorial Magisterio Español, 1975.

Iraizoz, Carmen. *Belzunegui. El ocaso de una familia.* Pamplona: Editorial Gómez, 1969.

Kent, Victoria. *Cuatro años en Paris (1940–44).* Buenos Aires: Sur, 1947.

León, María Teresa. *Memoria de la melancolía.* Buenos Aires: Losada, 1970.

March, Susana. *Algo muere cada día.* Barcelona: Planeta, 1955.

Martín Gaite, Carmen. *El cuarto de atrás.* Barcelona: Destino, 1978. English trans., *The Back Room.* Trans. Helen R. Lane. New York: Columbia University Press, 1983.

Masoliver, Liberata. *Hombre de paz.* Barcelona: Jaime Libros, 1969.

———. *La retirada.* Barcelona: Peñíscola, 1967.

Matute, Ana María. *Los Abel.* Barcelona: Destino, 1948.

———. *En esta tierra.* Barcelona: éxito, 1955.

———. *Fiesta al noroeste.* Barcelona: Pareja y Borrás, 1959.

———. *Los hijos muertos.* Barcelona: Planeta, 1958.

———. *Las luciérnagas.* Prohibited by censorship, ca. 1951. Revised, cut, and published as *En esta tierra.*

———. *Primera memoria.* Barcelona: Destino, 1960.

———. *Los soldados lloran de noche.* Barcelona: Destino, 1964.

———. *La torre vigía.* Barcelona: Lumen, 1971.

Medio, Doleres. *Atrapados en la ratonera: Memorias de una novelista.* Madrid: Alce, 1980.

———. *Diario de una maestra.* Barcelona: Destino, 1961.

———. *Nosotros, los Rivero.* Barcelona: Destino, 1953.

Mieza, Carmen. *La imposible canción.* Barcelona: Plaza y Janés, 1962.

———. *Una mañana cualquiera.* Lérida: Prisma, 1965.

Montseny, Federica. *Cent dies de la vida d'una dona.* N.p.: n.d.

Mora, Constancia de la. *Doble esplendor. Autobiografía de una aristócrata española, republicana y comunista.* Barcelona: Crítica, 1977. English trans., *In Place of Splendor.* New York: Harcourt Brace. 1939.

Palencia, Isabel de. *En mi hambre mando yo.* México: n.p., 1939.

Rodoreda, Mercè. *La plaça del Diamant.* Barcelona: Club dels Novel-listes, 1962.

———. *Quanta, quanta guerra.* Barcelona: Club Editor, 1980.

Rubio y López Quijarro, Carmen. *El precio del perdón.* Bilbao: Editores Comunicación Literaria de Autores, 1981.

———. *La rebeldía de los hijos: Historia de una familia (1933–1966).* Aranguren, Vizcaya: El Paisaje, 1982.

Salvá, María Antónia. *Lluneta de Pagès.* In *Obres de Maria Antónia Salvá,* vol. 5. Palma de Mallorca: Llibres del Moll, 1948–55.

Torrente Ballester, Gonzalo. *El golpe de estado de Guadalupe Limón.* Madrid: Ediciones Nueva época, 1946.

Tusquets, Ester. *Siete miradas en un mismo paisaje.* Barcelona: Lumen, 1981.

Notes on the Authors

PETER BARTA, a native of Hungary, received his early education in Europe before coming to the United States. He earned the Ph.D. in comparative literature at the University of Illinois at Urbana–Champaign in 1986. Since then, he has been assistant professor of Germanic and Slavic languages at Texas Tech University. His research and publications have centered around the works of Tolstoy, Joyce, and Andrei Bely.

ALFRED CISMARU, professor of Romance languages at Texas Tech University, earned the Ph.D. at New York University. He is the author of three books and more than one hundred articles in scholarly journals, and has delivered some two hundred papers at domestic and international meetings.

LUIS F. COSTA, a native of Spain, earned the B.A. in mathematics from the University of California–Berkeley, M.A. degrees in mathematics and Spanish from Fresno State University, and the Ph.D. in Spanish and Portuguese from UCLA. He is currently dean of arts and humanities and professor of foreign languages at California State University, Fresno. His research interests are in modern poetry and the novel, especially on the Generation of 1927 and its relation to the ideas of José Ortega y Gasset. His studies on the novel focus on very recent narratives, with emphasis on the nontraditional forms. His special interests are the works of Juan Benet and the new women novelists. He has completed a book on León Felipe and is at work on a book on Jorge Guillén. He has published essays on Guillén, Benet, Moix, Ortega y Gasset, Fuentes, and others.

THOMAS DEVENY is associate professor and chair of the Department of Foreign Languages at Western Maryland College in Westminister, Maryland. He earned the B.A. from the State University of New York at Albany, the M.A. from the University of Florida, and the Ph.D. from the University of North Carolina at Chapel Hill. Deveny has published works on Spanish literature, Brazilian literature, and language pedagogy, in numerous journals, including *Hispania, The Journal of Hispanic Philology, Romance Notes, Hispanófila,* and *Discurso Literario.* He is currently working on a book on contemporary Spanish film.

SALVADOR J. FAJARDO, professor of Spanish at State University of New York–Binghamton, holds the Ph.D. in Romance languages from the University of Chicago, where he studied French and Spanish literature. He has spoken at national conferences and contributed numerous articles to scholarly journals on the topics of contemporary Spanish poetry and Cervantes. His most recent book-length publication is *Multiple Spaces: The Poetry of Rafael Alberti.* His articles include "The Enchanted Return: On the Conclusion to Don Quixote, I," *Journal of Medieval and Renaissance Studies,* and "Hacia una iconograña del exilio en la poesía de Rafael Alberti," *Hispanic Journal.* His *The Word and the Mirror* was published recently by Fairleigh Dickinson Press.

CHRISTOPHER G. FLOOD teaches French studies and is convenor of the graduate program in European area studies at the University of Surrey, England. He also contributes to a graduate course in literary theory at St. Mary's College, Twickenham. He holds a D.Phil. from Oxford University, and has taught previously at the universities of Oxford and Paris X. He was a visiting scholar at Michigan State University in 1983–84. He is the author of a number of articles relating politics to literature, as well as contributions on Emile Boutmy and Louis Marin for a biographical encyclopedia of French politics, to be published by the British Association for the Study of Modern and Contemporary France. Currently he is completing a book, titled *Paul Claudel: Literature, Ideas, Ideology,* and is carrying out research for a study of political ideologies in contemporary France.

RICHARD J. GOLSAN, assistant professor of French at Texas A&M University, taught previously at Case Western Reserve University in Cleveland, Ohio. He earned the Ph.D. at the University of North Carolina at Chapel Hill. He has published on André Malraux, Henry de Montherlant, René Girard, and others in *Romance Quarterly, MLN, Essays in French Literature, Helios,* and elsewhere. His book, *Service inutile: A Study of the Tragic in the Theatre of Henry de Montherlant,* is forthcoming. His current interests include the relationship between French politics and literature in the l930s and Poetic Realist Cinema.

CHARLES KING earned the B.A. from the University of New Mexico and the Ph.D. in Spanish from the University of California. He taught at Louisiana State University before serving as a grantee of the United States Information Agency in Bolivia, Uruguay, Columbia, and Iran. He was a specialist for language institutes for the U.S. Office of Education in Washington, D.C., and only recently has he retired as a professor of Spanish from the University of Colorado, Boulder. He was editor of *The Modern Language,* 1970–79. His doctoral thesis, "An Exposition of the Synthetic Philosophy of Ramón Sender," was the first to be written on the Aragonese author. He has written a book on Sender and *An annotated Bibliography of Ramón Sender, 1928–1974.*

JEFFREY MEYERS, professor of English at the University of Colorado, is the author of several works on T. E. Lawrence and George Orwell; biographies of Katherine Mansfield (1978), Wyndham Lewis, and Ernest Hemingway; *Fiction and the Colonial Experience, Painting and the Novel, A Fever at the Core, Married to a Genius, D. H. Lawrence and the Experience of Italy, Disease and the Novel,* and *Manic Power: Robert Lowell and His Circle.* He has also edited several volumes of original essays: *Wyndham Lewis: A Revaluation, The Craft of Literary Biography,* and *D. H. Lawrence and Tradition.* He has been a Guggenheim Fellow and is a Fellow of the Royal Society of Literature.

EDOUARD MOROT-SIR is William Rand Kenan, Jr., Professor of French emeritus at the University of North Carolina at Chapel Hill. Former Cultural Attaché and Permanent Representative of the French Universities of Bordeaux and Lille, he has taught French literature in various American universities. Among his books are *La Philosophie française d'aujourdhui* (1971), *La Métaphysique de Pascal* (1973), *La Pensée négative* (1947), and *Du Surréalisme a l'empire de la critique,* coauthored with Germaine Brée (1984). He has written numerous articles on twentieth-century French literature, on the problem of the relation between literature and philosophy, and on the theory of criticism. He is currently working on two books, one on the philosophy of reference and the other on the practice of language in Pascal's *Pensées.*

ABE OSHEROFF, a veteran of the Spanish Civil War, served in the Abraham Lincoln Brigade along with some three thousand other Americans who volunteered to defend the Republic. He has made his living as a carpenter, but is a life-long "history major." His award-winning documentary film on the Spanish Civil war has been shown in various parts of the world, on public television, and at about three hundred universities in the United States. He was historical consultant for the Spanish segment of "Between the Wars," and has lectured at almost two hundred universities on this subject. For the last seven years, he has taught a seminar, "The Spanish Civil War, Origins and Aftermath," at UCLA. He has been a visiting scholar at Boston College, the University of Washington, and other universities.

JANET PÉREZ holds the M.A. and Ph.D. in Romance languages from Duke University. She taught at Duke, Trinity College (of Catholic University), Queens College (City University of New York), and the University of North Carolina at Chapel Hill before coming to Texas Tech, where she is Paul Whitfield Horn Professor of Spanish and associate dean of the graduate school. Her books include volumes on Ortega y Gasset, Ana María Matute, Miguel Delibes, Gonzalo Torrente Ballester, and a forthcoming study on contemporary Spanish women writers. A past or present member of some thirty editorial boards, she has edited or coedited nearly one hundred volumes in the Spanish section of the Twayne World Authors Series. Her articles have appeared in many professional journals: *Hispania, Romance Notes, Hispanófila, Kentucky Romance Quarterly, Revista de Estudios Hispánicos, Journal of Spanish Studies: Twentieth Century, The American Hispanist, Cuadernos hispanoamericanos, Estreño, World Literature Today, Anales de la Narrativa Española Contemporánea, Crítica Hispánica, Hispanic Journal, Revista Canadiense de Estudios Hispánicos, The Review of Contemporary Fiction, Discurso Literario, América Indígena, Anthropos (Barcelona),* and *Hispanic Review.* She is currently vice president of the Twentieth Century Spanish Society of America, a member of the national Board of Trustees of Sigma Delta Phi, and a consultant to the Council for International Exchange of Scholars.

JOSEPH SCHRAIBMAN was born in Havana, Cuba, and came to the United States where he received the B.A. from Brooklyn College and the Ph.D. from the University of Illinois. He has taught at Princeton University, the University of Indiana, and Washington University, where he is presently professor of Romance languages. Most of his published research concerns the Spanish novel of the nineteenth and twentieth centuries. His interest has centered particularly around Benito Pérez Galdós, as reflected by his book *Dreams in the Novels of Pérez Galdós* and more recently by a collection with Brian Dendle of political articles by Galdós in the *Revista de España.* Schraibman has also published articles on Martín-Santos, Ferres, Baroja, Matute, Clarín, Balzac, Camus, Marsé, and other writers. In recent years, he has been tracing Judeo-Spanish themes in Hispanic literature and the interrelationship between history and the novel.